Library of
Davidson College

The Confessional Fictions of Charles Dickens

Wrapper illustration. From *David Copperfield*.

THE CONFESSIONAL FICTIONS OF CHARLES DICKENS

by
Barry Westburg

NORTHERN ILLINOIS UNIVERSITY PRESS

Library of Congress Cataloging in Publication Data

Westburg, Barry, 1938-
  The confessional fictions of Charles Dickens.

  Bibliography: p.
  Includes index.
  1. Dickens, Charles, 1812-1870—Criticism and
interpretation. 2. Confession in literature. I. Title.
PR4588.W45   823'.8   76-14713
ISBN 0-87580-065-3

Copyright © 1977 by Northern Illinois University Press
Published by the Northern Illinois University Press
Dekalb, Illinois 60115
Manufactured in the United States of America
All rights reserved

Must not D. C. confide himself to the broad pinions of Time?
—from Julia Mills's private diary
(*David Copperfield*)

When I went to Lunnon town sirs,
   Too rul loo rul
   Too rul loo rul
Wasn't I done very brown sirs?
   Too rul loo rul
   Too rul loo rul
—song from *Great Expectations*

For the Two Tittlebats,
Jennifer Kingsley and Catherine Elizabeth

Contents

Acknowledgments
xi

INTRODUCTION
The Confessional Trilogy
xiii

ONE
Oliver Twist:
A Predevelopmental Fiction
1

TWO
David Copperfield:
"The Prismatic Hues of Memory"
33

THREE
David Copperfield
and the Aesthetics of Education
73

FOUR
Great Expectations
and the Fictions of the Future
115

FIVE
"A Cobweb Meant Expectations":
Pip and the Act of Confession
159

CONCLUSION
Dickens and the Art of Confession
179

APPENDIX
Confidence Game:
Oliver Twist, A Child's History,
and the Failure of Autobiography
189

Bibliography
207

Index
215

Acknowledgments

Many people helped me with this book—directly and indirectly, wittingly and unwittingly. Among them are M. H. Abrams, Jonathan Bishop, George Ford, Robert Garis, Richard Gollin, Bruce Johnson, James R. Kincaid, Catherine Maitland Jones, Mary Livingston, Carey McIntosh, J. Hillis Miller, Roger Porter, Edgar Rosenberg, Leroy Searle, David Tarbet, and Deborah Thomas Westburg. Special thanks go to students, over the years, in my preceptorial, "Literature and Growing Up." I was assisted at one point by a faculty summer research grant from the University of Rochester.

The Appendix appeared in somewhat briefer form in *Studies in the Novel* (Spring 1974) and is reprinted with the editors' permission.

Barry Westburg
Adelaide, South Australia

INTRODUCTION

The Confessional Trilogy

> *To have been young, and then to grow older, and finally to die is a very mediocre form of human existence; this belongs to every animal. But the unification of the different stages of life ... is the task set for human beings.*
> Kierkegaard, Concluding Unscientific Postscript

In Kierkegaard's view human beings must understand time as growth, and growth in turn as structure—that is, as a system of stages which, while remaining distinct enough in themselves, comprise a whole course of life. This differentiated whole we might call the truth of a life, as traditionally explored in confessional literature. This truth does not rest in the single fact, as for instance in the good or evil deed, or there would be no confessional literature, only a form of notation in which deeds are evaluated, if at all, by preexisting norms. Confession, typically written as a self-conscious narrative of personal development, reveals the system of truth, where events acquire significance by relation to one another and to the constellation of events forming the whole of a life. Confessional truth, from this standpoint, is a relational, not a normative construct. Like many other nineteenth-century writers, Charles Dickens would have agreed with Kierkegaard's notion of the need for seeking unity in individual life, a structural unity which, particularly in the form of a self-conscious developmental narrative, takes time and growth fully into account. Dickens was evidently more interested in this kind of personal truth than in inherited cultural truths. And of course he was more interested in gaining a human perspective on events than in contemplating the banal successiveness of an existence without perspective at all. Every novel he wrote deals in some fashion, of course, with time as growth (or as non-growth) and sketches out portions of life-histories, though in only three works did he ever penetrate deeply enough into the significance of individual stages, or treat thoroughly enough the connections of the various stages in the life of one character, to offer us the truth of a whole life in the way that more recognizably confessional writings do. But the three works where Dickens does become most markedly confessional are among his very best. This suggests that confession (in a general sense, as well as in more specific senses) was one of his central projects. Three major confessional novels, finished at approximately the beginning, middle, and end of Dickens's career— *Oliver Twist* (1838), *David Copperfield* (1850), and *Great Expectations* (1861)—are radical probes into growth, time, and life-structure and deserve study together as keystones of Dickens's creativity.

Two of these novels, *Copperfield* and *Great Expectations,* are pseudo-autobiographical narratives of personal development and deal with virtually the whole range of growth, from childhood to adulthood. The autobiographical pretense, along with the developmental emphasis, adequately attests to the confessional burden of these novels. Indeed, the reflexive first-person narrative stance is an obvious confessional marker by itself. There is some point to thinking of these novels as Dickens's own confessions, as long as we do not take the unwarranted step of thinking that, because these are pseudo-autobiographical, first-person, and developmental, they are also disguised autobiographies of Dickens himself. Goethe claimed that all of his own works were fragments of one Great Confession, and thus gave currency to the notion that every writer's every work is somehow confessional (which may be true but not interesting). Unfortunately, some readers of literature ignore a certain distinction between autobiography and confession lurking in claims like Goethe's. For it is—or has been—a common enough belief that literary works are disguised *autobiography,* which is a much more troublesome position to defend than that they are variants or portions of *confession.* Confession can be autobiographical, as in *Dichtung und Wahrheit,* or it can be fictional, as in *Wilhelm Meister,* though one could make a good case that confession in the form of a developmental fiction is more effective than autobiography in transmitting the truth of a life in terms of total structure—which is what interested Kierkegaard and many novelists, including Dickens.

The Confessional Trilogy

Certainly, confession as pseudo-autobiography made possible sharp focus on imaginative programs that were important to Dickens, as the novels themselves testify. In working these programs through, Dickens may have accomplished what many men hope to succeed at in their direct autobiographies. The excursion into fiction no doubt offered Dickens the chance to see things steadily and whole; otherwise perhaps he would not have bothered to write at all. But the study of his confessional novels is not significantly furthered by appeals to either the supposed autobiography or the biography of Dickens, unless admittedly at the level of speculation. Shortly before writing *Copperfield* Dickens tried to write actual autobiography but could not go through with it. This might be one of a few significant facts. Nevertheless, the important issues reveal themselves in fiction as structures of events that are significant to everybody: the author, fictional character, and, no doubt, reader. Thus one of the ways Dickens could deal with, say, a purely personal dissatisfaction would be to pass beyond the content and occasions of his own problem and to derive confessional gratifications rather more fully from fictional structure than from autobiographical fact. He could represent Pip's dissatisfaction so that both he and Pip shared a common structure, and not the mere occasions, of dissatisfaction. Dickens evidently did not need to write autobiography; he could instead write confessional narratives of development in which the perspective on growth and time widens, by successive acts of discrimination and inter-reference, into a fictional image of an individual's truth of life.

Of course it is not possible to speak unequivocally of fiction writing as a form of confession. The act of writing fiction introduces some ambiguity into confessional projects. First-person fictions are impersonations; impersonation is a form of deception or lying; and lying does not seem to accord well with confession—not unless we recall that Saint Paul was willing to believe Epimenides the Cretan's affirmation that "all Cretans are liars." Epimenides' truth is formal, not absolute. In absolute terms, perhaps, all men, like Cretans, are liars, and we must not believe them even when they say they lie. But formal truth has scant relation to absolute truth and can be attained by liars, or at least divined by those who are good at listening to liars. Epimenides did not say "I lie." He was not that close to his confession. He was not autobiographical. "All Cretans are liars" gains its truth, gained Saint Paul's assent, by its laconic, artful distance from the speaker. In order to get away with saying "they (Cretans) are liars" Epimenides had to impersonate a truth-teller and let this alterego speak as he could only paradoxically speak in his own person. By choosing to believe Epimenides, Saint Paul respected a form of imaginary construction, a mode of impersonation. The same considerations held for Dickens. He wrote three confessional novels, each situated at a progressively greater distance from himself as speaker. The requirement of truth-at-a-distance helps explain why Dickens had to write as many as three novels in order to realize a project that might be supposed to need only one text. The existence of three texts implies both failure and success, both the compulsive repetition and the strategic renewal of a single creative act. Dickensian confession began as something literal, a deceptive approximation to actual autobiography in *Oliver Twist* (see Appendix). Gradually Dickens advanced beyond this remarkable attempt to represent his own life in the form of an elaborate code towards an objective confession, a formalized truth attainable only at such a remove from the accidents of his own personality that the final work, *Great Expectations,* has the shimmer of pure aestheticist contrivance. This is an important shift of perspective in Dickens's work: a shift from representational, mimetic art to a kind of abstraction, an art of pure construction, an art of internal rather than external reference. Thus the confessional demand for self-distancing coincides with a shift in the aesthetics of these novels. A change in one feature entails change in others as well.

If we examine family resemblances and significant differences between and among these three confessional novels it becomes quite clear what Dickens's own discovery procedure in writing them was: He developed as a writer most radically each time he posed development itself as his theme. He developed by means of fruitful comparisons, resourceful transformations, and progressively apposite displacements of whatever stood at any moment of composition as the prior text in his own developmental canon. Some buried, personal "text" no doubt stood behind *Oliver Twist,* which later in turn became the pre-text for *David Copperfield,* which, in its turn, became the pretext for *Great Expectations.* The novels obviously are systematically

The Confessional Trilogy

related, so that it quite impoverishes them simply to study each in isolation, as has so often been done. For Dickens, meaning is partially a product of the very differences that hold among his novels. The whole process of movement in them from autobiographical imitation to aesthetic revelation is one of progressive displacements. Each work preys upon, in order to deconstruct, its immediate predecessor in the confessional series. And each is like a juncture or crisis in the process of growth itself—a liminal work, a place where boundary-problems get solved by the creation of new perspectives, new orientations. Viewing Dickens's confessional novels this way, we can begin to grasp his confessional history as a series of forms and functions. What was once living and functional in an earlier work becomes an object, a kind of fictional solid, to be decomposed so that a newer function appears.

Dickens initially transforms what are actually two pre-texts—his own life story and eighteenth-century picaresque narrative—into *Oliver Twist*. *Copperfield* displaces this initial naive interest, divided between life in general and art, with a new interest in a single life as creative, the artist's life. The aesthetic education of David is a much more intelligible theme than the vague kind of growing up postulated at the end of *Oliver Twist*. An admirable series of modulations at the opening of *Copperfield* leads us from an unthematic, global approach to life-experience into the artist theme proper. Here we can tangibly feel Dickens decomposing his original subject, inherited from *Oliver Twist*, in favor of a new line of investigation that leads away from the details (the nonartistic details) of his own life, as if he had discovered that the representation of general life is not interesting for its own sake, but that, for those who value the creative process enough to write or read novels, the growth of an artist is a worthy theme. But next, in *Great Expectations,* the artist's life is decomposed in favor of the activity of art itself. What comes into the foreground is not the artist's life but the behavior of the artwork. Pip lives not as a writer of novels; he lives as an inhabitant of novels; he is somebody written up. *Great Expectations* confesses itself as a fiction about fiction-making, and in this sense it is self-critical. It parades its own irreality, confides its intricate though morally neutral abstractness (abstract partly in the sense that it lacks meaningful reference to the real world). Pip's life story, which transforms David's, is in turn the pre-text for this final self-commentary, the end of a long line of Dickensian self-interpretations. Here pre-text and the interpretation of it appear simultaneously in the same work. If I am right in drawing this conclusion, we can place *Great Expectations* near the beginning of a great modernist tradition—embracing Flaubert, Proust, James, and, more recently, Jorge Borges, John Barth, and Vladimir Nabokov—which affirms that the true ethical dimension of fiction derives from the ability of narrative to demystify itself by means of self-commentary. *Great Expectations* exposes the fiction-making process to its readers; in this sense it is Dickens's confession extrapolated from the level of moralizing ethics, personal experience, and worldly wisdom to that of self-conscious aesthetic experience.

Dickens's strategy of revising and thus transforming his developmental narratives is similar to a process shown in individual novels. For each novel in some fashion deals with a protagonist who needs to transcend his earlier life and to meet new conditions of living with a changed outlook. Each protagonist interprets his own progress (whether he is looking at it from the position of grown-up narrator or whether he is still in the process of growing up when he thus views it) by means of differential judgments—that is, he interprets his life dynamically and structurally. Most important, this form of interpretation institutes time itself as the ground of meaning—whether this be the time we see at work in Dickens's career, wherein he indulged the luxury of three narratives about the same problem; the time which the narrator uses to gain a perspective on himself as hero; or the time in which the hero gains a reflexive vision of his own experiences while he is actually growing up. In fact, to grasp the series of structurings both among and within these novels means as well to perceive an entire system of fictional time much more vividly than is normally possible. Time is a construct just as fiction is a construct, and study of one presupposes study of the other: indeed, time, growth, identity, and fiction are mutually implicated in self-conscious developmental narratives, in confessional fictions.

In carrying out this kind of study, it is necessary to observe Dickens's own increasing emphasis on special kinds of developmental problems associated with the acts of fiction-making and fiction-

The Confessional Trilogy

consuming in themselves. The novels suggest he initially thought he could—by showing at length the role played by fictions in his protagonists' lives—find clues to his own identity as a maker of fictions. This meditation on fiction is a deepening theme in his works and led to the creation of a supreme fiction, *Great Expectations.* What I mean by the word *fiction* should, like many terms I use, become clearer only in my use of it; but generally I employ it in two ways: to refer to a broad range of things encountered, invented, or, more generally, experienced, by a character in a novel (visions, dreams, play-acting, deceptions, and so forth); and also, more narrowly, to refer to Dickens's novels themselves. But, since the progress of a Dickens hero is directly related, in the developmental narratives, to his discovery of, and judgments about, the illusoriness of what he once took to be real, there is a dynamics to the word *fiction* as used here. For the narrator-protagonist, real things perpetually become fictions, while fictions themselves can become real as useful tools, devices, constructs, enabling the hero to live and the narrator to write. This process embraces many of the entities that we, in everyday life, do not normally call fictions—such as legal procedures, special languages and dialects (thieves' argot, priestly cant, advertising slogans, journalistic jargon), sartorial fashions, class distinctions, social rituals, eroticism, good and evil, and even, as I suggested, time itself.

David, Pip, and even Oliver, to some extent, articulate for themselves a knowledge of life by means of progressive differentiations. In this manner the construction of what will be reality happens at the same time that fictions are discovered. Judgments about reality and fictiveness are not absolute, but relational and reciprocal. This diacritical process applies to identity-formation in general (what Jung called individuation) in these novels. Identity is the result of the differentiation of the character from his own body, from his world, from other people. He constructs an identity gradually out of acts that reveal, for instance, other people as outside, as beyond himself. Without this outside or beyond there can be no inside, no personal self. Identity is relationship. No I exists without its thou. Dickens even imagines a stage of growth (which I call "aestheticist" and "narcissist") in which a kind of simulacrum or false self plays the role of other person. This image, until repudiated as false, behaves as a transformer of identity. In the context of the education of the artist hero, this stage is of primary importance, since it brings to a focus symbol-making and fiction-using as such. Only by working out the meaning of his relation with himself and his symbols can the artist-hero move on to explore more or less unambiguously his relation with other people.

Even an apparent technical device, the assumption of the narrative "I," in these confessional narratives poses from the outset certain interlocking problems of personal relationships. There are several immediately implied relationships, all of which in their overlap offer the reader the impression of a total structured truth of a life: the narrator's relation with his imagined reader; the narrator's relation with himself as hero of events that have supposedly already occurred in his memorial past; the hero's relationship with others within that past; and so on, into relationships that include Dickens and his readers. No doubt it is significant that the number of relationships suggested by confessional fictions seems greater than that offered by actual autobiography. Where there is greater possibility of structure there is greater likelihood of ambiguity and of the need for interpretation. Nevertheless, interpretation of the central system of relationships, embracing the hero and his acquaintances, is obviously the most essential. Within this central system the confessional project explicitly figures large. For instance, in *Great Expectations* the main characters use confession to establish intimacy with one another. The closeness they achieve in confessing is a function of the very differences among them that are the subject of their confessions. This kind of confession could almost be defined as speech in which the speaker uses the account of his problematical differences and past deviations to transform and deepen his relations with other people who choose to listen and absolve. The three novels were all along leading up to such acts. The novels themselves, though, confess something which, as I have suggested, is quite distinct from the characters' confessions.

The distinction between what the characters' behavior means among themselves and what the novels mean as a whole is quite important to bear in mind. Dickens gradually abandoned fiction that was mimetic and moralizing in favor of artificial, abstract, and non-moralizing fiction. This change as it appears in the area of character-psychology is most interesting. When he began creating his characters, at the time of *Pickwick* and *Oliver Twist,* Dickens appears to have been trying to represent actual human identities (sometimes, in coded form, his own). But later, at several important points, using characters who display surprising mental characteristics, he implies a distinction between real human psychology and what Ortega later called "imaginary psychology."[1] The freedom to do this was accorded by the initial strategy of first-person narration, for such narration when applied to time and growth opens up vast possibilities in the area of psychological construction. Almost anything might be predicated of a narrating subject, and psychological realism, even if such a thing were possible, is hardly necessary. Furthermore, as if to open up even more possibilities of imaginary construction, Dickens took as his main subject two kinds of mind which could be explored differentially: the child's and the criminal's. Both of these creatures as usable in fiction are remote in quite interesting ways from the sphere of everyday consciousness that might serve a more forthrightly mimetic artist as a source of invention. Child and criminal are alien enough to an artist to offer him rare opportunities for the improvisation of identity. It is interesting to see what use Dickens makes of this freedom, when employing child and criminal as speculative instruments of confessional art. The Dickens child and criminal might in some respects be derived from prior literary images, but the inherited images have been transformed into characters with special kinds of self-consciousness, unique ways of experiencing time and change, and distinctive forms of relationships with other characters of their world.

Dickens's various confessional strategies, whether they involve handling of point of view, characterization, or theme, all depend ultimately on a general technique of progressive differentiation which, in the course of his career, produced quite elegant results. For over twenty-three years, the time between the writing of *Oliver Twist* and *Great Expectations,* Dickens maintained a remarkable creative continuity with respect to the problems of time, growth, fiction, and identity. But in the overlap of these problems and themes it might be difficult to identify the significant trends in Dickens's art without directing analysis rather pointedly to his treatment of time at the level of an invented developmental psychology. At this level, time is more than a fictional event; it appears as an organized notion—a notion systematic enough to be regarded as a psychological theory of time, though the "theory" is mainly expressed in images and actions rather than in purely discursive terms. The whole theory of time is central to the confessional novels and plays an important role elsewhere. It was constructed and made gradually explicit through the usual differential procedure. The contrast of child and criminal in *Oliver Twist* elicits its rudiments, though the theory does not emerge clearly until past, present, and future are examined, in *Copperfield,* as mutually dependent aspects of a total life-time. At the level of psychology this total life-time is the time of memory, perception, and imagination— or, to render it more functionally, the time of remembering, perceiving, and imagining. Each of Dickens's three confessional protagonists lives this time in a related, but distinctively weighted fashion. *Oliver Twist* emphasizes eternity and a present of muddled, discontinuous perceiving, *Copperfield* emphasizes the problems of remembering, while *Great Expectations* emphasizes the problems of imagining. But no matter how it is weighted, in terms of psychological time, the confessional narrative written by Dickens seeks to embrace all functions of time and manages to formulate appropriate laws for the whole system. And while the whole system of time in Dickens is, indirectly and teleologically speaking, a theory of the imagination, more directly and genetically speaking, it is foremost a theory of memory. This theory of memory helps us understand the significance of Dickens's entire confessional-developmental project.

Notes

1. "There exists in psychology, just as in mathematics, an evidence a priori. Because of this imaginary construction in either field is possible.... Because this is not recognized the psychology in a novel is taken to be identical with that of real life, and it is assumed that the author can do nothing but copy reality. So coarse a reasoning lies at the bottom of what is currently called 'realism.' " José Ortega y Gasset, "Notes on the Novel," in *The Dehumanization of Art and Other Writings on Art and Culture* (Garden City, N.Y.: Anchor Books, 1956), p. 94.

The Confessional Fictions of Charles Dickens

"Oliver Asking for More." From *Oliver Twist*.

ONE

Oliver Twist:
A Predevelopmental Fiction

In *Oliver Twist,* the problems of time, growth, fiction, and identity appear mainly in contrast to the other two confessional novels. *Copperfield* and *Great Expectations,* both genuine developmental novels, transform notions first projected in *Oliver Twist,* which hindsight prompts us to examine less as work in itself than as a predevelopmental fiction. The topics appropriate to the study of this novel will prove useful in studying the other two. *Oliver Twist* is a curious exercise in double-think in that it mixes static (non-developmental) and developmental modes of treating experience and of viewing it ethically. But the main interest the novel has for us here is in those features that betray, much more than *Pickwick* does, the beginnings of Dickens's developmental thinking, and more specifically, the beginnings of his psychological treatment of time.

I. The Child Without Qualities

Childhood is the starting point of Dickens's temporal imagination. His second novel, *Oliver Twist,* is the first English novel of any stature to take a child as its protagonist.[1] Whereas earlier English novels had given only passing attention, if any, to childhood, this one deals with it almost exclusively. This is an important step in the history of the fictional treatment of time, growth, and identity. Dickens derives his entire imaginative scheme of narrative time from the notion of childhood first projected in *Oliver Twist.* Here he enters relatively unexplored territory, territory which had been entered only a few decades earlier, for the first time extensively, in the poetry of Blake and Wordsworth. The discovery of childhood made possible the developmental novel as we know it today; for the notion that an individual's life is a history, a course of development, a process of transition from one stage to another (childhood to adulthood), could not arise without a rather extensive imaginative exploration of childhood.

Historically speaking, the widening of the temporal range of the novel to include childhood was partly the result of an attitude that had begun to form in the eighteenth century. "Nature wants children to be children before they are men. If we deliberately depart from this order we shall get premature fruits which are neither ripe nor well flavoured and which soon decay.... Childhood has ways of seeing, thinking, and feeling peculiar to itself: nothing can be more foolish than to substitute our ways for them."[2] When Rousseau wrote this he was flying in the face of the assumptions of most people of his period, both on the Continent and in England. The common assumption was that children virtually did not exist except to the extent that they happened to display adult characteristics. Childhood itself was not really a time of life. Portraits of earlier times show children dressed in adult costume, with heads and hands shaped to adult proportions, and eyes gleaming with skeptical adult intelligence.[3] The difference between children and adults was assumed to be quantitative; children were seen as scaled-down adults. This is evident, for example, in the notion of the homunculus that is bandied about in *Tristram Shandy:* this tiny creature, shaped like an adult being, swims in the seminal fluids and later grows up merely by expanding. This linear, quantitative notion of growth seems to have prevailed in the thought of men living before the organic notions of the late eighteenth century (eventually articulated, in England, by Coleridge in the early nineteenth century) began to replace mechanical models of life. Certainly, though, childhood took on much of its importance, for the nineteenth century, because it lay at the beginning of life; for in the midst of rapidly changing times people began to assume, as Carlyle said, that "in every phenomenon the beginning remains always the most notable moment."[4] The beginning remains *always.*

In that it offers an extended serious treatment of a child's life,

A Predevelopmental Fiction

Oliver Twist is a pioneering book. In other respects, though, it clings to narrative conventions so much as to appear anachronistic in form and meaning. Its image of life in time is almost as static as that in *Tom Jones*.[5] *Oliver Twist* represents—or projects—childhood at some length, but only hints at its evolutionary, temporal possibilities. Childhood has meaning as a state in itself but the process of growing up means very little. The novel shows us a picture rather than a process, being rather than becoming, the spectacle of something fixed and permanent rather than the growth of something new and changeable. The prevailing stasis implies a tendency to think of identity in a fictive mode appropriate to the authors of *The Vicar of Wakefield* and *Roderick Random,* who assume that the world is more stable than Dickens's could have been. Nevertheless, Dickens does manage to touch on developmental motifs—and eventually he became foremost among nineteenth-century writers who scrapped static fictions of identity.

Oliver Twist begins, at least, with the birth of a child, and thus seems to promise a treatment of the process of growing up, of the complexities that arise in an individual who changes in the midst of a time that represents both problem and possibility. Here is the beginning:

> Among other public buildings in a certain town, which for many reasons it will be prudent to refrain from mentioning, and to which I will assign no fictitious name, there is one anciently common to most such towns, great or small: to wit, a workhouse; and in this workhouse was born: on a day and a date which I need not trouble myself to repeat, inasmuch as it can be of no possible consequence to the reader, in this stage of the business at all events: the item of mortality whose name is prefixed to the head of this chapter. (1)

Images of beginnings often engage Dickens's imagination profoundly, so that sometimes we can gain interpretive leverage by considering the way he uses them in *Oliver Twist, David Copperfield, Great Expectations,* and elsewhere. Dickens's large-scale "personal histories" (his first-person developmental novels) are preoccupied (even obsessed) with beginnings, and whatever unity a narrator can see in his life is the result as much of his attempt to encompass beginnings as of his resolve to project a future. With Oliver's beginning, however, we sense right away how much of a blank it is—so much a blank that the hero could never be called upon to know it as his own. This is a beginning accessible neither to remembrance nor to any other act of imagining or perceiving. The hero has, at first, no location, no ancestors, no authentic name. The absence of locating coordinates hints that his identity is not a function of his temporality or spatiality. As for his name, a matter of great significance, of course, in developmental fictions, it is soon to be simply imposed upon him according to the "alphabetical" routine of the beadle. Oliver, "half-baptized," does not own his name.

What we get at the very first, in this void, is only the disembodied, normative, narrative voice, busy erecting a show of relations between itself and its audience, itself and its materials. James R. Kincaid has observed, in his excellent analysis of this paragraph, that it "seems to have been written by the head of the Circumlocution Office," and contains "some highly facetious banter about death and nothingness."[6] For the time being there is no being, only emptiness waiting to be filled by more than words. Oliver's childhood, too, is a time of waiting for proper identification. The grotesque Cruikshank illustration, "Oliver asking for more," makes visible the blankness of the character. Initially, Oliver is an aboriginal "something" with no voice and no right to speak; the narrator is a "nothing" with a privileged voice like that which calls into existence "the first ray of light which illumines the gloom" and "obscurity" of the origins of "the public career of the immortal Pickwick" (1). In *Pickwick Papers* that original voice separates light from darkness and throws light on subsequent events. The voice that begins *Oliver Twist*, on the other hand, appears as if to create darkness only.[7]

To the extent that Oliver does exist he is a thing, a "millstone" around the parish neck, an "item of mortality," "badged and ticketed." The sinister, meandering sentence that begins the novel establishes the ontological priority of the workhouse, which seems to displace Oliver's parentage (his real mother is not mentioned until later). Human origins for Oliver are being ironically undervalued, and he apparently issues from some nonhuman substratum of the world. In the Dickens world, reification and dehumanization—which we find virtually everywhere, but never more significantly than as a

A Predevelopmental Fiction

theme in the developmental novels—are among the major horrors of life. (The opposite horror, of flux and change, plays a large part, too, though not in *Oliver Twist.*) At any rate, the emptiness at the beginning of *Oliver Twist* is a "compositional" void, created with an eye to the demands of narrative strategy (a strategy the narrator takes pains to point out). This is not the beginning of Oliver so much as the beginning of a story; Oliver will shed his thinghood and symbolically gain his limited identity after he has been employed for a time as an occasion for a series of adventures. Dickensian narration is already moving in the direction of abstraction, geometry, interplay of forms—for far above the hero is a layer of expository speech in which we detect the activity of an intellect that Oliver can never know about. The "item of mortality" and the narrator's disembodied intelligence will never meet. This is important, because it means that two fictional identities have been invented, neither of which separately can arrive at the relational knowledge so essential to forming the truth of life. We have an all-knowing narrator who cannot effect anything but narration and an all-suffering hero who cannot know why he suffers. By comparison with the later developmental novels this division of function seems needless. The narrator lacks the insight that is forged out of the urgencies of action's partial blindness, while the hero lacks the reflective distance from action that teaches how temporary suffering might be. Both are incapable of putting any two things, ideas or actions, together. Narrator and actor remain stuck in their respective categories, whereas crossing the categories would help lead to a sense of totality.

II. Dickensian Adventure

What holds true for the relation between narrator and hero holds true as well for the hero's relation to himself; although Dickens does try to tie Oliver's experiences together at a few points, for the most part he remains fragmented, as the novel's full title suggests. In the earliest bound edition of *Oliver Twist* (1838), the subtitle was *The Parish Boy's Progress.* In all British editions after 1846 that Dickens had a hand in preparing, the title was changed to *The Adventures of Oliver Twist.*[8] His decision to use "adventure" rather than "progress" in the later editions suggests that Dickens (a man who was, as we know, exceedingly fussy about the titles he gave his books) drew a distinction between the two words, thus defining two basic modes of representing experience. The notion of progress suggests that a character can become something different from what he was at the beginning, as presumably in Bunyan's allegory, which was no doubt in Dickens's mind when he was originally concocting his title.[9] But the conception of life as adventure (as chance encounter, for example) implies that change, real change, is not an issue. Adventures we can view as events that are always in a suspended present, and not productive, necessarily, of long-term effects; when an adventure is over it is simply time for another one. Were we to discover inner relationships (that is to say, an inherent structure) between what a novelist has designated as adventures, we would probably ourselves choose to speak not of adventures but of a kind of continuous experience—such as, indeed, a progress or a decline and fall. Where there is no continuity, or where, more emphatically, there is simply unresolved discontinuity, we can speak of "adventure" or—as we say nowadays, generically—"picaresque."[10] Picaresque presents the conventional static identity characteristically found in the fictions of Dickens's predecessors in the eighteenth century.

Noncontinuity and discontinuity appear typically in picaresque fictions, where action is often a string of adventures and the basic logic tends to be an external logic dictated by compositional strategies of contrast, variety, and the like. For Oliver Twist, life is a series of discontinuous adventures, in that one moment of action usually cancels a previous one utterly. There is little sign that the hero's consciousness can do anything to connect events to one another, though of course the narrator can articulate everything quite neatly. This discontinuity is important to bear in mind when comparing *Oliver Twist* to large-scale developmental novels. Like many a picaresque hero Oliver takes away from almost every adventure little more than what he brought to it. The almost anecdotal, atomistic experiences of Oliver suggest the impossibility of continuous character development, life being merely "one thing after another," a pure succession; banal, by Dickens's time, as a temporal image.

For Oliver, events have no direction: something he seeks to es-

A Predevelopmental Fiction

cape in his immediate situation drives him into an obscure future—a future rarely probed by imagination, a future which reveals itself as it becomes transformed haphazardly into a mere succession of events surprising to the hero. Temporally, Oliver is thus little more than a silhouette. This impression derives partly, of course, from the absence of an inner view of Oliver. We cannot intimately and continuously observe a self either perceiving events as they happen or directing its attention toward past and future. A fiction of growth, of becoming, would imply a temporal perspective in which past and future would be differentiated as dimensions of the self. Such a fiction would almost by necessity have to offer, more continuously than in *Oliver Twist,* a view of the inside, as well as of the outside, of the central character.

The absence of spatial order is another feature of the fragmentary, disordered quality of Oliver's experience. Space, for Oliver, is the space of the open road and a series of separate enclosures (shelters, prisons), few of which he can relate topographically to one another. London, which the narrator can trace so expertly,[11] is for the boy a "labyrinth." When one thinks of the almost geometrical clarity with which the spatial world is laid out for David and Pip, the disorder of Oliver's seems remarkable. Sometimes we are shown Oliver's inner life, but rarely do we see in this innerness any sign of his making sense of the world by discovering the relationships of things. "He was . . . much confused by the earnest cunning of Fagin's looks" (20). "Hosts of bewildering and confused ideas came crowding on his mind" (28). "Oliver was in a flutter of agitation and uncertainty which deprived him of the power of collecting his thoughts, and almost of speech" (51).[12]

Partly, Oliver's bewilderment derives from the dichotomy in his experience between the two radically different worlds he comes to inhabit. There is seemingly no connection between them; they are as different as being and nothingness so far as Oliver is concerned. Thus he is incapable of taking anything he learns from one of the worlds into the next. And so experience does not accumulate. Steven Marcus notes that "suffering has no consequences in the character of the child."[13] The static notion we get of Oliver's character might have something to do with the pecularity of Dickens's own outlook, early in his career, regarding the relation (or nonrelation) of the underworld of criminality to the overworld of innocence. "It was principally the idea of the two masses of good and evil that held me fast and stifled me," wrote Saint Augustine in the *Confessions,* and the same is evidently true for Dickens, who hypostasizes two such masses in *Oliver Twist*—the world of the thieves and that of the Good People, the night-world and the day-world.[14] This is essentially a moral compartmentalization, but it is realized in almost every concrete aspect of life. Thieves have a language different from that of the Good People, different dress, different manners, and they occupy a different region of the world. In the course of the novel Oliver twice descends into the Inferno of thieves and rises to the Paradise of the Brownlow-Maylie world. Whenever he passes from one to the other there is a sudden and complete change. Oliver is a creature of Brownlow; he leaves on an errand, turns a wrong corner, and suddenly falls into the hands of Fagin's accomplices. The change is so rapid as to bewilder Oliver: "Stupefied by the blows and the suddenness of the attack; terrified by the fierce growling of the dog ... what could one poor child do! ... In another moment, he was dragged into a labyrinth of narrow courts: and forced along them, at a pace which rendered the few cries he dared to give utterance to, wholly unintelligible" (15).

Oliver's consciousness does not confront a new world in terms of its experience of a previous one; Oliver simply dies to his prior environment and is reborn (with an appropriate change of clothing) into a new one. This static dualism is alien to any systematic notions of personal growth. Evidently, in order to depict growth one must show structure—the connectedness, for some consciousness, of all experience, so that even the experience of a strange reality can be one more event, preferably a significant event, in a process viewed as monistic and dialectical. With a monistic view, conflict, encounter, and engagement are all parts of a process that is whole but temporarily divided within itself. Obviously, an effective strategy would be to abandon the omniscient narrator and to "descend" to first-person narration, where the narrator is in the world and yet can attempt to contain it in his words. Dickens tried this later. One of the results was a more complex delineation of moral issues; good and evil, insofar as

III. Experiential Order Versus Plotted Order

There is one occasion, important if viewed in the light of the later developmental novels, when we see the possibility of a real orientation for Oliver, when we see him at least momentarily begin to tie his experiences together. What is most important for us to notice is Dickens's creation of a temporally complex, because recursive, structure. After Monks (Oliver's scheming half-brother) has been apprehended by Mr. Brownlow, and Oliver is taken back by carriage to the town of his birth, the boy sees again his earliest surroundings, this time by travelling in the opposite direction over the old roads; he views again the once forbidding buildings, now "smaller and less imposing in appearance than he remembered" and "somehow fallen off in grandeur and in size" (51). "The whole current of his recollections ran back to old times" (51). But this orientation is only momentary, and, in this repetition and reversal, Oliver is freed forever from the darkness of that anonymous town, which had been passed off on him as "origin" at the beginning of his life. Fittingly, Oliver's true parentage is revealed upon his return to this town of spurious origins. At the "chief hotel," a building he had never entered before, he finds he is not of the town, that he has human origins, and for both Rose and Oliver "a father, sister, and mother" are "gained, and lost, in that one moment" (51). Instead of being a creature born of the mud and fog—in the manuscript Dickens had at first named the town "Mudfog"[16] (his favorite fictional name for Chatham)—instead of coming out of the nonhuman earth, and thus being unfit for the society of Brownlow and the Maylies, Oliver can repudiate all that is inferior on the Chain of Being (including the "devil" Fagin and the "wild beast" Sikes). He must undergo the psychically significant experience of return in order to achieve all this. This return, seen here in Dickens's favorite image of the river of life[17] as a reversal of the current, is an "orientative" return depicted again in both *Copperfield* and *Great Expectations,* where return is structurally important.

In spite of the typical disorder of events for Oliver (except for the above occasion), there is order on another level, as revealed notably in the two major "chance" occurrences of the novel.[18] Oliver, taken as a suspect in the theft of a handkerchief, accidentally meets Mr. Brownlow, who "happens" to have been his father's closest friend. And Rose Maylie, whom Oliver also meets accidentally, following the second crime, happens to be his aunt. Obviously there is a force at work in the novel that is neither true happenstance nor normal causality. From the vantage point of anyone in the novel, this series of chiming events could be attributed to Providence—as Mr. Brownlow says, the events reveal a "stronger hand than chance" (49). But from the reader's standpoint this orderly feature of the novel has different implications.

Oliver lives a providential myth; this myth is the traditional discovery story (we see it classically, for example, in *Tom Jones* and find it parodied in *Great Expectations*) in which the hero, bastard and orphan, after first undergoing various trials, discovers his true parentage and at that time comes into his long-delayed inheritance. Such a story expresses a definitely static notion of human existence. Any plot selected for such a story has special structural implications, as well. For instance, Dickens's discovery plot is definitely biased "against" time. Dickens's time-scheme is actually a static design which implies that there is no "real" time in the sense that Bergson defines it. Temporality, for Bergson, is antithetical to discovery—if we mean by discovery "the uncovering of what was *there* but hidden all along." Time is, as Bergson says, "invention or it is nothing at all."[19]

A discovery plot is appropriate to what Edwin Muir calls the "novel of character." In such a novel, he says, "the action [does not] spring from an inner development, from a spiritual change in the characters. It need not show us any new quality in them.... All it need do is to bring out their various attributes, which were there at the beginning: for these characters are almost static ... the alteration they undergo is less a temporal one than an unfolding in a continuously widening present. Their weaknesses, their vanities, their foibles, they possess from the beginning and never lose to the end; and what actually does change is not these, but our knowledge of them."[20]

At the moment we discover Oliver's real origins everything is granted that was withheld before by the narrator. The hero "becomes" what he had secretly been all along, there being no dynamic, continuous process of passage leading him from his original apparent nothingness to the full being (in accord with the symbolism of inheritance) we see him acquire at the end. There is no temporal depth. Oliver is an empty vessel given its shape at the moment of manufacture; it gets scratched and buffeted a bit in the course of its adventures but never changes shape; at last the rarity of its make is discovered, and it is filled with the precious things it was designed to hold. A human being, fixed in all essentials of character, is shown moving about in space, and only this movement—for instance from country to city and from the city, finally, to the country—is what "happens." This is a form of picaresque novel—not a *Bildungsroman*—in sum, a novel in which space is essential, time accidental. Oliver does not need time in which to become what he already is; the narrator needs only a portion of narrative time in which to unfold his story.

IV. Static Education

"I wished to shew, in little Oliver," Dickens said in "The Author's Preface to the Third Edition," "the principle of Good surviving through every adverse circumstance, and triumphing at last." In short, this is a study of opacity, of the immunity of character to time. Oliver's basic equipment is similar to Tom Jones's goodness of heart, which age cannot wither nor thieves break in to steal.

> "I saw it was not easy to train him to the business," replied the Jew; "he was not like other boys in the same circumstances."
> "Curse him, no!" muttered the man, "or he would have been a thief long ago." (26)

Monks and Fagin are realizing here what the narrator pointed out some time before, that "nature or inheritance had implanted a good sturdy spirit in Oliver's breast" (2).

Not only is Oliver's nature present (but temporarily invisible) at his birth, there is also a suggestion in this novel, as J. Hillis Miller has pointed out, that Oliver had an existence prior to his earthly one.[21]

This can be glimpsed in the dim sensations he has of some transcendent world of being. When Rose's tears fell on his forehead:

> The boy stirred, and smiled in his sleep, as though these marks of pity and compassion had awakened some pleasant dream of a love and affection he had never known; as a strain of gentle music, or the rippling of water in a silent place, or the odour of a flower, or even the mention of a familiar word, will sometimes call up sudden dim remembrances of scenes that never were, in this life ... and which some brief memory of a happier existence, long gone by, would seem to have awakened. (30)

In this passage, as well as in others like it[22] (there are several in *The Old Curiosity Shop,* as well), we discover a super-memory which suggests a time-transcending identity reaching into eternity. If identity is really anchored beyond time, then of course the temporal world dwindles in importance. And how does one think about growth and becoming when there seems to be an assurance of eternal being?

A final indication of a permanence of Oliver's identity is at the conclusion, where Mr. Brownlow is shown providing an education for Oliver. With this so-called education Oliver could not change in any significant way; it simply increases his knowledge. Though at first his head had been empty of the general knowledge that furnishes out a gentleman, by the end of the novel he is on his way to stocking his mind with the "stores" of matter that Mr. Brownlow is pleased to put into it:

> How Mr. Brownlow went on, from day to day, filling the mind of his adopted child with stores of knowledge, and becoming attached to him, more and more, as his nature developed itself, and shewed the thriving seeds of all he wished him to become—how he traced in him new traits of his early friend, that awakened in his own bosom old remembrances, melancholy and yet sweet and soothing—how the two orphans, tried by adversity, remembered its lessons in mercy to others, and mutual love, and fervent thanks to Him who had protected and preserved them—these are all matters which need not to be told. (53)

The notion of education is thoroughly conservative and static. The boy is formed on the lines of his father and is, curiously enough, a "living copy" of his mother, as well: "The eyes, the head, the mouth; every feature was the same" (12). Oliver is completely in the hands of his mentor, becoming just what Brownlow wishes him to become—

that is, what he has virtually been all along, the avatar of his father. The cultural tradition, as he absorbs it, will prepare the initiate for living in the future, because the future will in essential respects resemble the ancestral past (before it was troubled by the vapors of error and crime), just as Oliver is and will be like his father. At the end of a book about a child we would expect to see something new on the horizon, some intimation of change instead of reenactment, even if this reenactment will presumably be of the best that has been. The orphans spend their days conning the "lessons" of what Dickens, elsewhere, in a letter to Maria Beadnell, called "the changeless Past."[23] Meanwhile the guardian is busy with his remembrances and his visions of repetition. In the midst of this looking backward, the survivors (that is what they are) thank God for their "preservation." The novel sees the permanent as having more reality than the changing and implies that what is changing is irrelevant to human nature. Self is a constant; education does not create new forms of consciousness in Oliver but only activates latent ones, "just as," says Bergson in a highly appropriate simile, "on the night of a fête we light up one by one the rows of gas-jets which already outline the shape of some building."[24]

V. Education Through Crisis

Dickens's use in fiction of what is now so familiar to us (thanks to the writings of Erik Erikson) as identity crisis transforms the narrative of pure adventure, picaresque, into narrative of the divided self, where the confessional "I" must face as its identity problem the need for finding a relation between the "before" and "after" of the initially divisive experience. To invent crisis is to discover psychic dividedness, which leads to the novel configurations of psychological time that contribute so much to the texture and meaning of developmental fictions. This complex, nuanced time gives developmental narrative its layers, its depth; by comparison picaresque can seem flat, linear, univocal.

Mr. Brownlow's successful "education" of Oliver has as its counterpart in the underworld Fagin's unsuccessful attempt to educate him. In spite of the failure of Fagin's pedagogy, certain things meanwhile happen to Oliver that hint at a deeper initiation than ever life among Brownlows and Maylies (the Good People) could make possible; in fact, we can see, at one point, a sketch of an identity crisis. The implications remain buried, but obviously Dickens has begun to conceive of crisis, and in quite subtle terms.

Much of the suspense of the novel turns on the question of whether Oliver will become a thief; the possibility of this, at least, has to seem real. The possibility is suggested in the stipulation in his father's will that denies the boy his inheritance should he change and prove unworthy of his parentage. Edwin Leeford's legitimate son Edward had "premature bad passions," and, as well, had been "trained to hate" his father. There was thus some question about the perpetuation of worthiness. But to "mark his confidence" in the principle that like begets like, Edwin willed the bulk of his estate to his bastard son Oliver "only on the stipulation that in his minority he should never have stained his name with any public act of dishonour, meanness, cowardice, or wrong." Certainly, though, the boy "would share [Agnes's] gentle heart and noble nature" (51). The sequel proves the father right, but before then heredity cannot be taken entirely on faith; the boy must ring true when tested. The developmental novel shows passage, transformation, but this novel is designed to show simple endurance of trial. Leeford's will reflects the usual inheritance notions, which assume—or assumed—a symbolic transaction in which the essence of the parents passes on directly to the child.[25] In effect this is an ahistorical view; time and change do not exist; the past repeats itself in the present and will doubtless repeat itself in the future again. The special clause of the will also shows, however, some recognition of the possibility of change, and thus of truly developmental time. Dickens tries to have things two ways: Oliver's inheritance is a reward for trials undergone, temptations and evil resisted; but it is also a confirmation of what he was before any trials—a copy of his parents—and thus is not a reward but a rightful inheritance. He proves he is what he always was—which is what his parents were.

But in the course of his second "imprisonment" by Fagin, Oliver is exposed to the most serious of his trials. If he is going to change at all, Fagin's regimen will effect it. "Once let him feel that he is one of us; once fill his mind with the idea that he has been a thief; and he's ours!" says Fagin (19). If Oliver accepts the *idea* that he has been

A Predevelopmental Fiction

a thief, he will then be ready for crime—a sophisticated notion, indeed. If certain laws of relationship hold for Oliver's mind, he will come to define himself as the others around him both define themselves and seek to define him.

> The wily old Jew had the boy in his toils; and, having prepared his mind, by solitude and gloom, to prefer any society to the companionship of his own sad thoughts in such a dreary place, was now slowly instilling into his soul the poison which he hoped would blacken it, and change its hue forever. (18)

Dickens is beginning to envisage subtle aspects of transformation. Fagin recognizes a discontinuous rhythm of isolation and communion as necessary to radical character change. (Note, by the way, Dickens's imagery of the *"blackening* poison" and recall that the name of this evil character was borrowed by Dickens from Bob Fagin, who had worked with Dickens in the infamous *blacking* warehouse.) Isolation is especially important as Dickens shows again and again in many of the character changes in his other novels. Isolation is a crucial phase of the process of becoming, and the main form it takes in Dickens's novels is, of course, imprisonment. The importance of imprisonment to Dickens's imagination is well known, and such critics as A. O. J. Cockshut have given us something of a phenomenology of the prison,[26] as it was seen by Dickens; but no one has dwelt on the role of imprisonment in the whole process of psychic growth.[27]

It is in solitude that the imagination gets busy, as Fagin knows, so he leaves Oliver with what is meant to be an educational tract, "a history of the lives and trials of great criminals." What then ensues is of some interest, for we see the closest thing in the novel to a genuine educational crisis for Oliver, even though the outcome is not what Fagin anticipated.

> Here, he read of dreadful crimes that made the blood run cold; of secret murders that had been committed by the lonely wayside: and bodies hidden from the eye of man in deep pits and wells: which would not keep them down, deep as they were, but had yielded them up at last, after many years, and so maddened the murderers with the sight, that in their horror they had confessed their guilt, and yelled for the gibbet to end their agony.... The terrible descriptions were so real and vivid, that the sallow pages seemed to turn red with gore; and the words

upon them, to be sounded in his ears, as if they were whispered, in hollow murmurs, by the spirits of the dead.

In a paroxysm of fear, the boy closed the book, and thrust it from him. Then, falling upon his knees, he prayed Heaven to spare him from such deeds; and rather to will that he should die at once, than be reserved for crimes, so fearful and appalling.... [And prayed that] if any aid were to be raised up for a poor outcast boy, who had never known the love of friends or kindred, it might come to him now: when, desolate and deserted, he stood in the midst of wickedness and guilt. (5)

We rarely see Oliver more terrified than he is here, even though he lives through some frightening things, and these things are not merely in books. Here the written word is astonishingly powerful, opening up a whole world of evil unimaginable to Oliver before and forcing him to participate imaginatively in that evil.[28] The word becomes as if real and embodied and fills his isolation with terrifying life. It is not unusual in Dickens's novels of growing up to see this potency of the word expressed in the image of the word coming to life, becoming tangible and standing over against the initiate with its alien menace. Evidently the word can say more than reality is, and thus, as here, can amplify the sense of transgression and punishment to gigantic proportions. Oliver's terror, at the same time that it appears to be brought about by his sense of the reality of these fables as they might be lived by himself, is the result of an imaginative transcendence involving participation in an alien identity. He quickly recoils, however, from the words that would contaminate—or poison—him, and restores himself to himself in the act of praying. With this verbal countermagic he can rediscover the good but limited self he had been temporarily separated from as his eyes had roamed across the terrifying pages. This return is accompanied by a recognition of himself as occupying an isolated center of things, an image implying some access of self-consciousness. He is an island of purity surrounded by what is seemingly an oceanic, limitless evil. Oliver, a criminal in thought for a few minutes, becomes once more Oliver the victim. After a temporary self-alienation, he is able to return to his old, innocent self.

Dickens leaves open the possibility of two conflicting interpretations of Oliver's saving recoil. We can attribute it to Oliver's innate knowledge of good and evil, which makes him see the wrongness per

A Predevelopmental Fiction

se of crime; or we can explain it as his crossing a boundary to participate in the mental experience of fictional criminals—a verbal terror, but also a psychological terror which reveals the awful subjective cost, for the miscreant, of crime. The narration prevents us from deciding which interpretation to support. On the one hand Dickens seems to be giving yet another demonstration of what he claims he set out to show: "the Principle of Good, surviving through every adverse circumstance." But if he had only slightly shifted his emphasis, we could see the episode purely as a practical lesson in morality, as taught by unusual (fictional and criminal) experience. Were we treated to the spectacle of Oliver discovering personal reasons for eschewing evil actions, we would have had to speak of this as a truly educational experience, in a very modern sense. For Dickens would not have been appealing to eternal notions of right and wrong, but to an ethics based on self-interest and imaginative sympathy awakened by the rhythm of crisis itself.

The highly fictionalized histories of famous criminals seem to have taught Oliver that their victims return to haunt them, even if these victims remain buried for many years. Anyone familiar with Dickens's works will doubtless recognize here two motifs often appearing together: the motif of the reappearance or surfacing of what was hidden (hidden underground, underwater, in a dungeon, etc.) and that of the haunting of the present by something out of the past. Dickens was fascinated by these motifs, essentially motifs of frightening replication, which appear everywhere in his works, but nowhere with so much importance as in his developmental novels, where they are linked with the problems of becoming in time. In *Oliver Twist* these motifs are also important and appear in what are, psychologically, the most interesting events of the novel.

The arrival of Nancy immediately after Oliver sinks down in prayer (in the above passage) is enough to show us that the imaginary world of crime that Oliver has just experienced is linked to the actual world of crime, for the most horrible crime in the book, of course, is the murder of Nancy, and this murder is followed by psychological effects identical to those described in the lives of the famous criminals: both Sikes and Fagin are haunted. The evil past returns, wraithlike, and drives both of them to the point of madness. In both cases, the crime as it returns redoubled to the imagination is more horrible than the actual crime had seemed. Crime is committed blindly, unhesitatingly, but then the act intrudes upon the imagination, until its reverberations bring about the madness and often the destruction of the criminal. The present for him is the time when he relives his past involuntarily, except that this haunting past is not as it *was* lived; it is transformed grotesquely. For the criminal, imagination and time are the real obstacles in life.

The only possibility of *becoming* in this novel is the possibility of becoming a criminal. Becoming an adult means departing from the innocence of childhood and going wrong. Dickens ignores, for the most part, any positive value to growing up. The real point of this novel seems to be "hold out as long as possible," "remain what you were to begin with." Good adults, like Mr. Brownlow, are good because they have run the gauntlet of experience huddling to themselves an original purity. Thus we get that curious mixture of childlike adults and adultlike children, the former of which find their apotheosis in the polymorphous Cheerybles of *Nicholas Nickleby,* and the latter of which find their model in the prematurely corrupted Artful Dodger, who "had about him all the airs and manners of a man." It was not until much later in his career, in his developmental novels, that Dickens could represent the transition from childhood to adulthood in such a way that both phases of life had their own distinct reality and yet did not have such a gap between them as that between good child (or child-adult) and evil adult (or adultlike child). In his characterizations in *Oliver Twist,* Dickens reveals that he had not yet managed to envisage those features of imaginary childhood that he was to display so masterfully in *David Copperfield,* nor those of adulthood that he was to delineate so convincingly in the final pages of *Great Expectations.*

As far as the criminal himself is concerned, Dickens's attempts to characterize him as fully as possible reveal, in its earliest form, a notion of becoming—the pathogenesis, really, of criminality. Whereas Henry Fielding, for example, could at times view sinfulness as an immutable trait of a "criminal" personality, capable even of being passed on hereditarily (Blifil, Tom Jones's half-brother, is the moral simulacrum of his father), Dickens mainly seems to think it an acquired trait. (In *Oliver Twist* we discover innate, inherited goodness and acquired criminality, but Dickens hedges on the matter of inherited criminality and does not bother much with acquired goodness.) In the preface to the third edition of *Oliver Twist,* in the longish passage where he attempts to justify his portraits of depraved types, Dickens shows just how wary he was then of saying outright that a person is evil by nature and thus permanently cut off from the rest of mankind.[29] In spite of the fact that Dickens separates the good and evil worlds in this novel, his moral view is more complex than that of a Fielding. The view he is developing is that goodness is simple, badness is complex, and goodness is prior to badness, closer to origins. Only in later novels could Dickens entertain the possibility of complex adult personalities that were not necessarily criminal.

VI. "Deformation of Character": Concealment and the Underworld

Oliver's encounter with the underworld leaves much to be desired by anyone looking for signs of growth through experience, but Dickens nevertheless pictures his underworld as a place where growth might take place. In some respects the underworld is a negation of the Brownlow-Maylie world, and it thus provides something of the negative, hellish landscape that the traditional hero of a developmental fiction must traverse in the process of becoming. Standard properties of such a region do appear, as well as the most important concerns. The overriding concern, as one might imagine, is the concern with identity itself. In the sphere of the Brownlows and Maylies identity is conclusively fixed for the main characters. Identity becomes the concern of these satisfied people only when they find Oliver; they want to determine whether he is a rightful member of their world. In the underworld, on the other hand, identity is perpetually in crisis; for identity depends on certain relationships (such as, primarily, the relationship of the self to others and to itself), relationships that, for the thief, cannot be maintained unambiguously or for any considerable duration. Many aspects of thieves' behavior illustrate and symbolize the problems of identity.

We can see this if we begin with the obvious: a thief lives by the secret act of theft and its concomitant secrecies, hiding and telling lies. The thief (especially the confidence-man) is thus an appropriate figure to confront if one is concerned with telling the truth and writing confessional fiction. He is in a negative relation to everything: his "portable property" is always stolen property, his home is a hideout, his very language is false, a form of concealment. But this relation, curiously enough, intensifies *this* world, the phenomenal world, for him. Things become his fetishes; property, which he appropriates at risk of death, becomes, by his manipulation, the ambiguous and magical receptacle of his "soul," as is implied especially in the passage where Oliver, half awake, sees Fagin handling his concealed treasure:

> He then drew forth: as it seemed to Oliver, from some trap in the floor: a small box, which he placed carefully on the table. His eyes glistened as he raised the lid, and looked in. Dragging an old chair to the table, he sat down; and took from it a magnificent gold watch, sparkling with jewels....
>
> The Jew once more deposited the watch in its place of safety. At least half a dozen more were severally drawn forth from the same box, and surveyed with equal pleasure; besides rings, brooches, bracelets, and other articles of jewellery: of such magnificent materials, and costly workmanship, that Oliver had no idea, even of their names.
>
> Having replaced these trinkets, the Jew took out another: so small that it lay in the palm of his hand. There seemed to be some very minute inscription on it; for the Jew laid it flat upon the table: and shading it with his hand: pored over it, long and earnestly. At length he put it down, as if despairing of success.... (9)

For the thief his concealed loot both is and is not, as is the thief himself, whose life and death are linked to the objects he conceals. The loot is Fagin's "source," crystalline and deceptively durable, which he needs to exhume from time to time in order to assure himself of his own reality. But he cannot rest comfortably with this sense of existence, for to have his treasure he must keep it hidden. There is always this fatal doubleness that invalidates his attempt to secure himself in his possessions. The "glow" of Fagin's buried treasure is partly the result of the very contingency implicit in the purely negative way it is possessed. Brownlow and the Maylies have things too, but they enjoy public possession and do not invest in them psychically to the extent that the thieves do. Practically the only

A Predevelopmental Fiction

"things" we see (e.g., the Maylies' plate) in the Good World are those that are threatened by the thieves. When things are not threatened they remain invisible, preserving what Heidegger calls the "inconspicuousness of the ready-to-hand."

Identity cannot be anchored "magically" in matter, but there are other strategies open to the thieves, which are mainly little more than attempts to provide a duplicitous exterior behind which the soul can dwell safely. Consider, for example, the two dandies in the novel, the Artful Dodger and "flash" Toby Crackit. The dandy is important to developmental novels, as can be seen in *Copperfield* and *Great Expectations*. In *Oliver Twist* he is a self-conscious figure who pretends to pass off his exterior as everything. By doing this he appears to be free, to have sportively fabricated himself, to have consciously and playfully assumed his role. And he conceals himself in his display; this is a form of hiding characteristic of the gentleman thief, who is at once invisible and "well-known to the authorities." But dandyism remains, after all, merely a role and not an identity. Identity escapes the dandy. The self that retreats behind the carapace of dress and swagger remains pathetically immured, and in the dandy's attempt to live as he thinks his audience expects him to, his freedom vanishes. He becomes trapped in his persona, within what Dickens shows to be a "false-self system."[30] What is at first of life-affirming value—as can sometimes be seen when such a role is lived temporarily as one stage of identity-seeking—becomes in the end mortifying.[31] The attempt of the Dodger to mitigate (or rather transcend) his situation as a "taken" felon, by playing his role to the limit before the court, peters out into comic gestures meant to impress his audience with the fact that he is choosing what they have dished out to him: " 'Here, carry me off to prison! Take me away' " (43). Dickens puts a fine, Joycean malapropism in the Dodger's mouth when he accuses his witnesses of "deformation of character" (43).

Clothing, which ideally expresses the socially integrated person as it does for the primitive, who periodically undergoes divestment and reinvestiture during his rites of passage, becomes for the Dickens dandy an antiself, an armor imprisoning the inner man (such as he is). What is usually mere dress becomes costume, and eventually disguise, as it does also for those who, using techniques similar to the dandy's, play other false parts. Toby Crackit abandons his dandyism to do this, when he "cases" the Maylies' house, for instance. Fagin, Nancy, and Noah Claypole also assume disguises on occasion. Fagin is the keeper of many costumes and, in one of the later developmental fictions, would serve as a symbol of the fluidity and, at the same time, of the self-consciously improvisational quality of identity. The encounter with Proteus is a typical event in such fictions, especially when it is associated with play-acting, as happens in *Great Expectations*.

A more significant form of hiding than disguise—and such concealment complicates the time and space of the novel's world—is the verbal concealment that takes place in the underworld, a concealment that the narrator, too, takes part in. Orientation to language is important—perhaps of first importance—in fictions of growth, which of course are verbal projects to begin with. In Dickens's confessional narratives, orientation is never complete until the negative aspects of language are discovered and then used, ideally to further the characters' deepest wishes. It is quite amazing, when one considers the numerous accounts of growing up written in the last two centuries, how often lying figures (along with theft, of course, which we find playing a major part at least as early as Augustine's *Confessions*) in accounts of developing self-awareness. The discovery of the lie has tremendous ontological reverberations, as we will see later. This might be because, as Jean Gênet says, "Guilt gives rise, first, to individuality." In *Oliver Twist* the concealments that language makes possible are numerous: there are lies, there are euphemisms, there are private languages, and there is even the deliberate use of silence, the denial of language that in fact affirms its potency, that is in fact a form of language. In the underworld "things are best unsaid," for this is the repository of dark secrets, where the binding social principle is the agreement "not to tell." The major offense among the thieves themselves is "playing booty" with someone (telling on him). Sometimes people in this world have aliases—Artful Dodger, Morris Bolter, Monks—or they are shorn of full names—Fagin, Nancy.[32] For admission to the lairs of the underworld one uses a "watchword or signal"; "making a sign to a man at the bar, Fagin walked straight upstairs" (26). Here information is gathered in a highly indirect manner: "She

A Predevelopmental Fiction

guessed what had been passing in his thoughts" (20). To speak is often to risk violence: " 'Hush! Every word from you is a blow for me' " (20); " 'if you speak a word . . . if you *do* make up your mind to speak without leave; say your prayers first' " (20); " 'you'll prevent his ever telling tales afterwards by shooting him through the head' " (20). Even the narrator is part of this: Although the denizens of this world swear terrible oaths, the narrator gives us, as the worst, "damme." "He then in cant terms, with which his whole conversation was plentifully besprinkled, but which would be quite unintelligible if they were recorded here, demanded a glass of liquor" (13).

" 'Hullo, my covey, what's the row?' " Thus the Artful Dodger speaks when he first meets Oliver. Language is of great importance in the chapters where Oliver is among the thieves. The London underworld has its own argot that insulates it from the speakers of the King's English, which is the "authentic" language. Oliver receives an on-the-spot language drill.

> "I suppose you don't know what a beak is, my flash com-pan-i-on."
> Oliver mildly replied, that he had always heard a bird's mouth described by the term in question.
> "My eyes, how green!" exclaimed the young gentleman. "Why, a beak's a madgst'rate; and when you walk by a beak's order, it's not straight forerd, but always a-going up, and nivir a-coming down agin. Was you never on the mill?"
> "What mill?" inquired Oliver. (8)

And so on. (See also, for example, Chapter 18.) It has often been remarked that Oliver never speaks anything but the purest English no matter what his surroundings happen to be, which is a good sign of his inability to adapt to life in the sphere of humanity in which he finds himself much of the time. Had he learned the language of thieves he would also have assumed their alienated outlook. What would the Maylies or Brownlow have thought of little Oliver had he learned to speak like the Artful Dodger? As Ben Jonson wrote, *"Language* most shewes a man: speake, that I may see thee. It springs out of the most retired and inmost parts of us, and is the Image of the Parent of it, the mind. No glasse renders a mans forme or likenesse so true as his speech."[33] Fortunately Oliver was not keen about learning new languages.

VII. Crime, Time, and Psychological Complexity

Now let us consider the criminal from another angle. A criminal is complex in that he chooses a complex strategy for living. Jerome Bruner speaks of two basic types of "mythic plot" in people's lives: "the plot of innocence and the plot of cleverness—the former being a kind of Arcadian ideal, requiring the eschewal of complexity and awareness, the latter requiring the cultivation of competence almost to the point of guile."[34] (The criminal of course lives the latter plot well beyond the point of guile.) The plot that Dickens wrote so often for his beloved characters, in the first half of his career, especially, is the plot of innocence. The second plot appears over and over again in counterpoint with the first. In the former plot, the characters are simple and whole, like Oliver, Mr. Brownlow, Mrs. Maylie. In the latter, the characters are double, divided against themselves, against their society, or both (Monks, Fagin, Nancy). At one point Nancy says about Oliver that "the sight of him turns me against myself" (26).

By choosing guile the criminal comes in effect to believe that this world is more real than the "eternals" he is alienated from. Furthermore, opting for this world means opting for himself, and thus for self-awareness in at least a crude form. The practice of guile is partly what induces in him the self-consciousness that opens up an inner world for the criminal. This private world—the result of the fact that, as Fagin says, "Every man's his own friend"—is vastly more ample and continuous than that of Oliver, whose self-consciousness is at most a momentary phenomenon. It is not until *Great Expectations*, however, that Dickens shows in detail how self-consciousness can be a direct outgrowth of "guile."

His imaginings about the complex mental life of criminals mark Dickens's earliest fictional explorations of the psyche. These explorations—or, rather, constructions—paved the way for the psychological treatment of character in the developmental novels. Dickens's earliest attempt at construction of a psyche is the powerful evocation, in *Sketches by Boz,* of a condemned man's last days alive ("A Visit to Newgate"). This much admired sketch is by far the most interesting

A Predevelopmental Fiction

one in terms of Dickens's later development, when we consider all the later times he wrote about imprisonment and what might happen to the mind subjected to it, especially when death is on the horizon. But we immediately think, in our present context, of Fagin's last nights alive, as well as of the other event with similar psychic meaning and structure, Sikes's flight. There is, in the latter, the isolation of the guilty conscience, the inwardness that produces a consequent distortion of the outer world, resulting in a picture of high and vivid color, which attains much of its power from the profound evocation of a crime that cannot but remain as if doubly present no matter how frenzied the murderer's attempt to escape it: "There came the room with every well-known object—some, indeed, that he would have forgotten, if he had gone over its contents from memory.... The body was in *its* place, and its eyes were as he saw them when he stole away" (48). In this abortive attempt to escape he is "flying from memory and himself." His own self appears as an alien, threatening phantom which he carries with him, so that escape in space is impossible. His inner space is all that counts, and he is permanently imprisoned there. And consequent upon this involuntary, hallucinatory memory is a destruction of everyday time, such that time is simultaneously long in suffering and short in "objective" duration. "There were twenty score of violent deaths in one long minute of that agony of fear" (48). This "haunted" flight comes to an end in the scene where Sikes is finally trapped on a roof above "the tiers and tiers of faces" (50), an image that must be compared with Fagin's vision of the courtroom "paved, from floor to roof, with human faces" (52). They are both imprisoned in their own space, a space isolated, hollowed out in the midst of the crowd. In this distorted form the Dickens criminal experiences his public identity—a moment of verification soon followed by annihilation. The guilty thing is brought into the light only to vanish.

I'll quote at some length from the chapter on Fagin's last nights alive, because it shows Dickens depicting consciousness in a way that made possible later the writing of "personal history," developmental narrative, like *David Copperfield.*

> As it came on very dark, he began to think of all the men he had known who had died upon the scaffold; some of them through his

> means. They rose up, in such quick succession, that he could hardly count them....
> Some of them might have inhabited that very cell.... The cell had been built for many years. Scores of men must have passed their last hours there. It was like sitting in a vault strewn with dead bodies—the cap, the noose, the pinioned arms, the faces that he knew, even beneath that hideous veil—Light, light! (52)

Oliver "remembered" a heavenly eternity, but Fagin's memories are earthbound. His past (and the past of the cell itself) comes alive, but as an entirely new thing composed by the urgencies of a tortured and isolated imagination. Past crimes, criminals resurrected in their death agony—a kind of hallucination brings them, cinematically, into the severely constricted present of the prisoner. The images overflow all determinations of the mind and appear as a fluid blur of superimposed forms. These phantoms, risen from their graves, summoned by a guilty conscience, rush into the vacuum of Fagin's isolation. Such an involuntary, oppressively expanded memory is associated frequently in this novel with a guilty conscience.

> Then came night—dark, dismal, silent night. Other watchers are glad to hear the church-clocks strike, for they tell of life and coming day. To the Jew, they brought despair. The boom of every iron bell came laden with the one, deep, hollow sound—Death....
> The day passed off—day! There was no day; it was gone as soon as come—and night came on again; night so long, and yet so short; long in its dreadful silence, and short in its fleeting hours. At one time he raved and blasphemed; and at another howled and tore his hair....
> Saturday night. He had only one night more to live. And as he thought of this, the day broke—Sunday. (52)

Dickens first contrasts two experiences of clock-time: the time for the outside public and that for Fagin. Fagin wants the night both to be and not to be an eternity; he wants to live time in contradictory ways. There are, for Fagin, only nights between him and death. The simplest of the cycles that provide ordinary orientation (that of day and night) has been destroyed. Days shrink down to become instants separating, punctuating, the nights that are "so long, and yet so short." Fagin's consciousness is distributed randomly throughout the intervals: "At one time he ... and at another he ...." As it sounds the

A Predevelopmental Fiction

hour, the clock usurps the entire interval Fagin's mind had been wandering in. A night of torment is in retrospect only an instant. This is a remarkable interplay of retrospection and direct perception. There has been an unquestionable duration, measured by Fagin's suffering. He is experiencing time as such, a naked, what must be called *real* time that is intimately his measure. He feels his existence, as Coleridge would say, "momently"; his nonexistence he feels, while his past, as retrospective vision, devours him. Here there is none of the invisibility, the "automatization" of time that is the common experience of the man-in-the-street. And yet Fagin does not just perceive time, or try to measure it; it is more accurate to say that he lives time, and time only.

> He cowered down upon his stone bed, and thought of the past.... His eyes shone with a terrible light; his unwashed flesh, crackled with the fever that burnt him up. Eight—nine—ten. If it was not a trick to frighten him, and those were the real hours treading on each other's heels, where would he be, when they came round again! Eleven! Another struck, before the voice of the previous hour had ceased to vibrate. At eight, he would be the only mourner in his own funeral train; at eleven— (52)

Now by a kind of inversion of the previous situation, Fagin's past is where he exists, his present is where he is being devoured. There is no content to the present except the voice of the clock, just as the future, too (thinking of which caused Saturday night to pass so unheeded and thus so quickly), has less and less content as the hours hurry by elusively. The clock now sounds its continuous emergency. Fagin attempts to follow himself to his last moment; but he is squandering his future while he explores it. To look for the future is also to consume the past and the present; to explore (or encounter) any region of time is to use up the others prodigally. He should be in all of them at once, idly tasting of past, present, and future and thus putting things off. But his time, no matter what the exertions of his consciousness, has only one direction—past, present, and future form a total and yet irreversible sequence.

In this episode we see Dickens creating, in a remarkably subtle, if melodramatic, way, a subjective and intensely real time that he establishes within objective time. This time is supple but not infinitely malleable. (Fagin's imagination cannot here triumph over death.) The fact that it is not thus malleable, that it has limits, and that it implies, in some form, a relationship of a past, a present, and a future is enough to provide a basis for the later developmental novels, which found themselves on time and the fatality implicit in it. For Dickens, the sense of this time arises in conjunction with guilt, secrecy, horror, impending death—any negative experience which cannot be shared with other men. To the extent that one lives in such a time he is an individual, different from others, with an individuality that is tormenting. At the root of this time-consciousness is the character's sense of his boundaries and, beyond, his own nothingness. *Oliver Twist* is organized so that, generally, no real developmental time is shown as passing. The novel deals with at least two eternally juxtaposed spaces: the underworld of the criminals and the overworld of Brownlows and Maylies, with their direct access to eternal essences. But in the lower depths, in the imprisoned space of the criminal, appears the personal sense of time so important to *David Copperfield* and *Great Expectations*.[35] The criminal knows himself as lower than and different from the blandly unconscious Good People, and he knows his days are numbered; his is the mind in crisis attempting to forge connections among the many facts, phantoms, and limits that make him up. He has the rudiments of a mind able to order a discontinuous montage of events into significant processes.

Notes

1. There were, of course, books written for and about children that appeared before *Oliver Twist.* Thomas Day's *Sandford and Merton* (1789), a moralizing tale about children, was perhaps the most popular. Among other writers who used fictional accounts of children for educational and propagandistic purposes were Maria Edgeworth (*Parent's Assistant,* 1800) and Mary Sherwood (*The Fairchild Family,* 1818). But these writers did not produce serious fiction about the child in the sense that Dickens did in his novel.
2. Jean-Jacques Rousseau, *Emile* (New York: Columbia University Press, 1962), pp. 38-39.
3. Peter Coveney says that "art provides no more pathetic sight than the portraiture of the [the eighteenth] and the previous century with its little Dutch and English children starched into lace and taffeta before their time." *The Image of Childhood: The Individual and Society: A Study of the Theme in English Literature* (Baltimore: Penguin Books, 1967), pp. 43-44. See also Philippe Ariès, *Centuries of Childhood: A Social History of Family Life,* trans. Robert Baldick (New York: Vintage Books, 1962).
4. *Sartor Resartus,* ed. Charles Frederick Harrold (New York: Odyssey Press, 1937), p. 81.
5. A novel that George Ford, in his introduction to *David Copperfield,* assumes to be a *Bildungsroman.* In my view it is every bit as much a revelation of what Ford in a later essay calls a "space world" as Smollett's novels are. George H. Ford, "Dickens and the Voices of Time," in *Dickens Centennial Essays,* ed. Ada Nisbet and Blake Nevius (Berkeley: University of California Press, 1971), pp. 46-66. The picaresque novel, like *Tom Jones,* shows movement as a "tour"; the *Bildungsroman* deals with what Ford says characterizes Dickens's novels after *Pickwick:* "movement in time, as well as movement in space" (p. 56).
6. *Dickens and the Rhetoric of Laughter* (Oxford: Clarendon Press, 1971), pp. 50, 55.
7. Here I have in mind Steven Marcus's brilliant essay, "Laughter into Structure: Pickwick Revisited," *Daedalus* 101, no. 1 (Winter 1972): 183-202. Consider especially p. 187.
8. See *Oliver Twist,* ed. Kathleen Tillotson (Oxford: Clarendon Press, 1966), pp. xlviii-liv. Subsequent references will be to this edition, and chapter numbers will appear in parentheses.
9. Steven Marcus, *Dickens: From Pickwick to Dombey* (New York: Basic Books, 1965), stresses Bunyan's influence, but rather too strongly, if my subsequent argument about *Oliver Twist* is correct.
10. Claudio Guillén, "Toward a Definition of the Picaresque," in *Literature as System* (Princeton, N.J.: Princeton University Press, 1971), asserts that "the picaresque is based on a situation, or rather, a chain of situations," but he includes in his definition of the genre a definite educational experience for the hero, stressing "the lessons he learns

from his adventures" (p. 87). Thus he seems to make of the picaresque novel something of a *Bildungsroman,* and his definition perhaps loses its point, if a definition is best used to draw a distinction.

11. It is possible to trace on a contemporary map of London precisely the route Oliver takes when he enters the city, and, later, when he leaves it with Sikes to journey to "the crib at Chertsey" where the Maylies live.

12. J. Hillis Miller, *Charles Dickens: The World of His Novels* (Cambridge, Mass.: Harvard University Press, 1965), pp. 36-84, discusses this aspect of Oliver's perception. In my treatment of *Oliver Twist* —particularly in this section of my chapter—I depend much upon Miller's definitive reading of the novel.

13. *From Pickwick to Dombey,* p. 83.

14. In their books, Marcus, Miller, and Kincaid all mention this feature of the work as significant.

15. Graham Greene, "The Young Dickens," in *The Dickens Critics,* ed. George H. Ford and Lauriat Lane, Jr. (Ithaca, N.Y.: Cornell University Press, 1961), p. 251; Greene was, I think, the first to attest to the Manichean world of *Oliver Twist.*

16. See Tillotson's edition, p. 1, n. 1.

17. This river appears in almost every Dickens novel, with especially frequent appearances in *Dombey, Copperfield, Dorrit,* and, of course, *Our Mutual Friend.* John Henry Raleigh, "Dickens and the Sense of Time," *Nineteenth-Century Fiction* 13 (1958): 130, points this out as an instance of Dickens's use of "great natural phenomena as symbols of time."

18. Marcus, *From Pickwick to Dombey,* pp. 78-79, discusses coincidence in *Oliver Twist.* The second of the coincidences I mention above, according to Marcus, "beggars the very notion of accident," showing that "coincidences in *Oliver Twist* are of too cosmic an order to belong in the category of the fortuitous."

19. As quoted by Hans Meyerhoff, *Time in Literature* (Berkeley: University of California Press, 1960), p. 67.

20. Edwin Muir, *The Structure of the Novel* (London: Hogarth Press, 1963), pp. 24-25.

21. *Charles Dickens: The World of His Novels,* pp. 78-79.

22. Notably in chaps. 32 and 35.

23. Letter to Maria Winter, 10 February 1855, in *The Letters of Charles Dickens,* ed. Walter Dexter (Bloomsbury: The Nonesuch Press, 1938), 2:626.

24. Henri Bergson, *An Introduction to Metaphysics,* trans. T. E. Hulme (New York: Bobbs-Merrill, 1955), p. 59.

25. Montaigne once wrote, "What a wonderful thing it is that the drop of seed from which we are produced should carry in itself the impression not only of the bodily form, but even of the thoughts and inclination of our fathers." Norman O. Brown, *Love's Body* (New York: Random House, 1966), illuminates this notion of "the magical metamorphosis of living persons into reincarnations of the dead" by quoting from Henry Maine (*Ancient Law*) to the effect that in Roman inheritance laws, " 'the notion was that, though the physical person . . . had perished, his legal personality survived and descended unimpaired on his Heir.' " Brown, on the same page (101), quotes Roheim (*The Riddle of the Sphinx*): " 'What is the basis of inheritance? A retention of the past. The great man is not dead; his psychological identification with his son is taken to be real.' " Gibbon, in his *Autobiography,* wrote, with an interesting reversal

A Predevelopmental Fiction

of perspective, "We seem to have lived in the persons of our fathers." (Gibbon of course, *meant* that word *seem.*)

26. *The Imagination of Charles Dickens* (London: Collins, 1961), especially in the chapter, "The Expanding Prison," pp. 26-49.

27. See Philip Collins, "Murder: From Bill Sikes to Bradley Headstone," in *Dickens and Crime* (Bloomington: Indiana University Press, 1968), pp. 256-89. Collins sketches the psychic disruption of criminals who are self-immured in their own evil actions, but his interest in his particular topic, no doubt, leads him to ignore the general developmental implications of crime and punishment.

28. Father Arnall's vivid evocation of the torments of hell, during the Retreat for Saint Francis Xavier, in James Joyce's *A Portrait of the Artist as a Young Man* (New York: Viking Press, 1956), resembles Oliver's reading about criminals. Joyce shows us the full developmental meaning of such verbal thunder, however.

29. Dickens writes, in part: "It has been objected to Sikes ... that he is surely overdrawn, because in him there would appear to be none of those redeeming traits which are objected to as unnatural in his mistress.... I will merely say, that I fear there are in the world some insensible and callous natures that do become, at last, utterly and irredeemably bad. But whether this be so or not, of one thing I am certain: that there are such men as Sikes, who, being closely followed through the same space of time ... would not give ... the faintest indication of a better nature. Whether every gentler human feeling is dead within such bosoms, or the proper chord to strike has rusted and is hard to find, I do not know; but that the fact is so, I'm sure."

30. R. D. Laing, *The Divided Self: An Existential Study in Sanity and Madness* (Baltimore: Penguin Books, 1965), chap. 6.

31. See Jean-Paul Sartre's analysis of dandyism in *Baudelaire,* trans. Martin Turnell (New York: New Directions, 1950), especially p. 146: "He created the parasite of parasites—the dandy who was the parasite of a class of oppressors; beyond the artist, who still sought to create, he projected a social idea of absolute sterility in which the cult of the self was identified with the suppression of oneself. That is why J. Crepet could rightly say, that 'suicide is the supreme sacrament of dandyism.' Better still, dandyism was a 'suicides' club,' and the life of each of its members was simply the carrying out of a permanent suicide."

32. In the Appendix I discuss these names in another context of secrecy—but the secrecy is Dickens's own, not that of his characters.

33. "From *Timber, or Discoveries,*" in *Critical Essays of the Seventeenth Century,* ed. J. E. Spingarn (Oxford: Clarendon Press, 1908), p. 41.

34. "Myth and Identity," in *On Knowing: Essays for the Left Hand* (New York: Atheneum, 1965), p. 37.

35. Compare Fagin's experiences with those of Barnaby Rudge in prison (77), Jonas Chuzzlewit (47), Carker in flight in *Dombey and Son* (55) and with the frightful experiences of numerous other guilty and imprisoned Dickens characters. The *Rudge* passages are strikingly similar to those at the end of *Oliver Twist.*

"Aunt Betsey at Blunderstone Rookery." From *David Copperfield*.

TWO

David Copperfield: "The Prismatic Hues of Memory"

I wrote a story with a purpose growing, not remotely, out of my experience.

I. Origins: The Double Consciousness

To begin my life with the beginnings of my life, I record that I was born (as I have been informed and believe) on a Friday, at twelve o'clock at night. It was remarked that the clock began to strike, and I began to cry, simultaneously.[1]

"To begin . . . with the beginnings" is naturally the first step in any attempt to grasp life *sub specie temporis.* The naive attempt to know life temporally involves no more orderly a principle of organization than the deployment of events as they naturally occur, in the sequence "earlier-later." One locates the beginning and constructs the series from that point. But where is the beginning? Samuel Butler began *Ernest Pontifex* and D. H. Lawrence began *The Rainbow* with synopses of several generations of family life preceding the birth of the central characters. As we have seen in *Oliver Twist,* a novel that displaces existential beginnings, the true beginning of the hero is prior to his birth, in the parental identity whose nature is concealed until the end of the novel. *Great Expectations* does begin at the beginning, but there the beginning is the moment of the hero's "first consciousness of the identity of things," a moment deferred in *Copperfield* until the second chapter. As Thomas Mann recognized, in sounding the "well of the past," which is really of infinite depth, one comes to accept fictional beginnings for oneself. "There may exist provisional origins, . . . and memory, though sufficiently instructed that the depths have not actually been plumbed, yet . . . may find reassurance in some primitive point of time and, personally and historically speaking, come to rest there."[2] Or again, according to George Eliot, "Man can do nothing without the make-believe of a beginning. . . . No retrospect will take us to the true beginning: and whether our prologue be in heaven or on earth, it is but a fraction of that all-supposing fact with which our story sets out."[3] One manufactures a self in the very act of looking for it in its origins. In the act of retrospection that produces autobiography we create the fiction of ourselves. The same goes for David Copperfield.

There is no narrative reticence blurring the facts of the hero's beginnings as there was in *Oliver Twist;* David candidly appears with his own voice to locate himself clearly in time and space. True, he claims to be born at the kind of moment that is invariably shrouded in folk superstitions: midnight of a Friday. Consequently, for David, there are predictions: "I was destined to be unlucky in life; and . . . I was privileged to see ghosts and spirits" (1). The future *already awaits* this child of destiny; a little society of "sage women" surrounding the nativity is able to declare what will happen to him. And there are other predictions made around the time of his birth. Aunt Betsey has "a presentiment that it must be a girl" (1) who will be born. Furthermore, David is born with a caul and is thus destined to be safe from drowning, so long as he keeps it. Unusual circumstances surrounding birth inevitably provoke predictions from the superstitious, who are comfortable only with a sense of foreknowledge of some already established divine scheme.

But the purest forms of developmental narratives (beginning, no doubt, with Rousseau's assertion of his absolute uniqueness on the first page of his *Confessions*) found themselves on the notion of the innovative and fundamentally surprising operation of time. There is a respect for the unique event in itself as an irreducible part of the texture and meaning of a life continuum and a tendency to regard predictive schema as no doubt necessary, in their ubiquity, but as essentially false. Foreknowledge is alien to the consciousness which grounds itself in a confession of "personal history" and eschews as corrupt fictions those formulations about life which envisage repetitious patterns or destinies.[4] Consider *Copperfield.* Though it opens

"The Prismatic Hues of Memory"

with intimations of destiny, this destiny is immediately called into question. Aunt Betsey was wrong in her prediction; the caul, after being unsuccessfully offered for sale, is raffled off. As for the prediction that David was "privileged to see ghosts and spirits," the narrator says, "I will only remark, that unless I ran through that part of my inheritance while I was still a baby, I have not come into it yet." But the prediction that he was "destined to be unlucky in life" the narrator leaves up in the air: "I need say nothing here on [that] head, because nothing can show better than my history whether that prediction was verified or falsified by the result."

Tom Jones ("born to be hanged") and Oliver Twist ("born to be hung") are also the subjects of unpleasant prediction, but the narrators, from the very outset, are presumably in possession of essential information, which, when it is "discovered," will subvert the negative predictions in a classic reversal of fortunes—a reversal, however, which the reader expects because of his familiarity with the numerous rhetorical cues that advertise a traditional discovery plot. (The initial cue is the presence of the omniscient narrator.) Expectation is gratified, and one's faith in plots of discovery, and perhaps also in the providential arrangement of so-called history, is once again justified. But in *Copperfield* the narrator assumes the prerogative of withholding advance comment on his destiny, though not because he needs to keep things from the reader that he can later reveal so as to stagger us in a peripeteia (which was the basis of the manufactured mystery in *Oliver Twist*). In the case of David there is simply no single piece of information that could be given us in advance to help us decide about his luck. We have to view everything as in a temporal continuum of events.

"Whether I shall turn out to be the hero of my own life, or whether that station will be held by anybody else, these pages must show" (1). This initial question becomes associated with the one about whether David is destined to be unlucky, for if destiny is really operative, heroism is negligible, the "hero" being mainly shaped and acted upon by some more powerful agency than himself. Oliver, whose fortunes were directed by a Providence which arranged events so as to assure his preservation, could by no stretch of the imagination be called "the hero of his own life." David, who views heroism as a possibility, is thus rejecting both the Twistian and the Zolaesque views of destiny and identity. Oliver was the child of a destiny that manifested itself by working counter to natural laws of probability and normal causality. His novel is deterministic in precisely the opposite sense of, say, *L'Assommoir,* a model of Zolaesque naturalism. The heroine Gervaise was not able to rise above the force of circumstances and natural laws, while Oliver certainly never sank low enough to feel their operation. Transcendental forces shielded his inner being and guaranteed his fate; the fate of Gervaise was assured by immanent powers of life that were, however, equally extraneous to her consciousness, to her ability to remember, perceive, or imagine.

Does David have any right to his own name? "These pages must show." "Nothing can show better" than his history (the total narrative of his life-in-time) what the answer to this important question is. Dickens would have us pretend that we are not reading a novel so much as following the narrator as he carries out a project he initiates for himself: he will recite his whole story, from birth to adulthood. No single event will reveal his heroism any more than it will reveal his destiny, but each event must be recited; a temporal process cannot easily be telescoped, collapsed into a static summary. The narrator recognizes this at the outset, but as he draws toward the end (which is really the middle of his life viewed as end) he attempts to come to conclusions, and, with his increased knowledge, he manages to find some that satisfy him as confessions. These conclusions are not as important to the student of developmental-confessional fictions as the process that leads to them, for in it Dickens dramatizes with a great deal of originality the dynamism of a kind of mind that was no doubt as familiar a phenomenon in the middle of the nineteenth century as it is today. He shows certain activities of a particular consciousness and is not afraid to break the ordinary laws of external (natural, realistic) probability in order to create an image of the temporal structure of that consciousness. It is my assumption all along, incidentally, that Dickens's improbabilities of plot and incident are not merely forms of rhetoric or "theatre," but that they are unique means of expressing notions of psychic process.

In *Oliver Twist* the hero's adventures were shrouded in unreality. The criminal world appeared as a bewildering collection of phenomena to Oliver, as a fiction unable to make an impression on the fixed nature of the hero. His history among thieves was a ghastly nightmare from which he eventually could awaken. Oliver was indeed a pure "substance." R. G. Collingwood's critique of eighteenth-century historians applies quite well to the early Dickens—for them "human nature was conceived substantialistically as something static and permanent, an unvarying substratum underlying the course of historical changes and all human activities."[5] For a character with a fixed nature, history itself is mere appearance, and events are either vapors that interfere with one's perception of the underlying realities or merely occasions for their predictable display.

The closest we come to substance in *Copperfield* is the mind of the narrator, but it is not a substance in the same sense that human nature was for the eighteenth century.[6] This mind—as distinct from the mind of the hero, which obviously changes—grows even as it narrates its story. In the step-by-step rehearsal of his life, the narrator reforms his adult consciousness while at the same time tracing its formation. After this second voyage of self-discovery, he ends up in a different state of knowledge than before, especially as regards the historical basis of his relation to Agnes, and this different state of knowledge is, in effect, a new state of mind. One can see this change in the gathering force of David's hymn to Agnes, which reaches its peak in the last words of the novel, where a vision of the significance of his life seizes the narrator at the moment when he and the hero are for once unequivocally the same person. What began as an inquiry into the self ends as a paean to the eternal feminine as manifest in Agnes. *Copperfield* is obviously a developmental novel in two respects; it recounts the development out of childhood by the hero and superimposes upon this the development of the narrator. But neither development is complete in relation to criteria suggested by the novel itself.

The double view that results from "autobiographical" self-reflectiveness is suggested in the full title of the novel:

The Personal History, Adventures
Experience, & Observation
of
David Copperfield
The Younger

Of Blunderstone Rookery
(Which He never meant to be Published on any Account.)

The narrator is ostensibly writing both *about* and *for* himself. Later on David says, "This manuscript is intended for no eyes but mine" (42). The motive is similar to that in Dickens's story "George Silverman's Explanation" (1867), in which the narrator, only slightly more inclined than David to publication of his deepest thoughts, says, "I pen [this story] for the relief of my own mind, not foreseeing whether or no it will ever have a reader." The narrator's relation to himself is not to be seen as mediated by his awareness of any audience. Presumably the truth is to be got at directly:

> I search my breast, and I commit its secrets, if I know them, without any reservation to this paper. (44)
>
> In fulfilment of the compact I have made with myself, to reflect my mind on this paper, I again examine it, closely, and bring its secrets to the light. (48)
>
> I have made it, thus far, with no purpose of suppressing any of my thoughts; for, as I have elsewhere said, this narrative is my written memory. (58)

In spite of the humility implied here—humility, however, before the facts of one's *own* life, before one's *own* memory—this book is apparently meant to be seen as reflecting an attempt to define the self individualistically, exclusive of the evaluations of other men. Writing this kind of autobiography is an attempt ultimately to substitute oneself for one's parents, for one's community, perhaps even for one's God—in Spinoza's terms to become *causa sui* by co-opting language from others and attempting to create oneself in it for oneself. This assertion would not apply to *Great Expectations,* which is presented as having a different narrative motive behind it than *Copperfield,* but David does seek to become "the hero of his own life" through words —and to a point he succeeds. He is shown as responsible at least for the unheroic vision of himself that appears at the end.

What is rather odd about the title of this novel is the variety of terms Dickens chooses as categories for David's life: personal history, adventures, experience, and observation. Forster lists numerous variants of the title that Dickens proposed, once he had decided to give the hero that name of which, as Forster pointed out to a "startled" Dickens, "the initials were but his own reversed."[7] Six of these variants, contrived once the name of the hero was settled, contain the phrase "personal history," and four of them add "experience" to that. The worksheets that Dickens used in sketching out the contents of the serial numbers were headed for Number 1, "The Personal History and Adventures of David Copperfield," but in the second number the word "Adventures" was deleted and replaced by "Experience," which remained Dickens's working title at the head of all further number plans.[8] It is clear that he is not using these words casually. If we remember how appropriate "adventures" was to the title of *Oliver Twist,* we can surmise that here "experience" might be the best word for what happens to the hero. Forster notes that it was not until after Dickens had finished the second chapter that he adopted the final title and rejected, among others, *The Copperfield Survey of the World as It Rolled.* This suggests an original picaresque rather than developmental intention. And picaresque is based on observation (or present perception) more than on imagination and memory. "His completion of the second chapter defined to himself, more clearly than before, the character of the book; and the propriety of rejecting everything not strictly personal from the name given to it."[9] The first chapter offers circumstances of birth; objective, "communal" knowledge of origins that the hero himself never remembers experiencing, and a comic-pathetic situation for which the hero merely provides the occasion. In the second chapter subjectivity predominates; it is an evocation of the earliest rememberable awareness, of the earliest consciousness not obliterated by infantile amnesia. The narration of the first chapter is appropriate to recounting adventures—his birth as an adventure for other people, perhaps—while the narration of the second is suited to rendering individual inner experience with all its resonance.

Dickens's term "personal history" evidently refers to his story as something told by the narrator, the story as story. It is the self-conscious "narrative" category. "Adventures, experience, and observation" are the elements of the life of David as hero, which are usually distinct from the narrator's life as narrator. The hero has adventures just as Oliver does; some things happen without having much impact on identity. And he experiences: certain things sink in and transform his consciousness as they become structurally related to rememberings and imaginings. Finally, in accord with Dickens's theory about the observational powers of children, the young David (at any rate) is a good observer of "the world as it rolls." "Adventures, experience, and observation" are modes that apply existentially to the hero's life-time, but "adventure" and "observation" are less relevant modes than "experience" (which was the term that, for Dickens, swallowed up the others, as a glance at his worksheet shows). Experience is a depth-term, implying time's articulation of remembrance, perception, and imagination. "Personal history" is the self-conscious, narrative category.

II. Childhood's Book of Repetition: "Adventures, Experience, and Observation"

David is shown in transition from childhood to adulthood. Evidently, the point of the developmental novel is to achieve a verbal account of the process of mediation by means of which one such stage changes into the next. Apparently, in the developmentalist view, childhood can hardly be seen as nothing more than a reduction in scale of adulthood—the child as *petit homme* or, as John Earle, in his *Microcosmography*, calls him, "a man in a small letter."[10] Nor can adults be seen as blown-up children (like Dickens's own Cheerybles). Both views are based on a notion of pseudo-change, change in quantity and not in quality. Adulthood must instead be seen as different from and yet continuous with childhood. It is true, incidentally, that every means yet devised for representing both the continuity and the difference evident in a process of change contains an ineradicable element of mystery. No matter how a developmental fiction deals with process, it is unable to avoid perpetuating this mystery—and that is one sense in which it is fiction.

To speak of stages of life, like childhood and adulthood, is of course to indulge in another kind of fiction, even though we can be fairly certain of what we mean when we use such words, which designate relatively stable periods of life typically seen as separated by crises. Interpreting developmental accounts involves noticing both the static stages and the crises, but especially the latter, which some writers, like D. H. Lawrence, show as happening all the time. (As Lawrence says, in a famous statement, "You mustn't look in my novel for the old stable ego of the character. There is another ego, according to whose action the individual is unrecognizable, and passes through, as it were, allotropic states which it needs a deeper sense than any we've been used to exercise, to discover are states of the same single radically unchanged element.")[11] In *Copperfield* childhood is seen as the most important stage of life, as the time when one really existed; but it is a time early doomed to disruption. But, because of memory and the protagonist's use of it, in Wordsworth's phrase, to perceive "similitude in dissimilitude," he is able to perpetuate many of the features of childhood beyond crisis. Furthermore, even the plot of the novel is designed to make it possible for David to live by repeating earlier experiences. Before going on to consider the major crises, we must look—as we did with Oliver—at childhood and the repetitive, static elements of David's novel.

One form of repetitiveness, as we have seen, is heredity. The hero is "David Copperfield the Younger," which hints at the "like father like son" hypothesis that was tested and proved in *Oliver Twist*. Thanks to his father, David is born gentle, and he has the same trusting nature, of a passive and "poetical" turn. Toward the end of the novel, Mr. Chillip says, "There's a strong resemblance between you and your poor father, sir!" (54), a statement mainly suggesting, however, that David has merely grown up. Dickens does not make enough of this form of repetitiveness for us to consider it as significant in the novel. David will seek his own identity, which he will try to base as much as possible on his personal past. Growing up for him will be, except for the real crises, a series of incremental repetitions or variations on the themes of childhood. Kenneth Burke's term "repetitive form" would define this important aspect of the structure of *Copperfield*. It is a structural characteristic of almost all the novels Dickens wrote for serial publication,[12] but in this novel this form perfectly expresses the conservative tendency of the hero's consciousness.

"Being starts with well-being," says Gaston Bachelard.[13] David, unlike Oliver and Pip, lives childhood first as well-being. Danger intrudes soon after the earliest moments, but it is a danger that at first merely adds piquancy to the sense of shelter. Dickens reveals the structure of the child's being and growth by unfolding its primitive understanding of space, especially of the original home. Bachelard, whose *Poetics of Space,* in particular, is useful to keep in mind when reading the second chapter of *Copperfield,* says that "there is ground for taking the house as a *tool for analysis* of the human soul."[14] Dickens uses houses in *Copperfield* as tools for construction of complex psyches. The earliest effective sphere of action, the first space, for David is simply the two-dimensional line between his mother and Peggotty, as he learns to totter "unsteadily from the one to the other" (2). The second structure, the second shape to "come out of the cloud" is the interior of the house felt as a sheltering sphere. David first knows his house exclusively from within, and as divided, differentiated affectively into regions expressive of consciousness: the comfortable places and the places to be avoided, certain of them sacred, certain profane, some mysterious, some familiar. "There are . . . two parlours; the parlour in which we sit of an evening . . . and the best parlour where we sit on a Sunday; grandly, but not so comfortably" (2). There is the center of heat and nourishment, "Peggotty's kitchen," in structured opposition to the sinister, "dark store-room" giving off the "long passage" from the kitchen, "a place to be run past at night; for I don't know what may be among those tubs and jars" (2). And while the front door might lead into an infinite public world, the back door (as the child looks out) opens onto the more limited animal world—a wasteland of vacated shelters, yet teeming with threatening life that is a microcosm of a human world not yet encountered. Just behind this wasteland is its opposite, the true childhood Eden "where the fruit clusters on the trees, riper and richer than fruit has ever been since, in any other garden" (2). There seems to be in all this, and what follows, an instinctive polarization, a rudimentary form of differentiation that is initially dualistic, with the child behaving from the beginning like a little Manichean—and Dickens unfolds his spaces so as to suggest this tendency, while still managing to suggest the as yet undisclosed presence of meaningful structure. Here, but in *Great Expectations* especially, psychic growth is envisioned as the overcoming of this initial emergent dualism in favor of something more like monism—that is, the perception of a total structure in experience. In other words, it follows the pattern of Augustine's *Confessions*.[15]

For the child there is a basic differentiation between inner and outer; again and again within a few pages we see David on the inside looking out at what is mysterious to him. Through the window he sees his father's grave:

> There is something strange to me ... in the shadowy remembrance that I have of my first childish associations with his white gravestone in the churchyard , and of the indefinable compassion I used to feel for it lying out alone there in the dark night, when our little parlour was warm and bright with fire and candle, and the doors of our house were—almost cruelly, it seemed to me sometimes—bolted and locked against it. (1)

One Sunday he hears the story of "how Lazarus was raised up from the dead." "I am so frightened that they are afterwards obliged to take me out of bed, and show me the quiet churchyard out of the bedroom window, with the dead all lying in their graves at rest" (2). Here he tactfully does not reveal that he fears the revival of his father—but David the Elder is after all buried a good safe twenty-five feet deep (9). In this imagery of outer and inner we see primitive distinctions made between the "I" (here at the center, inside) and the "not-I." The house is the membrane that mediates between inside and outside in the same way that the body, clothing, and language are shown to do. When David is in church he looks out and sees his house from the outside, thus putting himself for the first time in the position of an observer of a piece of "himself." "Outside" beings cannot be kept separate from the self, as David hopes: The original shelter comes soon to be invaded; but in a sense, after he goes "outside," on his return he himself is in the position of an alien—as is presently shown in Murdstone's treatment of him—and gradually comes to be denied access to his original nature.

There are literary parallels, incidentally, to Dickens's imaginary constructions here. Malte Laurids Brigge, Rilke's pseudo-autobiographical hero, expresses clearly a logic of alienation from his original home that augments the Copperfieldian vision. For Malte, the house is inside the self and yet fragmented by an adult memory which, in the act of reaching back seeks—unsuccessfully—to appropriate the original home in its prelapsarian unity: "As I recover it in recalling my child-wrought memories, it is no complete building; it is all broken up inside me; here a room, there a room, and here a piece of hallway that does not connect [them]. . . . in the obscurity of which one moved as blood does in the veins; the tower rooms, the high-hung balconies . . . all that is still in me and will never cease to be in me. It is as though the picture of this house had fallen into me from an infinite height and had shattered against my very ground."[16]

George Orwell said of the early passages of *Copperfield* that "the mental atmosphere . . . was so immediately intelligible to me [as a nine-year-old] that I vaguely imagined they had been written *by a child.*"[17] And truly, these passages come closer than perhaps any in literature to avoiding the appearance of what Bachelard calls that "*invented childhood,* with which novels abound." "For novelists often return to an invented childhood which has not been experienced to recount events whose naiveté is also invented. This unreal past . . . so often conceals the actuality of a daydream which would assume all its phenomenological value if it were presented in really actual naiveté. But the verbs *to be* and *to write* are hard to reconcile."[18] If they ever can be reconciled perhaps they are here, in this daydream of childhood which reveals so much "actual naiveté." Does Joyce achieve more at the beginning of *A Portrait of the Artist* where he invents naive language and thought?

In one respect David's movement into spaces more and more remote from home is an exile or alienation, which he begins to sense as early as the time he squirms in his pew at the church, the church which originally he had only seen from its outside, from the window of his home. But he is also able to perpetuate the first world in the greater world, so that what sometimes appears to be an advance in comprehending new things often is an imaginary reconstruction of them along the lines of the old things, in order that an easy transfer of affect can take place. And even the original way of seeing things perpetuates itself, often in spite of intervening crises. We can see an original attitude diffusing itself as a continuous structure in Dickens's progressive manipulations of what might be called a good-evil dichotomy. David can comprehend his church by means of homology: it is to the home what the Sunday parlour is to the daily one. Further, good and evil have their temporal as well as spatial axis; time is organized in weekly units—there is Sunday in opposition to the rest of the days, all forming a two-phase cycle of comfort and discomfort. Sunday is the day with its special places, clothing, behavior. (This is the day of the week that Dickens himself never forgave until the end of *Great Expectations;* a good example of an early attitude perpetuating itself throughout life.)[19] Sunday and church next come to be associated with Murdstone, whom David first sees walking his mother home from church. The courtship continues on Sundays, and the first disruption that Murdstone creates at David's own hearth happens on the night when David first mentions the prophetic little work-box of Peggotty's with its view of St. Paul's Cathedral, a miniature, and a symbolic foretaste of the London to which Murdstone exiles David. That night David and Peggotty have their first "adult" discussion, of marriage (also of course associated with the unpleasantness of churches), followed by their attack with renewed zeal on the Crocodile Book—for, significantly, this famous book also makes its first appearance on this unhappy occasion. The Crocodile Book, which David reads to Peggotty, rather than the other way around, is a prophetic miniature of David's own art—his autobiography. He says later that his "own infant face" looked up at him from the pages of this book, as if it were a kind of mirror. Appropriately, the stressed sounds in the word "crocodile" are the consonants C and D—can it be that Charles Dickens is once again playing a game with his own initials? This little book gives David his very earliest opportunity for role-playing using fictions; the role he plays is principally that of a savage who outwits Murdstonian monsters: "... we left their eggs in the sand for the sun to hatch; and we ran away from them, and baffled them by constantly turning, which they were unable to do quickly, on account of their unwieldy make; and we went into the water after them, as natives, and put sharp pieces of timber down their throats; and in short we ran the whole crocodile gauntlet" (2).

Fittingly enough, when Murdstone comes to take the place of David's father, he changes the whole current of life in the house, reversing it, directing it into the tabooed Sunday parlor, the one which David said had for him a "doleful air" because it was associated in his mind with the story of his father's funeral. Murdstone's seizure of the sacred parlor is both a sacrilege and the exercise of a privilege, since Murdstone is both the loathsome antithesis of the real father and a continuation of him. Lazarus has come from the dead, and the name "Murdstone" with all of its rich portmanteau meanings is proof of it. He is, like Headstone in *Our Mutual Friend,* the "dead" man who could cause death.[20] When David is told "You have got a Pa!" he says, "Something . . . connected with the grave in the churchyard, and the raising of the dead, seemed to strike me like an unwholesome wind" (3). When two of his associates greet Murdstone they say, "We thought you were dead!" (2). He is dark of dress, skin, and whisker and professes a mortifying religiosity. Here again is Dickens's motif of the evil rebirth and haunting resurrection of what was thought to be safely dead and buried in the past. Murdstone is the resurrection of death itself, of life's primal antithesis, of evil (since death threatens to halt the comforting—at first—cycles of infinite repetition) as time's limit.

Examples of the perpetual diffusion of David's original attitudes, even his original being, into later life occur when rooms intimate to himself offer continuity in the midst of his change. He is able to transfer feelings from one beloved room to the next, keeping intact all the while the sense of original shelter. The bedrooms—at the Yarmouth "Beein," at Peggotty's house, at Aunt Betsey's, at the Wickfield's, and so on—all are that original bedroom at Blunderstone. There is even a binary pattern of defilement in which, eventually, several of these are invaded by alien figures whose presence clearly is a desecration that symbolizes violations of the self by others. When Murdstone comes to live at the "Rookery" he ousts David from his original bedroom: "My old dear bedroom was changed, and I was to lie a long way off" (3). (He is first an exile *within* his own home.) Years later a madman comes to occupy that first room. In later life, Heep's intrusions repeat Murdstone's. Heep occupies David's bedroom in Agnes's house and worms his way into his London lodgings for a night, as well. Were these rooms not so thoroughly identified with his very being, occupancy by others would not have the awful significance that it seems to have.

In spite of these reconstructive powers and this analogical thinking, David's actual originals are more real than the ones he manufactures for himself. This explains the need for return to the places of his origins. After his first excursions to Yarmouth and Salem House there are homecomings highly charged with emotion. Even though Blunderstone Rookery has become desecrated, he sees it as a photographic negative from which he tries to print in memory a picture of his origins, which now have the super-reality of dream: "Ah, what a strange feeling it was to be going home when it was not home, and to find that every object I looked at, reminded me of the happy old home, which was like a dream I could never dream again!" (8). Paradoxically, this closeness to origins awakens the sense of distance from them. Later, after the Murdstones have left, David abandons himself to a nostalgic meditation in which he imagines that the light of his origins has gone out.

> God knows I had no part in it while they remained there, but it pained me to think of the dear old place as altogether abandoned; of the weeds growing tall in the garden, and the fallen leaves lying thick and wet upon the paths. I imagined how the winds of winter would howl around it, how the cold rain would beat upon the window-glass, how the moon would make ghosts on the walls of the empty rooms, watching their solitude all night. I thought afresh of the grave in the churchyard, underneath the tree: and it seemed as if the house were dead too, now, and all connected with my father and mother were faded away. (17)

In this we have some of the same poetry of the abandoned house as that which Virginia Woolf evokes at the beginning of the "Time Passes" section of *To the Lighthouse*. But here, especially, the house's desolation and disrepair represent a corresponding condition of the self momentarily deprived of Eden, where the "weeds [are now] growing tall."

David's origins are not dead to his memory, however. When he and Steerforth visit Yarmouth in later days, when they are both out of school and a new gap has opened in David's life between schooldays and the next stage in his career, he returns home. "I had naturally an interest in going over to Blunderstone, and revisiting the old familiar scenes of my childhood."

> My occupation in my solitary pilgrimages was to recall every yard of the old road as I went along it, and to haunt the old spots, of which I never tired. I haunted them, as my memory had often done, and lingered among them as my younger thoughts had lingered when I was far away.... I walked near [the grave beneath the tree] by the hour.... My reflections at these times were always associated with the figure I was to make in life.... [as if] I had come home to build my castles in the air at a living mother's side. (22)

For "more than a fortnight" he lurks and lingers about his native place, "haunting" it as if he were himself merely a ghost now, but soaking up the atmosphere, recharging spiritual batteries all the while. At almost every important hiatus in his life he must make a progress through the scenes of his past; again and again he passes over old, familiar ground. The London–Canterbury–Dover road hardly ever fails to stir up the remembrance of his original unhappy pilgrimage from London; the London–Yarmouth road perpetually awakens memories of his first trip from home. "It was curious and interesting ... to be sitting up there, behind four horses [now he is on the Canterbury-London road]: well educated, well dressed, and with plenty of money in my pocket; and to look out for the places where I had slept on my weary journey. I had abundant occupation for my thoughts, in every conspicuous landmark on the road" (19). "In the imagination to go in and to come out are never symmetrical images."[21] By the same token Dickens exploits the asymmetries of departure and return—here, as in *Oliver Twist* and *Great Expectations,* to indicate development of the self as well as to hint at a pervasive stasis. In *Copperfield* what comes through the most is the hero's conservative engagement with the "first time," even when that time was unpleasant. But it is Dickens's irony that many of David's repetitions, which awaken the sense of the "first time," either show how far he is from those times he would like to repeat, or how near he is to those he would like to forget.

In some of the repetitions of *Copperfield* we see a picture no doubt representative of the Victorian mentality in its nostalgic phase. Cold, antinostalgic winds blow in later, astringent *Bildungsromane* like *Ernest Pontifex,* where the hero looks back only in anger. But in *Copperfield* the recoil from the sense of time and change reinforces a tendency to worship even the humblest objects associated with the past. There is a typically Victorian attention paid to forget-me-nots of all descriptions, an elevation of intrinsically worthless *things.* A gloss on this attitude is Strachey's splendid account, in *Queen Victoria,* of the Queen's passion for turning everything into mementoes.[22] We have seen how the "thing" in *Oliver Twist* was raised to awareness by being displaced from its everyday context and then being made to serve as a veritable concretion of the self. In *Copperfield* somewhat the same rule of perception applies, except that displacement is in memory: the thing is real to the extent that it is a souvenir, and the souvenir resurrects a past state-of-being.

The "things" that stand out in *Copperfield* are often relics associated with the *mysterium tremendum* of origins. Certain objects recollected from early childhood appear over and over to speak of sources. There are, for example, the Crocodile Book and Peggotty's sewing kit, which is nothing less than a "little house with a thatched roof, where the yard-measure lived," which is always accompanied by "her workbox with a sliding lid, with a view of St. Paul's Cathedral (with a pink dome) painted on the top," a brass thimble, and a "little bit of wax-candle she kept for her thread" (2). These items, catalogued so lovingly and in such unusual detail, and associated with Peggotty, are like the savage's churinga, which contain the past and the self as well in a concrete form. (Bachelardian reverie might be able to make a great deal of these particular objects, one a sacred, another a profane miniature shelter.) Home for the holidays during the Murdstone ascendancy, David is already in the attitude of a *passéiste:* he secretly finds occasion to "read Peggotty a chapter out of the Crocodile Book, in remembrance of old times." "She took it out of her pocket: I don't know whether she had kept it there ever since" (8). There is a hint of freemasonry about this, and, loyal to the usages of their little cult, Peggotty saves the book so that David can read it whenever he visits Yarmouth. Almost every time Peggotty happens to "turn up" in his life these objects are displayed. They are left in her care, and when he visits her he handles them, allowing them to awaken in him the past. At the end of the book, Peggotty sits among David's children, never to be seen "without a bit of wax candle, a yard measure in the little house," etc. And "there is something bulky in Peggotty's pocket." What can it be? "It is nothing smaller than the Crocodile Book, which is in a rather dilapidated condition by this time, . . . but which Peggotty exhibits to the children as a precious relic. I find it very curious to see my own infant face looking up at me from the Crocodile stories" (64).

People acquire similar hieratic value, which seems to derive less from their intrinsic virtues than from their contribution to the meaning of David's life by the mere fact of their repeated appearances. The people David knows from his childhood pop up repeatedly in his life and serve to quicken dormant regions of his memory. Some of these *revenants* even help him to measure how much time has passed since he saw them last. Take Mr. Omer, the Yarmouth undertaker, who is a combined souvenir, *memento mori,* and human clock for David. As if drawn to the funeral parlor by an irresistible magnetism, David visits it every time he is in the neighborhood. We thus get a series of snapshots of life going on in the midst of death. Omer's apprentice becomes a master and marries; later on we see his children; and near the end of the novel we see Omer in a wheelchair almost ready for the grave himself. Nearly an entire generation is shown to pass in the course of this series of visits. These people mark both the stability of the past and the inexorable advance of time. In the change of some of these characters (even the immortal Aunt Betsey and Peggotty take to spectacles and wither up a bit in old age) we catch a glimpse of universal time-passing. But David's memory is always opposed to the strong current pulling him willy-nilly into the future. For him even writing an autobiography must be seen as an expression of his desire to repeat the past for repetitions's sake, and not just to gain self-knowledge. He is after self-recapture as well as self-knowledge. Dickens has created a consciousness with a double motive and a redoubled time-sense, in that David wishes to be at once literal about his past (to be representational) and creative of himself in the present. David's situation to some extent reinforces my view that Dickens confronts, in this novel, his own gradual shift from an art of representation or mimesis to an art of abstraction, artifice, free creation—free that is, of direct reference to social or moral issues of the Victorian world.

"The Prismatic Hues of Memory"

Touchstone characters like Omer might change, but they are always fixed in their milieu, always there when David wants to consult them. They all coexist in a kind of eternal suspension, ready to go into their acts whenever the hero needs them. David needs to have his past on tap, and the plot is such that he can have it that way much of the time. Even when the finite space of the original home is replaced by the supposedly infinite space of the city, the city also seems to accommodate itself to the hero's desire to live infinitely in time (in the infinite repetition of the finite past). These are "coincidental" encounters, of course. The city is often the place one goes to in order to get lost, but Copperfield's city is a place where everyone can miraculously be found. The city is a vast external counterpart of the hero's obsessive memory. Whatever is important to that memory, whether unpleasant or pleasant, is bound to "turn up" at the appropriate time. Murdstone happens to be at the court getting another marriage license just when David and Peggotty are on the spot as well. And David is always bumping into Mr. Peggotty as the latter wanders in search of Emily, who is expected to come to London, for "where could she lose herself so readily as in this vast city?" (46). Martha, the "lost" woman, is found precisely when Mr. Peggotty and Martha herself most need the encounter (when she is on the verge of suicide). This network of magical coincidences, in which the city seems to labor hard to answer to David's conscious and unconscious wishes and fears, can be seen in two encounters with Agnes. Right after David has learned that his aunt has lost her fortune, the following meeting occurs:

> I was trying to familiarise my mind with the worst, and to present to myself the arrangements we should have to make for the future in their sternest aspect, when a hackney chariot coming after me, and stopping at my very feet, occasioned me to look up. A fair hand was stretched forth to me from the window; and the face I had never seen without a feeling of serenity and happiness ... was smiling on me.
> "Agnes!" I joyfully exclaimed. "Oh, my dear Agnes, of all people in the world, what a pleasure to see you! ... I want to talk to you so much!" said I. "It's such a lightening of my heart, only to look at you! If I had had a conjurer's cap, there is no one I should have wished for but you." (35)

As Tim Linkinwater says in *Nicholas Nickleby*, "Why I don't believe now . . . that there's such a place in all the world for coincidences as London is!" Again, when he gets drunk and goes with friends to the theatre, another chance-in-a-million encounter with Agnes takes place. There is a perfect appropriateness to her seeing him at his worst: she is his lifelong moral guide and represents the return of the repressed conscience. If there was anybody he would rather *not* have seen! The claustral nature of the city corresponds to the repetitious consciousness of the hero. London is like a mind that can never forget. In *Oliver Twist* serendipitous coincidence was used to symbolize the operation of destiny; in *Copperfield* it symbolizes a tendency of consciousness to conserve its world.[23]

David says, when he sees London for the first time, "What an amazing place London was to me when I saw it in the distance . . . I believed all the adventures of all my favourite heroes to be constantly enacting and re-enacting there" (5). This is merely a child's fancy, but we have seen how people and things have a great repeatability in this novel. Many of David's own adventures, like those of his "favourite heroes," are frequently reenacted. Consider for instance a very humble kind of event, eating dinner. In *Copperfield,* as in *Great Expectations,* we are treated to a good many episodes in which the hero does little more than to eat dinner. There is a pattern to these seemingly anecdotal episodes that seldom varies; it is soon possible to see why we are shown them. David sits down to dinner and something goes wrong: the waiter bullies him, the housekeeper bullies him—servants are generally recalcitrant in some way—and usually the food is ill-prepared. Somehow David's immaturity is shown in the fact that the everyday ritual of eating cannot be observed properly. The first time he has this trouble is on the way to London, when the waiter dupes him into giving up his dinner. When he gets older the simple tricks are replaced by subtler evasions, as at the first dinner party he gives at his bachelor's lodgings—and the second time, as well. Then there is Dora's dinner, with Traddles as guest. Caught up as he is in an unpleasant form of repetition, David takes an unconscionably long time in life just learning how to get a proper dinner.

Repetitiveness in *Copperfield* generally signifies stasis as created by a sense of overdetermination at the level of structure. Repetitiveness is banal structure, in that it is unrelated to finite time, transformation, or the problems of meaning-making that these engender. One form of it is the basis of most of Dickens's comic effects in character drawing: the repetition of gesture and phrase of such as Mr. and Mrs. Micawber ("I shall never desert Mr. Micawber." "Something is bound to turn up.") The characters who are distinguished in this way, who do not take into account feedback from the changing environment, are of course veritable mechanisms who do not seem to exist fully in finite time. The principle that assures their infinite survival in a world of changing circumstances is hard to divine, to say the least. Perhaps it is in their very thingness that they find the source of their durability.[24] " 'If [Micawber] always goes on in the same way, he must be, virtually, about two hundred years old at present' " (54). These characters, as static as any created in seventeenth-century "character-books," provide a choral background against which we can measure the changes that occur in David.

III. Dickensian Psychology: The Theory of Memory

William H. Marshall, in discussing the narrator of *Copperfield*, says that "the writing becomes, rather than merely a record of the past, a description of his tranquil recollection."[25] It is important to recognize Dickens's accomplishment in creating a narrator who not only unfolds a remembered world but also reveals the process of remembering it (a process not always "tranquil"). To manage this Dickens veritably had to be able to imagine David's past and present as if he had not lived them, which is an achievement in inventing another consciousness seemingly more characteristic of, say, Conrad's four Marlow narratives than of Dickens's art. At this point, we engage Robert Garis's influential argument about Dickens's inability to render (or imagine) a character's inside.[26] Pursuing the "theatrical" Dickens, Garis thus emphasizes a point I should like to see this book partly discredit, even at risk of making too much of the subtlety of Dickens's imaginary psychology.

To a large extent Garis's argument depends upon an evidently constricted view of what inner life as presented in a novel might actually be. We can see this limitation in his comments on the two main incidents he selects as, presumably, among Dickens's best representations of the interior of the self: the thoughts and feelings of Lady Dedlock in *Bleak House* just before she begins her flight from Sir Leicester (55), and Fagin's thoughts while he is on the prisoner's dock (32). The first of these I don't really need to discuss because Garis admits—"as the exception that proves the rule"—Dickens's powers here. He comments, though, in order to dismiss this imaginativeness as incidental, that "Dickens' insight into Lady Dedlock's mind here represents a special act of the sympathetic imagination which is caused by Dickens' special interest in the psychology of guilt."[27] But though the psychology of guilt is a special Dickensian topic, it is indeed one he deals with in almost every novel and usually explores at the most critical moments of suffering, decision, and change—during what Karl Jaspers calls the "boundary situations." It is also a topic that is special to a great many other novelists, including Dostoyevsky, Kafka, and Conrad, to name only a few. Wherever a novelist strives for psychological vision this topic is almost bound to come up in some way, if the personal consequences of deviant action are to be explored.

As for the fine moment at Fagin's trial, Garis decides that, since Dickens shows Fagin's consciousness as a kind of blank, "no inner life, properly speaking, is taking place."[28] But to show a mind suddenly released from the praxis of existence to become for a moment an idle spectator of its own impending doom is to make an excellent supposition about the way a mind might actually function. Garis does not choose to explore, beneath the melodramatic surface, the further motions of Fagin's inner life as Dickens reveals them in the rest of the chapter, which, as the title tells us, is concerned particularly with "The Jew's Last Night Alive." Certainly guilt and the imagining of death (which are associated with one another in many of Dickens's other accounts of inner life) are psychic events important enough not to be thought merely "special," in the sense that Garis implies.

Of course, a defense of the view that Dickens was unable to deal adequately with inner life would have to depend upon analysis of *Copperfield* and *Great Expectations,* as well as of certain characters in the other later novels. As for the latter, as Garis says, "the careers of Arthur Clennam, of Bella Wilfer, of Eugene Wrayburn, and others represent ... another kind of exception to the rule."²⁹ In short, a good many of Dickens's most important developing characters are dismissed as exceptions, even though Dickens, admittedly with varying degrees of success, does explore their inner lives, too, and at similarly important moments. Supposedly, *Great Expectations* is "Dickens' masterpiece" because it is the apotheosis of the Dickens theatre and not because of Dickens's successful handling of inner life. (Success, in Garis's view, apparently means writing about inner life the way George Eliot does it.) Garis's discussion of this novel is subtle and displays Dickens's brilliant use of certain "theatrical" devices in order that his narrator might reveal more than a real middle-aged bourgeois could be expected to do, but the upshot of Garis's discussion is that Pip's hard-won objectivity about life is somehow brought into "the theatre" as: "the mature Pip's traditional attitude towards the history of his inner life."³⁰ "The tradition of the Seven Ages of Man is not far away"³¹ from this book in which, on the other hand, Graham Greene noticed the "music of memory that so influenced Proust."³²

In his interpretation of Dickens's treatment of the inner life, Garis goes wrong, I think, in two respects: First, he is apparently unwilling to admit the full force of what we all discover in interpreting the Brontës, Dickens, Dostoyevsky, Conrad, Kafka, and others—that various things outside the characters can "express" their inner lives and notions about inner life in ways that are sometimes more subtle and interesting than realistic or mimetic character analysis as offered by such as George Eliot. Even an author's handling of a traditional theatrical device, as when Dickens insistently uses "ghosts" to haunt his characters, can produce a quite complex statement about the structure and operation of consciousness. Taylor Stoehr has shown that Dickens's devices, from local aspects of his style to complete plots, are at least analogous to that most revelatory activity of the inner self, dreaming.³³ Certain of Dickens's effects are traditional, or lead us to traditional insights, but they are so in much the way Freud's basic insights are also traditional. Dickens is not Freud, and I am not the parlor analyst to propose that he might be. But where Dickens's theories, such as the important theory of memory, reveal themselves in action, as in his novels of growing up, a mere notation of the emergent structures and textures reveals much: Even when we do not admit any astonishing insight into actual psychology, we find a subtle imaginary psychology, which offers an interesting repertory of behavior for a consciousness threatened by change and time.

The second flaw in Garis's argument is his insistence that Dickens's first-person narrators are, as I take it, purely formal devices for getting a story told in what is still, somehow, the voice of the Inimitable himself. I deal further with this point in Chapter Four, in my discussion of the narrator of *Great Expectations.* Esther Summerson of *Bleak House* is, I suspect, the starting point for those who see in Dickens's other first-person narrators only "thin verbal mask[s]" that are not fully realized characters in their own right. For it is perfectly true that "we are not surprised to find our belief in the existence of Esther Summerson to be a very limited kind of belief."[34] As Garis shows, she is in many respects a rhetorical invention, a viewpoint for the "attack on system" that he sees as one main objective of the Dickens theatre. But *Copperfield,* which displays simultaneously two different stages of the same character's life (and which shows the narrator's psyche as fully as it does the hero's), is different. Garis does not discuss *Copperfield* except in passing, and he does not touch on Dickens's use of a fully realized first-person narrator in revealing the content of inner life. The self-examination that was presumably taking place in Dickens at the time of *Copperfield* is not important, says Garis, whose a priori judgment shows up clearly in the way he states the case: "The fact that Dickens never really developed a fictional mode suitable for self-examination suggests that what took place within him was not really self-examination at all."[35] The point is that for all practical purposes, what happened "inside" Dickens at the time and what happens in the novel are one and the same act of self-examination. Dickens's thought, insofar as we can ever know it fully, is to be known in his novel, where he was investing the major part of his energies. What remains to be decided is whether *Copperfield* serves as a "fictional mode suitable for self-examination." Garis refers to the ending of *Copperfield* unfavorably and then makes the interesting comment that "although . . . Dickens' former attitudes saw him through the actual composition of *David Copperfield,* everything that happened afterwards shows that an important change had taken place."[36] Garis says this much even though he would exclude the possibility that perhaps something important in *Copperfield* itself might have been responsible for the new direction Dickens's work took after this novel.

I shall not defend *Copperfield* as the turning point of Dickens's career, because to do so I would have to depart from my immediate concerns in order to dig into at least *Dombey and Son* (1848) and *Bleak House* (1853). It is enough to point out here that what is new in *Copperfield* is the exploration of the continuities and discontinuities of a single life in the context of a more or less continuous memory—for of course memory was extremely important in Dickens's psychological scheme. He dealt with it more fully than any other writer of his time (except possibly Wordsworth, whose *Prelude* was published the same year as *Copperfield*), while many of the crucial situations and characters in his novels were designed to present problems of memory. In his major attempt, in *Copperfield,* at envisioning a working memory, Dickens expatiated on psychological time with an emphasis which was quite special in his novels. He afterwards continued to depict memory as playing a major part in psychic growth, but did not emphasize again many of the problems he focused on in *Copperfield.*

It might be helpful in understanding the role of memory in *Copperfield,* and elsewhere, to examine *The Haunted Man,* a story Dickens completed for Christmas 1848. Here, as in so many of Dickens's shorter works, we can see, reduced to clear schema, the concerns of the longer novels. The story was finished after *Dombey and Son,* whose final number appeared in April 1848. Edgar Johnson says that the fragments of Dickens's soon-to-be-abandoned autobiography were "begun not long before or after *The Haunted Man* was conceived,"[37] and, considering the content of the latter, it certainly belongs with *Copperfield* as a fictional expression of what we can surmise to have been Dickens's confessional impulse at that time. It is about a famous chemist, Redlaw, who is burdened with unhappy memories to the extent that, when given the opportunity by an obliging phantom, he consents to have his memory erased. He is also invested with the power to cancel the memories of other people he comes into contact with. But this blessing, a variant of the Midas touch, becomes a curse to its possessor. Everyone he infects with loss of memory immediately becomes brutal, unsympathetic, or conscienceless; the sentimental ties that link husband and wife in the midst of common suffering are suddenly dissolved; fathers disown their sons, and sons curse their fathers. Finally, through the healing humanity—or perhaps the angelic power—of a woman, Milly, he is able to regain his memory. The conclusion of the tale is one of those Christmas dinners that embody so well Dickens's *philosophie de Noël;* the last words of the story are the prayer, "Lord, keep my memory green!"

Before he lost his memory, Redlaw went about "with a distraught air of reverting to a byegone place and time, or of listening to some old echoes in his mind ... [with] the manner of a haunted man."[38] This haunting of the present by the past happens often in Dickens's writings. Usually it awakens the self to the need for getting on the right terms with the misfortunes of the past. As it was for Scrooge, Christmas for Redlaw was only the sign of "another year gone! ... More figures in the lengthening sum of recollection that we work and work at to our torment" (255). He wants to cancel this negative aspect of memory, but by doing so he cancels as well its positive features, which are also part of "the intertwisted chain of feelings and associations, each in its turn dependent on, and nourished by, the banished recollections" (270). With the banishment of memory, identity itself becomes doubtful. "He looked confusedly upon his hands and limbs, as if to be assured of his identity ... for there was a strangeness and terror upon him, as if he ... were lost" (271). "My mind is going blind!" he says (294). He becomes a mere observer, a picaresque figure, a one-dimensional man, his eye the blank eye of a Blakean Ulro-dweller: "The time had been ... when not one of these objects, in its remotest association of interest ... would have been lost on Redlaw. Now, they were but objects" (295). "He stopped to listen to a plaintive strain of music, but could only hear a tune, made manifest to him by the dry mechanism of the instruments and his own ears, with no address to any mystery within him, without a whisper in it of the past, or of the future" (309–10). Abolish the past, and you abolish the present and future as well.

One of the few people Redlaw cannot infect with his "blessing" is a strange little street urchin, an unchildlike child, "a baby savage, a young monster, a child who had never been a child, a creature who might live to take the outward form of man, but who, within, would live and perish a mere beast" (272). As Kierkegaard would say, his "form of existence belongs to every animal." This child cannot be deprived of memory because he does not have any: "No softening memory of sorrow, wrong, or trouble enters here, because this wretched mortal from his birth has been abandoned to a worse condition than the beasts, and has, within his knowledge, no one contrast, no humanising touch, to make a grain of such a memory spring up in his hardened breast" (327).[39] According to Dickens, there can be no self without memory; that is, the total, differential memory built up out of two kinds of experience, good and bad. It is impossible to be whole without this whole, structured memory. Redlaw realizes this when he says, "In the material world, as I have long taught, nothing can be spared; no step or atom in the wondrous structure could be lost, without a blank being made in the great universe. I know, now, that it is the same with good and evil, happiness and sorrow, in the memories of men" (322). In a letter to Forster about this story, Dickens said, "Of course my point is that bad and good are inextricably linked in remembrance, and that you could not choose the enjoyment of recollecting only the good. To have all the best of it you must remember the worst also."[40]

In this rather schematic but significant tale Dickens gives us the essence of his theory of memory and shows us why the Dickens hero, as opposed to the Stendhal hero defined by Georges Poulet, cannot simply, at each moment, "*forget* what he was in order to become as he wishes."[41] Becoming is not quite so easy for him. Dickens designs an inverted theory of repression, which furthermore implies a distinction between willed and unwilled remembering; and the theory is an assertion of a more direct relation between character and experience than we saw in *Oliver Twist*. This is a kind of historicism based not on any firm notion of external causality, but on a "totalizing" law of the psyche that can run counter to external sequences by establishing its own priorities, its own "chain of feelings and associations." And in fact it is a law which points the way to freedom from what is at first appallingly sensed as external, deterministic sequence. Novelistically, this law justifies a certain freedom in designing character psychology. In *Oliver Twist* good and evil experiences were kept for the most part in separate spheres; in *The Haunted Man* the theory of memory, which provides the substructure of *Copperfield,* posits an identity built up out of good and evil experiences. Good and evil come into dynamic relation in the self rather than remain in static opposition to one another. Continuity in the self comes from the conscious acknowledgement of positive and negative phases of experience, phases once thought of not as phases but as "adventures" extrinsic, fundamentally alien to one another. This is now a definite beginning of a monistic, structured view that seeks unity out of the diversity of experience, which posits a complex, totalized self as an outgrowth of manifold (though, for memory, essentially two-valued) experiences. In his view of memory as fundamental to identity, Dickens thus explicitly recognizes his characters' essential temporality and offers the key to its structure.

Dickens distinguishes between two basic projects of memory in *Copperfield.* One is the hero's—and to a great extent the narrator's—attempt to experience the totality of life by repeating those good moments of the past which are the basis of his personal myth (his simplistic notion of his life-pattern). The second is the narrator's—and to a much lesser extent the hero's—attempt verbally to repeat his life in its entirety, not just for repetition's sake, but also for self-knowledge (and a self-remaking) that will allow him to turn away from the evils of the past.

The second project arises mainly because of the failure of the first. The first fails because of an early intrusion of evil, which comes so early as to demand to be itself included in the structure of the primary myth; but the hero never clearly sees the connection between the "good" part of the myth and the "evil" part. According to the theory of memory, if the hero were to see this connection he would immediately explode the myth (the naive little scenario of innocence) and enter a new, complex life. Kafka has a parable of a leopard that breaks in upon a holy place to despoil it again and again until finally the sacrilegious intrusions are made a part of the ritual of the place. This complex recognition and accommodation of insistent evil apparently is denied the Dickens hero; it is the phase of the parable that precedes accommodation that David experiences most of his life. David's memory-life consists of a disturbing oscillation between

"The Prismatic Hues of Memory"

"automatic" returns of at one time the good past and at another the evil one. His life contains both a desirable repetition and an unpredictable, undesirable repetitiousness—and we can perhaps best see the writing of the "autobiography" as partly an attempt to put an end to such instability, such repetitious unpredictability. The latter results from a specialization of memory that in effect partitions good and evil and *wills* to know only good. Many other Dickens characters make the same mistake through willing to know only evil, including Mrs. Clennam in *Little Dorrit* and Miss Havisham in *Great Expectations.*

Here is an example of the way David's memory, both as willingly and unwillingly activated (it is often not clear which), operates to segment the past, to condition it so that certain unpleasant things are either screened out of memory or else somehow kept apart from the pleasant things though they are able to exercise their disruptive vitality just the same. David says of Dora when she is dying, that "Ever rising from the sea of my remembrance, is the image of the dear child as I knew her first" (53). This is precisely the kind of language he used earlier, when speaking of the death of his mother: "I remembered her, from that instant, only as the young mother of my earliest impressions" (9). And further: "What Peggotty had told me now, was so far from bringing me back to the later period [of Murdstone], that it rooted the earlier image in my mind. It may be curious, but it is true. In her death she winged her way back to her calm untroubled youth and cancelled all the rest" (9). But in spite of the fact that he does not attempt to recall the image of his mother as an older, more experienced woman in her suffering (that word *image* is quite appropriate to David's static way of viewing her; the word *presence* is similarly applied to Agnes, later on), the scene of her funeral, by a kind of compensation, comes to oppress him: "Events of later date have floated from me to the shore where all forgotten things will reappear, but this stands like a high rock in the ocean" (9). And "the great remembrance by which that time is marked in my mind, seems to have swallowed up all lesser recollections, and to exist alone" (9).

David's usual tendency is to establish a hierarchy of experiences in which "earlier" is superior to "later." For much of the time, beginning when childhood is hardly over, his present becomes merely the time for remembering the past and for finding pastness in present events. The only present that had been fully real in and for itself was the time of the childhood idyll, the eternally recurrent present, when one was too young to imagine either a past or a future:

> The days sported by us, as if Time had not grown up himself yet, but were a child too, and always at play.... As to any sense of inequality, or youthfulness, or other difficulty in our way, little Em'ly and I had no such trouble, because we had no future. We made no more provision for growing older, than we did for growing younger. (3)

> What happiness (I thought) if we were married, and were going away anywhere to live among the trees and in the fields, never growing older, never growing wiser, children ever, rambling hand in hand through sunshine and among flowery meadows. (10)

Time present is fully time present only when one is a child; Angus Wilson is correct in saying that very little *happens* to David after his childhood is over.[42] Later, even when the present offers up new experience, sometimes it is deprived of newness, as déjà vu.

> We have all some experience of a feeling, that comes over us occasionally, of what we are saying and doing having been said and done before ... of our having been surrounded, dim ages ago, by the same faces, objects, and circumstances—of our knowing perfectly what will be said next, as if we suddenly remembered it! (39)

> [Heep] seemed to swell and grow before my eyes; the room seemed full of the echoes of his voice; and the strange feeling (to which, perhaps, no one is quite a stranger) that all this had occurred before, at some indefinite time, and that I knew what he was going to say next, took possession of me. (25)

Or an experience will refer back, in Proustian fashion, to an earlier one: Dora's ring is "so associated in my remembrance with Dora's hand, that yesterday, when I saw such another, by chance, on the finger of my own daughter, there was a momentary stirring in my heart, like pain!" (33). "The scent of a geranium leaf, at this day, strikes me with a half comical, half serious wonder as to what change has come over me in a moment; and then I see [again] a straw hat and blue ribbons, and a quantity of curls" (36).

But the past comes to occupy the present in a more subtle way, a way which does not bode well for the narrator, if he is trying to

"The Prismatic Hues of Memory"

avoid the repetitions that alternately shatter and restore him. There are moments in *Copperfield* when narrator and hero become virtually one.

> The influence of the strain [of music from Mr. Mell's flute] upon me was ... to make me so sleepy that I couldn't keep my eyes open. They begin to close again, and I begin to nod, as the recollection rises fresh upon me. Once more the little room, with its open corner cupboard, and its square-backed chairs, and its angular little staircase leading to the room above, and its three peacock's feathers displayed over the mantelpiece—I remember wondering when I first went in, what that peacock would have thought if he had known what his finery was doomed to come to—fades from before me, and I nod, and sleep. The flute becomes inaudible, the wheels of the coach are heard instead, and I am on my journey. The coach jolts, I wake with a start, and the flute has come back again, and the Master at Salem House is sitting with his legs crossed, playing it dolefully, while the old woman of the house looks on delighted. She fades in her turn, and he fades, and all fades, and there is no flute, no Master, no Salem House, no David Copperfield, no anything but heavy sleep. (5)

This is a complex, perhaps confused, moment of remembering. For one thing, both the narrator and the hero are remembering (observing the past, really), and their perceptions and memories are fitted one within the other. The hero gets sleepy, and the narrator also nods, as "recollection rises fresh"; but in the next sentence, when the narrator continues to nod, it has to be, by an almost imperceptible shift in viewpoint, the hero who falls asleep. The use of "I" as usual and the unusual use of the present tense bring hero and narrator together so closely that if we did not assume that the narrator has to be awake to narrate we would think that he has actually fallen asleep, too. When "the coach jolts" the hero awakens and immediately relives in an undistanced memory the events that the narrator is also now re-reliving in the telling, many years later. At such moments distinctions between past and present and narrator and hero become almost pointless. Elsewhere the narrator says, "There was that jumble in my thoughts and recollections, that I lost the clear arrangement of time and distance" (55). Insistently, the novel mentions facts of memory and perception, but as often as not it dissolves these states of mind into fields of rapidly reciprocating functions. There is no past and present, merely remembering and perceiving as a total, complex act. Consider this passage, where time relations become indeed complex.

> As I walked to and fro daily between Southwark and Blackfriars, and lounged about at meal-times in obscure streets, the stones of which may, for anything I know, be worn at this moment by my childish feet, I wonder how many of these people were wanting in the crowd that used to come filing before me in review again, to the echo of Captain Hopkins's voice! When my thoughts go back now, to that slow agony of my youth, I wonder how much of the histories I invented for such people hangs like a mist of fancy over well-remembered facts! (11)

One is perhaps first disoriented by a defeated expectancy of tense-continuity between "As I walked" and the beginning of the main clause, "I wonder"—an expectancy that persists in spite of or perhaps because of the seemingly momentary shift of tenses in the dependent clauses. Description of the past-as-past, followed by speculation on a present condition (of the stones), suddenly becomes a present meditation on the past. This meditation is displaced somewhat, at "these people," by the actual past, which keeps percolating into this sentence not as past, but as present. This past is pushed out by the distancing "used to come," but it then pops back at "in review again." "The echo of Captain Hopkins's voice," which is the first really concrete memory of the hero's that the narrator is able to gain direct access to here, is shared by hero and narrator in the present (by virtue of the "again," which is definitely in the narrator's as well as the hero's present). The original experience, "Captain Hopkins's voice," here comes to the hero as mediated (an echo), but the hero's memory comes to the narrator as unmediated. Once again the narrator's memory gives him present access to fields of rememberings instead of to original experiences. To remember remembering is to have, indeed, the "strong memory" that the narrator claims he has.

The above passages represent, I think, an achievement of Dickens's art; they work to suggest a certain specious wholeness of self, when the self-alienation, the temporal separation of hero and narrator, seems to vanish, and child and adult become as one. In these moments of mystification, what we have taken as the general objective of confessional narrative, which is to see the major phases of life as external to one another and yet as continuous, is not being

"The Prismatic Hues of Memory"

achieved. There is often, as here, no past *and* present, but instead a presentness of things and memories past. If David's "autobiography" is for self-knowledge and not simply self-recapture (which it ought to be according to the logic of the theory of memory), then the mystifications arising at such moments as those discussed above will not do at all. Taking into account those occasions, as well as numerous other ones when a strange kind of past displaces the present, we have in effect a dramatization of an unhealthy memory.

We can now understand better what I have designated as the second project of memory by considering the Memorial ("his own history") that Mr. Dick works at continually. An unpleasant episode in his past—his sister's abandonment of him—is the cause of his madness. " 'That was before he came to me,' " says Aunt Betsey. " 'But the recollection of it is oppressive to him now. Did he say anything to you about King Charles the First, child?' " (14). Like Miss Havisham's in *Great Expectations,* Mr. Dick's clock has stopped at the moment evil intruded into his life. His own identity has somehow become partly confused with that of the unfortunate king (" 'how could the people about him have made that mistake of putting some of the trouble out of *his* head, after it was taken off, into *mine?'* "). Consequently the King Charles head keeps appearing in the Memorial, which is meant to be about Mr. Dick. " 'It's not a business-like way of speaking,' said my aunt, 'nor a worldly way. I am sure of that; and that's the reason why I insist upon it, that there shan't be a word about it in his Memorial!' " (14). Since he cannot keep Charles the First out of his Memorial, even though "every day of his life he had a long sitting at it," the Memorial "never made the least progress" (15). Until the great evil of his life can be appropriately verbalized, Mr. Dick is condemned to eternal repetitiveness. Since the evil that the head of Charles the First "stands for" cannot be confessed to in a story about himself in a disguised symbolic form, it will never get said at all—and so it persists in his mind. Aunt Betsey's insistence on literalness is what perpetuates the writer's block and the kite-flying.

Mr. Dick's need to free himself from the past by an adequate confession is also David's need. Not inscribing one's own history condemns one to repeating, in thought, its evils. David must attempt to confess, and repeat all of his history, perhaps as literal autobiography, in order to be freed from having to repeat discontinuous, opposed parts of it over and over again; for whenever he uncritically actuates his personal myth of childhood,[43] the dark counterpart of that myth returns upon him as well. This other, presumably separate myth comprehends all the evil first times of childhood. David writes, remembering his departure for Murdstone and Grinby's wines and spirits warehouse, that "I now approach a period of my life, which I can never lose the remembrance of, while I remember anything; and the recollection of which has often, without my invocation, come before me like a ghost, and haunted happier times" (10). Here is an early evil often repeated hauntingly. As we know, Murdstone and Grinby's is the "allegorical way of expressing" Warren's blacking warehouse, scene of the first intrusion of evil into Dickens's childhood world, scene of the darkest episode of Dickens's early life. Like David, and Redlaw in *The Haunted Man,* Dickens, too, perhaps felt an evil event return upon him again and again. But, again, this is merely autobiographical extrapolation.

Certainly what we know of Dickens's response to another event that supposedly haunted him, the death of his beloved sister-in-law Mary Hogarth (7 May 1837), qualifies as a quite explicit contribution to the theory of memory and relates specifically to David's project in writing his autobiography. We have records of the response in at least three places (including Forster's biography), two of the accounts being almost identical and quite interesting. The first of these two is in a letter on dreams to a Dr. Stone (2 February 1851), and the second is in a semi-autobiographical story, "The Holly Tree" (1855). I shall cite here only the first as being rather the more revealing one, if analytic power is our criterion.

> Recurring dreams which come back almost as certain as the night—unhealthy and morbid species of these visions—should be particularly noticed. Secrecy on the part of the dreamer, as to these illusions, has a remarkable tendency to perpetuate them.
>
> I once underwent great affliction in the loss of a very dear young friend. For a year I dreamed of her every night, sometimes as living, sometimes as dead, never in any terrible or shocking aspect. As she had been my wife's sister and had died suddenly in our house, I forbore to allude to these dreams—kept them wholly to myself. At the end of the year, I lay down to sleep in an inn on a wild Yorkshire moor,

covered with snow. As I looked out of the window on the bleak winter prospect before I undressed, I wondered within myself whether the subject would follow me here. It did. Writing home next morning, I mentioned the circumstance, cheerfully, as being curious. The subject immediately departed out of my dreams, and years passed before it returned.[44]

What Dickens claims to have discovered about his own mental processes appears in his fiction as a matter for much more extensive treatment than his letter to Dr. Stone gave it. Evidently, for David Copperfield, the escape from morbid, repetitious visions (bad memories) is to be made by writing them down for himself. Pip, on the other hand, goes a great deal further in the direction that Dickens's letter suggests. It is not enough merely to write down bad dreams or bad memories; they must be confessed to and for other people. In *Great Expectations* the narrator confesses in writing for his unknown readers, while the hero (the younger Pip) confesses himself verbally to other characters within the novel. But as for Dickens himself, his claim that, in his letter home, he "mentioned the circumstances [of a recurrent dream he has already characterized as an 'unhealthy and morbid species of ... vision'] cheerfully, as being curious," might prompt us to beware of a certain indirection with regard to his more precious secrets. What we have to allow for, in interpreting his novels, is the presence of a fictional (and in that sense indirect) confession that is perhaps more useful to him than the direct, nonfictional confession that we call autobiography.

Notes

1. *David Copperfield,* ed. George H. Ford (Cambridge, Mass.: Riverside Press, 1958), p. 9. All further references will be to this edition, with chapter numbers cited parenthetically in my text.
2. *Joseph and His Brothers,* trans. H. T. Lowe-Porter (New York: Alfred A. Knopf, 1963), p. 3.
3. *Daniel Deronda,* chap. 1.
4. Bruce F. Kawin, *Telling It Again and Again: Repetition in Literature and Film* (Ithaca, N.Y.: Cornell University Press, 1972), p. 4, draws an excellent distinction between "repetitiousness" and "repetitive" in imaginative experience:

> *Repetitious:* when a word, percept, or experience is repeated with less impact at each recurrence; repeated to no particular end, out of a failure of invention or sloppiness of thought. *Repetitive:* when a word, percept, or experience is repeated with equal or greater force at each occurrence.

In *Copperfield* the impulse to be repetitive is consistently frustrated by the discovery that, owing to the recurring presence of evil, experience becomes repetitious.

5. *The Idea of History* (New York: Galaxy Books, 1956), p. 82.
6. See *Tom Jones,* Bk. 1, chap. 1, for a statement on "Human Nature" that reveals the eighteenth-century bias. As for my claim that the mind of Copperfield is in process, see William H. Marshall, "The Image of Steerforth and the Structure of *David Copperfield,*" *Tennessee Studies in Literature* 5 (1960): 57-65. Marshall emphasizes, in making his point, that *Copperfield* is the autobiography of *David,* not Dickens. Consider also Gwendolyn B. Needham, "The Undisciplined Heart of David Copperfield," *Nineteenth-Century Fiction* 9 (1954): 84.
7. John Forster, *The Life of Charles Dickens,* rev. A. J. Hoppé (London: J. M. Dent & Sons, 1966) 2:78.
8. John Butt and Kathleen Tillotson, *Dickens at Work* (London: Methuen, 1957), pp. 121-23. Also Forster, *Life of Charles Dickens,* 2:78.
9. Forster, *Life of Charles Dickens,* 2:79.
10. *Microcosmography; or A Piece of the World Discovered* (London, 1811), p. 1.
11. Aldous Huxley, ed., *The Letters of D. H. Lawrence* (New York: Viking Press, 1932), p. 200.
12. An elaborate treatment of Dickens's serialization procedures is Archibald C. Coolidge's *Charles Dickens as Serial Novelist* (Ames, Ia.: Iowa State University Press, 1967), though one questions the interpretive weight of Coolidge's initial "collection of some 25,000 separate facts about Dickens's novels" (p. vii).
13. *The Poetics of Space,* trans. Maria Jolas (New York: Orion Press, 1964), p. 104.

14. Ibid., p. xxxiii.

15. The pattern of the *Confessions* proceeds from division, reflected in Augustine's bewilderment over Manichean dualism, to a fervent monism in which opposites are reconciled in an experience of conversion that reconciles the narrator to the Lord's will. On the level of self, as M. H. Abrams shows, the " 'two wills, one old, one new, one carnal, one spiritual' " of the narrator are subsumed into a higher awareness, by the regenerative experience in the garden at Milan. *Natural Supernaturalism: Tradition and Revolution in Romantic Literature* (New York: W. W. Norton, 1971), p. 85.

16. Rainer Maria Rilke, *The Notebooks of Malte Laurids Brigge,* trans. M. D. Herter Norton (New York: Capricorn Books, 1958), pp. 30-31.

17. "Charles Dickens," *A Collection of Essays* (Garden City, N.Y.: Anchor Books, 1954), p. 67.

18. Bachelard, *Poetics of Space,* p. 138.

19. See Edgar Johnson's discussion of Dickens's caustic pamphlet, *Sunday Under Three Heads: As it is; As Sabbath Bills would make it; As it might be made* (1836) in which Dickens attempts to save Sunday as a day of enjoyment. *Tragedy and Triumph,* pp. 144-47.

20. See the story of Captain Murderer in "Nurse's Stories," *Uncommercial Traveller* (1860). Dickens says that "the first diabolical character who intruded himself on my peaceful youth . . . was a certain Captain Murderer. . . . His warning name would seem to have awakened no general prejudice against him, for he was admitted into the best society and possessed immense wealth. Captain Murderer's mission was matrimony, and the gratification of a cannibal appetite with tender brides." This figure, out of one of the stories that Dickens remembered best from his childhood, bears obvious resemblance to Murdstone.

21. Bachelard, *Poetics of Space,* p. 108.

22. Lytton Strachey, *Queen Victoria* (New York: Harcourt, Brace and Co., 1921), pp. 398-406.

23. Near the end of the novel, after he has returned from abroad, David says, "I went to London to lose myself in the swarm of life there" (61). But on one such trip, besides keeping in close touch with Traddles and menage, he also has occasion to encounter Creakle, his old schoolmaster, which in turn leads to a final meeting, in prison, with Heep and Littimer. As A. O. J. Cockshut, *Imagination of Charles Dickens,* says, in this book there is "no logic of cause and effect. . . . We are almost in Freud's territory of the omnipotence of thought" (p. 121).

24. Mary McCarthy, "Characters in Fiction," *The Humanist in the Bathtub* (New York: New American Library, 1964), p. 212, speaks of the "principle of eternity or inertia represented by the comic."

25. "Image of Steerforth," p. 57.

26. Robert Garis, *The Dickens Theatre: A Reassessment of the Novels* (Oxford: Clarendon Press, 1965).

27. Ibid., p. 59.

28. Ibid., p. 60.

29. Ibid., p. 62.

30. Ibid., p. 197.

31. Ibid., p. 196.

32. Greene, "The Young Dickens," p. 246.

33. Taylor Stoehr, *Dickens: The Dreamer's Stance* (Ithaca, N.Y.: Cornell University Press, 1965). See especially chap. 4, "The Novel as Dream."

34. Garis, *Dickens Theatre*, p. 108.

35. Ibid., p. 105.

36. Ibid., p. 95.

37. Johnson, *Tragedy and Triumph*, p. 659.

38. *The Christmas Books*, ed. Michael Slater (Baltimore: Penguin Books, 1971) 2:246. Further references will be to this edition, with page numbers in parentheses.

39. See Alexander Welsh, "Forgiveness," in *The City of Dickens* (Oxford: Clarendon Press, 1971). Welsh sees this passage as somewhat contradictory to what I would agree in calling the "doctrine of memory" presented in this tale (p. 104).

40. Forster, *Life of Charles Dickens*, 2:61.

41. Georges Poulet, *Studies in Human Time*, trans. Elliott Coleman (Baltimore: Johns Hopkins Press, 1956), p. 36.

42. Angus Wilson, "The Heroes and Heroines of Dickens," in *Dickens and the Twentieth Century*, ed. John Gross and Gabriel Pearson (London: Routledge and Kegan Paul, 1962), p. 7.

43. It would doubtless be possible to designate as "mythic" everything that has to do with the Dickens hero's past, while reserving "fictive" for his imaginative constructions in the present and the future—since the word "myth" is used to distinguish between unsophisticated, handed-down, ready-made fictions and more developed ones, used much more self-consciously.

44. F. W. Dupee, *The Selected Letters of Charles Dickens* (New York: Farrar, Straus and Cudahy, 1960), pp. 178-79.

"My First Fall in Life." From *David Copperfield*.

THREE

David Copperfield and the Aesthetics of Education

I. David Sees "Himself" in the Mirror

Many critics who discuss growth, crisis, and conversion in Dickens's novels choose to focus on explicitly "moral" themes, such as that of the "undisciplined heart" in *Copperfield*,[1] to the exclusion of what might be called the growth of consciousness, of which overt moral changes are the often rather sententiously announced outcome. Accordingly, when a critic with moral preoccupations looks for "change of heart" in Dickens's novels, he usually looks at adult crises and finds some rather crude stereotyped reversals and "gap[s] between the flow of events and the moral action."[2] If one's notions of moral change in novels are derived from the practices of George Eliot, evidently psychomimetic, then Dickens's practices are likely to seem unsatisfying and to demand some apologetics. But even if one manages to find an almost Eliot-like subtlety (as Gwendolyn B. Needham seems to do) in the "recognition" that characters like David Copperfield come to, emphasis on moral growth per se can lead to neglect of the childhood crises of consciousness that are Dickens's greatest achievements in imaginary psychology. These early crises establish postures of the self that play important parts in future development and influence moral growth itself. Some themes like the disciplining of the heart—the narrator's explicit discussion of it being one of the most forgettable parts of *Copperfield*—need to be seen as almost epiphenomena, or as generalized approximations to deeper imaginative concerns that reveal themselves persistently from the very first.

Copperfield is a drama of memory, but it is also a drama of the imagination. Imagination and memory are intimately connected in growth, transforming the present and helping to create the future. Since Dickens treats of imagination and memory for the most part as functions—remembering and imagining as differential functions—they are not always visible as discrete psychic states. We have seen how memory can contaminate perception (how the activity of remembering can intermittently displace that of perceiving). Similarly, the imagination contaminates perception. This happens most frequently at moments of crisis; for it seems part of the point of Dickens's imaginary psychology to center on moments at which ordinary conceptions of mental faculties prove unhelpful or lead to ambiguities for the reader who tries to think with them. Thus, as usual, Dickens chooses to exploit occasions where there is a certain opportunity for free construction. And, in general, in accord with this project of constructing an imaginary psychology, Dickens forecloses on the possibility of thinking about psychic growth with simple equations or structures in mind. For instance, the "theory of memory" is quite complex enough to dispel any simplistic notion that remembering as such is nondevelopmental. True enough, certain kinds of remembering can retard growth and turn the personality to stone, but others can foster growth in important ways. The same is true of imagination. Imagination helps David to deal with crisis, but it also offers him a questionable new identity. Crisis generates a symbolic thinking that is quite different from remembering but which can offer equally seductive pleasures, so that the initiate can merely exchange one static way of being for another. The pleasures of the symbol (or, if one prefers, more generally, the pleasures of the imagination) are bound up with the problem of narcissism, and Dickens explores narcissism as an essential obstacle to personal relationships.

Murdstone, who terrorizes with Order the sweet confusion of Blunderstone Rookery, intrudes into David's life and precipitates his first genuine identity crisis. The timeless pleasures of childhood thereupon come to be replaced by the cruel necessities of living in time, and the boy must change or go under. The most important episode of this crisis begins when David, upon provocation, bites

The Aesthetics of Education

Murdstone's hand, and is beaten viciously and confined to his room. In response to an evil action, he (with a vitality usually found only in the Dickens child) commits one in return. Violence begins by imitating violence. Oliver Twist's rage at Noah Claypole was a temporary and unique instance of rebellion and vanished like clouds after a storm, but David's rebellion put him permanently into a new position and a new frame of mind. Both boys have to leave the country and go to the city as a result of rebellion, a significant pattern; but in David we see the resulting mental adjustment that begins at the moment of rebellion itself. Here is part of the scene:

> He beat me ... as if he would have beaten me to death. Above all the noise we made, I heard them running up the stairs, and crying out—I heard my mother crying out—and Peggotty. Then he was gone; and the door was locked outside; and I was lying, fevered and hot, and torn, and sore, and raging in my puny way, upon the floor.
>
> How well I recollect, when I became quiet, what an unnatural stillness seemed to reign through the whole house! How well I remember, when my smart and passion began to cool, how wicked I began to feel.
>
> I sat listening for a long while, but there was not a sound. I crawled up from the floor, and saw my face in the glass, so swollen, red, and ugly that it almost frightened me. My stripes were sore and stiff, and made me cry afresh, when I moved; but they were nothing to the guilt I felt. It lay heavier on my breast than if I had been a most atrocious criminal....
>
> Long after it was dark I sat there.... I undressed, and went to bed; and there, I began to wonder fearfully what would be done to me. Whether it was a criminal act that I had committed?... Whether I was at all in danger of being hanged? (4)

The scene begins with the body as its "theme." In Dickens's novels the body is frequently (as in the developmental novels, and, with Esther, in *Bleak House*) discovered in pain, imprisonment, and guilt—that is, by and as limitation. Here the discovery of the body is connected with certain imaginative steps. First we note that in the symmetry of David's counteraction against Murdstone he is in a way testing his sense of a crude analogy: that Murdstone, the embodiment of otherness, is like him in that he can be hurt, too. Rousseau, Edmund Gosse, and many others have testified to the importance of the lesson that one's father is not a god. But if Murdstone is mortal, so, emphatically, is David. He is beaten further "as if he would have beaten me to death." Thanks to the unequal distribution of power, some actions do not evoke opposite and equal reactions. This failure on a purely physical level is something that many of Dickens's heroes seem to experience, a fact which transforms their imaginative life as they seek more effective means of response on higher levels. This scene occurs, incidentally, in David's bedroom; he is at the very center of shelter and yet can still be harmed by a force that cannot by walled out, and which can, by its intrusion, turn the house [and self] inside out, so that the shelter becomes a prison.

David's pain at first identifies his body with the self at "the center," but as soon as the body is felt from the inside the next step is to see the body from the outside, just as the child's house was first known from within and then was seen in an alienated vision from without. Dickens's use of a mirror in this scene has almost exactly the meaning of Charlotte Brontë's use of one in the very similar scene, published in 1847, in which Jane Eyre, because she lashed back at her tormentor, is imprisoned in the "red room." This is the way Brontë presents the moment:

> Alas!... no jail was ever more secure. Returning, I had to cross before the looking-glass; my fascinated glance involuntarily explored the depth it revealed. All looked colder and darker in that visionary hollow than in reality: and the strange little figure there gazing at me, with a white face and arms specking the gloom, and glittering eyes of fear moving where all else was still, had the effect of a real spirit.[3]

David, as well, momentarily sees himself as almost an alien being: "My face in the glass, so swollen, red and ugly that it almost frightened me." But the important step is the subsequent accommodation of the mirror, the recognition that that particular other is really oneself. Jacques Lacan, in his article on *le stade du miroir*, emphasizes the significance of this experience for infants—real infants. "L'assomption jubilatoire de son image spéculaire par l'être encore plongé dans l'impuissance motrice et la dépendance du nourrissage qu'est le petit homme à ce stade *infans,* nous paraîtra dès lor manifester en une situation exemplaire la matrice symbolique où le *je* se précipite en une forme primordiale, avant qu'il ne s'objective dans la dialectique de l'identification à l'autre et que le langage ne lui restitue dans l'universel sa fonction de sujet."[4] Lacan goes on to say that "le point important est que cette forme situe l'instance du *moi,* dès avant sa détermination sociale, dans une *ligne de fiction"* [5] (my italics). Dickens and Brontë offer the mirror-perspective to their children precisely at an early moment of suffering and "impuissance motrice." Both writers exploit the mirror experience fully and offer it as symbolic of a step in the development of the self—a self seen as growing in moments of imaginative transcendence.

The scene in *Copperfield,* after revealing the discovery of the body and the discovery of the complex, self-conscious self, leads to further effects, which can be compared with the effect on Oliver Twist of reading the Newgate Calendar. Bodily punishment by others leads to mental self-punishment. As David says, the bodily suffering is "nothing" to the guilt he feels. This remark distances the body from the deeper self which now feels a pain qualitatively different from that of the body. And just as David's awakened imagination now explores the parts of the house where he cannot be, so does this imagination explore for the first time the imaginative world of the others. By doing so he does not merely await judgment and definition by them, he unconsciously attempts to anticipate them and, in a way, to punish himself in advance in his imagination. He makes a rudimentary attempt at self-evaluation using the limited terms adults have given him; naturally these terms have a simplistic, either-or character to them. Was it "a criminal act that I had committed?" Was I "at all in danger of being hanged?" In his attempt at evaluation David has to go beyond his primitive stance in a new way by exploring the objective role of criminal; furthermore, he can do this only by trying to think the thoughts of the judge as well. Even to begin to think of himself as an "atrocious criminal," as he does, is to accept the supposed judgment of Murdstone, is to be Murdstone for himself. Before, David had been in no need of any justification; now he demonstrates that he feels the mithradatic necessity of internalizing Murdstone's probable notions, of standing apart within himself and seeing as provisionally real the David whom he imagines Murdstone has imagined. Imitating authority is perhaps the necessary preliminary to becoming one's own authority; if the process is successful, David can eventually (as an autobiographer, for instance) substitute his own judgments for those of the judges.

Returning to the mirror-event itself, we can see how the mirrors in *Copperfield* suggest that the hero functions as a kind of imaginative tool for exploring the limits of the artistic imagination. *Copperfield* is concerned with exploring the power of symbols, especially their role in self-development, and does this in an "erotic" context. That is, the narcissism of symbol-using is examined as an alternative to intimate human relationships.

In this sense the novel is about aesthetic education far more than about "erotic" education, though the two are of course linked. Only indirectly is it about "disciplining" David's heart, a thesis which once gained its authority (I think) from the widespread impression that, though David is ostensibly a famous writer, we actually hear next to nothing about his works. It is precisely this apparent absence of the "work" that misleads many readers into believing that the novel is about something more down-to-earth than aestheticism and artists. Need we be reminded that *Copperfield* itself is offered as the work written by David?

Six times, in similar and momentous circumstances, David sees himself in the mirror. Now the mirror is not simply an image, and in this I see its importance for Dickens's novel—for any aestheticist novel, perhaps. To the extent that it is an image, it comes as close as possible to imaging pure structure. The simplest of all structures is inherent in repetition, and the mirror is a static image of repetition. Further, it exists to frame or contain other images: it *images* (v. t.) or presents other images, and thus is the purest image we can conceive of for presenting the notion of image as such. In a novel, then, a mirror is not necessarily on the same level as other images; it tends to be estranged from everything else. To put a mirror into a novel— and novels have themselves been likened to mirrors, of course—is to create what in the passage from *Jane Eyre* is called a "visionary hollow," a hole in the work, which is imageless and yet which is also a form of *meta*-image in that it comments recursively on itself and upon the other images around it. Empty and irreal, the mirror can nevertheless derealize surrounding images, can put in question their reality.[6] It foregrounds itself. Thus, whenever a novel—especially a first-person, reflexive novel—uses mirrors insistently, it is commenting on itself, saying something it cannot say with other images, the rest of which (except those expressing the phenomenon of mirroring: doubles, shadows, reflections in water, plot redoublements, and the like) cannot be so readily about themselves and still be themselves at the same time. In reflecting suffering and love (the singular and plural aspects of real life) the mirror draws attention to its own power and thus to the power of the symbol over real life.

Consider further Jacques Lacan's claim that a real infant reaches a crucial stage of development when, at around six months of age, it suddenly and joyfully recognizes itself in the mirror; when, thereupon, "le je se precipite en une forme primordiale." Maurice Merleau-Ponty, in his essay "The Child's Relations with Others," substantiates this insight by drawing on objective psychological studies and developing a detailed theory of what he calls, on the symbolic level, "l'image spéculaire," and on the literal, "l'image du miroir."[7] Understanding these images evidently is central to understanding the growth of the real person. Dickens the novelist leads us through a gallery of mirrors, and they also are used, these seemingly humble images, to mark stages on life's way, to punctuate crucial moments for consciousness, as David moves from childhood simplicities to adulthood complexities.

In Dickens's use of mirrors, however, there is an emphasis on a circumstance not accounted for by Lacan or Merleau-Ponty. This emphasis is a clue to the way an imaginary consciousness can differ from a real one. To begin with, we cannot fully understand the imaginary consciousness created in *Copperfield* by using the basic "self/other" contrast of the psychologists. According to Merleau-Ponty, a real, ordinary child is shown the mirror by another person, can compare the person beside him with the image of that person in the mirror, and can then easily correlate the leftover image there with himself, so as to begin to learn about his own separateness, to discover his own space.[8] There is no mystery in this very simple imaginative act. But in literary examples of mirror-gazing, a different process is usually involved, as the writings of Dickens, Charlotte Brontë, Poe, Mallarmé,

Sartre, and others testify.[9] The fictive initiate discovers his mirror-image all by himself: therefore in a much more radically imaginative and mysterious act. Also, the typically fictional form of the mirror-experience is essentially negative, while real children supposedly react to the encounter happily (Lacan speaks of "jubilation"), and it is invariably beneficial to their growth. For normal people the mirror seems, indeed, to initiate symbolic activity, along with the awareness that it is only symbolic activity. But many artists seem to resent or even fear that image, perhaps because it cannot, for them, be so easily reduced to mere image and then generally ignored, as we are told is the normal case. Otto Rank has commented on the frequency with which "autoscopic" experiences occur for artists in their lives and in their art, as if the mirror image of the self haunts artists as it haunted primitive man.[10] Understandably, if there is a marked difference in this one respect between the experiences of artists and those of ordinary people, then one might expect the difference between fictive characters and ordinary people to be every bit as great.

Accordingly, much more useful than the self/other distinction for exploring mirrors in art is the subjective/objective polarity used by Jean-Paul Sartre in his meditations on artists who have had to wrestle with the paradoxes of narcissism. It takes a thief to catch a thief; Sartre, discussing Flaubert and *Madame Bovary*, speaks with precise abstraction of the "objectification of the subjective"[11] as a tendency of *homo faber*. Further, he speaks of "the moving unity of subjectivity and objectivity, those cardinal determinants of activity."[12] Dickens's several accounts of growing up (especially in *Copperfield* and *Great Expectations*) could be described as explorations of the ways that characters live through the subjective phase of growth, with its intermittent egocentric solitude (subjectivity), punctuated by times of thing-like manipulation by others (objectivity), so as eventually to accomplish their successful "objectification." Objectification for the narrator of *Copperfield* is envisaged, first, as the creation of a positive, definitive, even redemptive work of art. He seeks a form of personal knowledge and potency as well as an intimate communion with others, both to be made possible by art. Whether he can achieve either or both of these things is a central question in the novel. If, as Robert

The Aesthetics of Education

Langbaum says, "The whole conscious concern with objectivity as a *problem,* as something to be achieved, is . . . specifically romantic,"[13] then here Dickens again shows his affinity with the "modern tradition" of Romanticism. Substitute Sartre's "objectification" for Langbaum's "objectivity" and we have the appropriate terms. David's life can be described as a prolonged oscillation between the poles of subjectivity and objectivity, both of which are prior to any true objectification. Were this final stage attainable, interaction between self and other would pass beyond the subjectivity/objectivity oscillation altogether (that oscillation being essentially narcissistic, the drama of a person's relations with himself and his imaginings), and the hero would reach what Merleau-Ponty and many others see as the goal of maturity: a true non-narcissistic communication. This would not be the delicious commingling of identities that many lovers value, but rather a meeting with others as other. Other people would not serve as mere backdrops for the hero's projections of his own wishes, nor would they offer him the chance to copy, on the slate of his own bemused soul, their perhaps alien ways.[14]

Mirrors in *Copperfield* often suggest both the advantages and the dangers of self-awareness; mirrors provide orientation, but they can also come between oneself and others, causing communicative, even erotic, distortion. Though his hero does not develop adequately, Dickens at least shows with his mirrorings that he has begun to understand why David cannot be imagined into maturity. The central moment of the first crisis, as we have seen, produces the mirror image. The conflict with Murdstone began because David was not learning things fast enough (reading, Latin grammar, sums), but the conflict itself takes education to a much deeper level than before. In this "spot of time," Dickens penetrates to what, for a real child, would have been a crisis of early infancy—when, according to Merleau-Ponty, the most important issue is "consciousness of one's own body and the specular image."[15] Dickens shows us, as in a "time-warp," a moment of transformation, when infantile unity is replaced (through bodily pain and specular scutiny) by a new sense of distance, boundary, perspective; a split in the world that is also a split in the self. David must now "lie a long way off" (3) from his mother;

the mirror, which at first shows him himself as a stranger, records this decentering. The crisis brings about a qualitative leap in development—a veritable conversion of quantity to quality.

But decentering does not produce for David, as it supposedly does for real children, a true, objective view of himself. One can guess from David's excessive insistence on his guilt feelings that his rivalry with Murdstone has taken, if anything, an even more deeply subjective form. While he learns the lesson taught him by Murdstone and the mirror at one level—as is evident in some of his later facility in handling mirrors—at another level emerges the threat of a neurotic stasis and narcissism. The whole book, his whole life, seems to whirl around this moment, and the time-stoppage is reflected even in the repetitive structure of the novel, an appropriate formal analogue to the memorial circularities and obsessions of both child and adult Copperfield. (Prior to this crisis David had seen a mirror, though Dickens does not have him look into it. But according to one of my students, Elizabeth A. Burns, the event does qualify as a seventh instance of Dickens's critical use of mirrors in *Copperfield*. David's first impressions of the Peggotty household at Yarmouth include a view of the bedroom he will occupy at "the stern of the vessel." "It was the completest and most desirable bedroom ever seen ... with a little window, where the rudder used to go through; and a little looking-glass, just the right height for me, nailed against the wall, and framed with oyster-shells ..." [3]. The passage is quite resonant when thought of in proximity both with David's first and with his final mirror vision, the latter also at Yarmouth, involving shipwreck and the like. In both of the earlier passages mirrors and windows in bedrooms are side by side, while in the later one mirror and window, again in a bedroom, merge into one and the same image.)

According to Merleau-Ponty, for real children, "jealousy is overcome thanks to the constitution of a scheme of past-present-future. In effect jealousy in [a] subject consists in a rigid attachment to his present—that is, to the situation ... which was hitherto his own."[16] To study the profound role of memory and imagination in this novel is to recognize the importance of this early event involving the body, a father who is less a real person than an image out of projective fantasy, and the mirror. Recapture of the original childhood idyll, in an involuntary memory that distorts the objective "scheme of past-present-future" by coming forward to possess the present, is not at all rewarding, because the hard times of childhood come along with the good ones. Memorial regression would be fortunate indeed if only the eternally recurring childhood, so supple at insinuating itself into adult consciousness as pure perception, did not appear thus dyadic.

When he begins his autobiography David is a celebrated author and supposedly a mature man, but he is haunted by this dyadic childhood in which good and evil co-exist as if inseparable, though he wants to keep the good for himself and precipitate out the memory of evil, to make sure that the evil is "other." He wants to remember at will only the good times, but, like the hero of *The Haunted Man,* he cannot be selective. Unlike Dickens, who abandoned a real to write a fictional autobiography, David intends to use his sincerest art (the supposedly mimetic art that shows everything, as in a mirror) to complete his maturation and to orient himself to both art and love. He begins his self-researches by positing two deceptive alternatives: "Whether I shall turn out to be the hero of my own life, or whether that station will be held by anybody else." In short, am I self-made or made by others? Either alternative, if embraced fully, amounts to the same thing, which reflects a basic narcissism (solipsism and monism) not uncommon in artists who attempt autobiography. In both instances other people would have to be seen as either ciphers (mere phenomena) or symbols. In the former case (David Hero) the other would be internalized, while in the latter (David as Prisoner of Grace) the self would evaporate, and action and motive would be thrust upon symbolically dominant others, who can do anything, especially what the hero secretly most wishes to do. A realist critic of this behavior would say that David invents those others, whether they seem potent or vacuous. But the very fact that David begins by posing that truly existential question about his life means that he will direct his consciousness toward a specific end, and thus reduce the richness of his avowedly global memory in doing so. Even though he is not able consistently to maintain this posture, his autobiography will still be every bit as fictive as Dickens's pseudo-autobiographical novel. Without knowing it, David is writing a novel about his life, hopefully to create himself as his own hero, independent of others' definitions of him. This is one sense in which *Copperfield*, while appearing to be about mutual love and exchanges of nurture, is actually about narcissism and its related aestheticism.

David discovers his problematic objectivity while locked in his room confronting a stranger in his mirror; but the isolation from the world and the human community has also its corresponding subjective moment, so that we see for David a two-way split—from the world and also within himself. As early as *Sketches by Boz* ("A Visit to Newgate") Dickens viewed imprisonment as a psychological disturbance; later he always used it as an occasion for mental development or at least transformation. During David's imprisonment in his room he endures a subjective, solitary time ("the uncertain pace of the hours") and the sense of foreground-background reversal. He hears doors closing, footsteps, voices merely as voices—all the normally unperceived sounds. During this seemingly interminable imprisonment his personal world is a negative of the commonly shared one. It is as if he had passed through the looking-glass like Alice. He is thus complex, with an inside and an outside. But he finds his freedom in the eye, in the objective adult organ that enables him to explore his painfully limited body in the mirror. After all, he can direct his gaze, but he cannot close his ears. When he accepts the image there as somehow also himself, the mirror becomes a tool. This is use of metaphor: taking the emanation, his fictive projection, a ghost on the glass, as a reality. And temporarily this is an aestheticist stance that diminishes the hero, for himself, to the sum of his surfaces.

The second time David sees himself in the mirror is that "memorable birthday" when he learns of his mother's death, and, as he says, feels "like an orphan in the wide world." This is the first of four deaths that mark important stages in his life (Dora's, Ham's, and Steerforth's are the others). After exhausting his first tears, David says:

> I stood upon a chair when I was left alone, and looked into the glass to see how red my eyes were, and how sorrowful my face.... I am sensible of having felt that a dignity attached to me among the rest of the boys, and that I was important in my affliction.... I remember that this importance was a kind of satisfaction to me, when I walked

in the playground.... When I saw them glancing at me out of the windows, as they went up to their classes, I felt distinguished, and looked more melancholy, and walked slower. (9)

He looks to confirm his devastation; he has come far from that first accidental glimpse. The self-image has precedence over emotion. Instead of dwelling on the purity of reaction, Dickens shows how real suffering soon gives way to the public gesture. David tries to see himself as others will see him and models his imagined exterior for them. At the end of this scene David is placed (with Dickens's usual finesse) on the outside of the school looking in, while the others are inside looking out. During the first crisis while hiding from the imagined gaze of children playing outside his house, David felt segregation from others. Now he exhibits himself, asking that his suffering (birthday suffering, no less) be seen as his isolating, distinguishing feature. Exhibitionism is no less immature and subjective than hiding, though, and it is also a subtler alienation.

In most narratives of growing up there is at least one scene in which the hero, often with the aid of potions or dreams, journeys into strange regions of experience; this is important to the logic of such narrative, in that it tests perceptual norms and disrupts some of them enough to create new orientation. David, during his "first dissipation," accordingly befuddles himself with drink and strong tobacco:

> Somebody was leaning out of my bedroom window, refreshing his forehead against the cool stone of the parapet, and feeling the air upon his face. It was myself. I was addressing myself as "Copperfield," and saying, "Why did you try to smoke? You might have known you couldn't do it." Now, somebody was unsteadily contemplating his features in the looking-glass. That was I too. I was very pale in the looking-glass; my eyes had a vacant appearance; and my hair—only my hair, nothing else—looked drunk. (24)

Dickens then describes drunken confusions of time and space; for example, "I stepped at once out of the box-door [of the theatre] into my bedroom." (In the comparable "Circe" episode of *Ulysses,* Mr. Bloom observes that "drunks cover distance double quick.") Here part of David is Admonisher, part is Strayed Reveller, and there is perspective within perspective of him. Somebody is in the glass, somebody sees that somebody, and somebody sees that seeing; and the narrator's own vision subtends all this. Thus Dickens makes it explicit once again that point of view is an issue, that he is exploring aesthesis in a general sense. David has been trying to play the role of man-about-town for Steerforth and friends (one of whom, by the way, "always spoke of himself indefinitely, as 'a man,' and seldom or never in the first person singular"). In an alternating subjectivity and objectivity, David keeps losing and finding himself in the mirror, which seems also to take on a new function. It offers a critical view that almost is that of a real other person. Its illusory depth now, in the midst of this extreme identity diffusion, offers what must pass for truth. "I was very pale." Actually the mirror has been doing this all along, but in different contexts, so that what it is able to tell David is each time different. It earlier taught him about his body and the need for hiding; then it taught him the possibility of disguise and deception; but now it begins to suggest that it can turn against him and offer him a coldly objective image that cannot be managed for deceptive purposes. The mirror hints at the requirements of another who will not be fooled by images. The mirror is becoming a form of external knowing that is analogous to the perspective not of a superficial society but of a fellow human being.

In a passage canceled from the proof sheets of the novel (18), David is fully the self-bewitched fop, a fake eroticist, and the mirror for the last time offers genial criticism. Clearly, it serves to focus narcissist-eroticist ironies in the novel.[17] David tries to use his image seductively but finds himself unable to integrate his outside (as he images it) with an inside that does not even seem to know what it means. "Sometimes I am persuaded [Miss Larkins] must be aware of [my attachment to her] on account of my agitation and the expression on my face when I meet her; then I look in the glass, and getting up that expression as nearly as I can, doubt it, and suspect it may not reveal what I mean." The gentle, humorous self-depreciation in this passage shows that the narcissistic use of the mirror and the body-image is becoming more difficult, especially in relation to a person who insists on being herself while overlooking her admirer.

When "Doady" falls in love with the childish, inadequate Dora, another abnormal state of mind ensues, just as when he had suffered from Murdstone, from his mother's death, and from the confusion of being disguised in drink. "Lost in blissful delirium," he listens to the

The Aesthetics of Education

girl's singing. "When Miss Murdstone took her into custody and led her away, she smiled and gave me her delicious hand. . . . I caught a view of myself in the mirror, looking perfectly imbecile and idiotic" (26). This "objectivity" is still best understood as the narrator's hyperbolic self-criticism. But there is a greater than usual ironic distance: the narrator's presence comes to the fore, as he revives before himself, through memory aided by imagination, the earlier self which is now his *Seelenspiegel.* The mirror's mythic job is to tell the negative truth (as at the entrance to Dante's Purgatory), and so it begins to do, especially for that concerned, backward-looking narrator. But the hero, bright-fledged flâneur, whose cues are an imagined reflection in the eyes of others, persists in his folly of tight boots, at once bruising body to pleasure the Dandiacal Soul and sacrificing his real soul to the all-important exterior.

The last mirror in *Copperfield* appears during a most crucial period in David's development; the time when he is faced with a manhood crisis that corresponds to, and certainly is a thematic answer to, the childhood crisis initiated by Murdstone. The principal figure at this point in his life is Steerforth, who brings adult eroticism into temporary focus as Murdstone could never have done. David arrives at Yarmouth during the tempest (so emphatic as transformation symbol) that is about to destroy Steerforth. Once again, in this admirable episode, the mirror is associated (as at the beginning) with pain, alienation, and death—and again the context is covertly erotic. Copperfield is in his hotel room, pacing nervously about: "I got up several times, and looked out; but could see nothing, except the reflection in the window-panes . . . of my own haggard face looking in at me from the black void" (55). Dickens's use of reflection in this passage is significant, for it suggests interwoven narcissist-eroticist problems, and, more generally, it helps us to understand related identity questions that Dickens was exploring in mid-career. Jorge Borges says that "mirrors have something monstrous about them." The window as mirror appears now almost monstrously. The ordinarily clear relation between the indoors and outdoors becomes ambiguous, thus undermining our sense of David's safety, which might otherwise have been based on a feeling of the contrast between storm and the privileges of shelter. In this moment, the mirror becomes linked with the important network of images in the novel that are associated with houses. Dickens is a supreme poet and dreamer of buildings—for him (to transpose Heidegger's famous metaphor) houses are the language of being. In a continuing harmonics of open and closed dwelling-spaces Dickens elaborates the very process of becoming. This storm scene first hints at the interpenetration of a builded enclosure and an inhuman chaos, which, in terms of the personal crisis just beginning, symbolizes a deeper emergent ambiguity. For two interfused versions of identity figure here, and both are momentarily sustained as simultaneously valid: the clearly outlined self as derived from human relationships and the stress of community; and identity as self-derived (an isolated self which, by comparison with the communal, bounded one, is unbounded, chaotic, inhuman, faintly autochthonous). David is in a zero hour of the imagination: at this fork in the labyrinth of symbols he will choose either the path of mystification or that of lucidity. The one is narcissistic, leading by incessant circlings to a center of self which is illusory (and without circumference); the other leads into the community, where boundaries (as between the inside and outside, self and other) exist in support of identity. The narcissist takes mirror images and the images of other people as versions of himself, as symbolically potent. The ordinary consciousness takes such images not as powerful symbols but merely as images without much content, depth, or significance.

Dickens is evidently trying to imagine for David an unambiguous way out of the subjectivity/objectivity split, the narcissism, shown up to now. Since Steerforth, who has often been called, perhaps without too much thought about it, David's alter ego, is out there in mortal peril, David's "haggard" face, coming as if from out there, has in effect been substituted for Steerforth's. Dickens obviously suggests this; had he been a surrealist he would have shown Steerforth's face at the window. For supposedly David's identity is involved in Steerforth's fate, because the latter has selfishly abused Emily, the girl who had once been the object of David's own (infantile) erotic fantasy. From this point of view, Steerforth is a negative projection, after having served his earlier contrary purpose as a positive model for David. He lives out David's desire for aggressive adult sex and pays for it, leaving David with clean hands and innocent memories. The mirror-image serves to remind us of their symbolic association, their doubling.

But by using the window as yet another mirror in this scene, Dickens superimposes upon this projective drama another one of quite opposite meaning, in which Steerforth plays no role at all, certainly in which the Steerforth-David equation is questioned, and thereby all symbolic appropriations of others. In the projective drama "Steerforth" is looking in from outside, and David is symbolically a Steerforth, voyaging without really voyaging, from sin to punishment. But in what we might term the counterpoised realist drama, David is seeing himself in the act of seeing, or, rather, is looking at an image of himself looking inwards to himself. The makeshift mirror shows thus an image of David in the posture he has actually assumed; the image is quite literal, perfectly accurate; for the mirror-window does make it impossible for David to look out; in trying to look out, he must encounter his own simulacrum as another person might see it. The image signals to readers who have the quite natural tendency to construct symbolic equations and to perceive doublings everywhere (as the hero himself does) that David is not connected with Steerforth as alter ego. Indeed, it is precisely his tendency to think so which is related to his split within himself: he is unable to see others nonsymbolically as other and himself literally as himself. It is not quite clear at this point what additional act of imagination or what intrusion would help David grow up (into a literal-minded adult). I would venture Dickens is intimating that David must first see the mirror as mirror, and the image as image, before it can become the window it really must become. Looking-*at* rather than looking-*into* would reveal to him the banality, the emptiness of the mirror and the specular image. The mirror would show him that it showed him only himself, as a literal image that then could not further operate as an identity transformer. This would lead him to see that the mirror was the symbol of his predicament, had been his predicament, and that by seeing through the simultaneous literalness and fictiveness of the mirror, he could then look-*through* the window to others. Thus the mirror would teach that it teaches nothing: a considerable lesson.

Because, as his later behavior shows, he does not learn this lesson, David does not grow up; he marries a mother-sister-angel named Agnes who is merely more symbolic baggage. The business at the end about inner changes and Agnes's influence can be seen as a great deal of mystification designed to obscure the fact that David does not essentially change and that Agnes's presence indicates he need not change: for it seems to be Dickens's point in this novel not only that artists write fictions, but that their lives are fictions they have written themselves, stocked with gratifying images they have created out of real people who so miraculously feel the sway of imagination that they allow themselves to be used as screens upon which the self-absorbed artist can project symbolic variants of himself.

But the mirror shows that this is only a pleasant fancy of artists; doubtless it reveals up to this point, in Dickens himself, a real faith in the power of imagination to generate its own satisfactory objects—never mind whether in life or in art. Poetic faith is a biographical matter of some interest, but probably we can only point to it without proving it. But in novels mirrors are monstrous. Dickens learned enough about them in *Copperfield,* perhaps, to spare himself having to write works as shocking as E. T. A. Hoffmann's nightmarish tales, or, even more appropriately, Dostoyevsky's *The Double,* where the ultimate horror is the vision of one's own face everywhere. This horror derives from the sense that everybody else is symbolically a version of oneself.

In his preface to *Copperfield* Dickens says, "I am a fond parent to every child of my fancy, and . . . no one can ever love that family as dearly as I love them." The novel is, he says, his "favourite child." We can only guess what a test in aesthetic possibilities *Copperfield* was for Dickens, who no doubt left it behind him (if *Great Expectations* is any indication) as his own mirror-stage in his striving for identity as an artist and as a person. This is biographical speculation, but I think he saw the child-monster in the mirror of his art and saw his favorite child as that child could not see itself (since it is evidently others who complete seeing). David reveals his shortcomings when he repeats the assertion that "this manuscript is intended for no eyes but mine." This is a conventional way of establishing the sincerity of sentimental, self-conscious narrative. But it is also the mark of an artist (and perhaps Dickens was like this artist) who wishes to define himself in bypassing—or recreating—other people, an artist who will not venture himself, for to do so means simultaneously to abandon his own solipsistic distinctiveness and to admit the separateness and uniqueness of others. As Dickens later concluded, this is far from complete *confession,* which he came to see (in *Great Expectations*), as unsentimental, nonnarcissistic, and formally ruthless.

II. Language Games: True and False, Sinister and Dexterous.

Imprisonment is isolation and silence. Every confessional account of growing up deals with some form of imprisonment as an almost inevitable period of limitation. Imprisonment takes on positive values, in these accounts, only when viewed temporally, and when, in temporal perspective, it is seen to encourage new ways of encountering the world. Imprisonment involves an extreme specialization of the environment—much as in a laboratory—and a circumscription of motor and observational activity which of course intensify memory and imagination. Thus, in spite of the many imprisonments shown in picaresque narratives (e.g. *The Vicar of Wakefield* and *Pickwick*) imprisonment is actually anti-picaresque. Isolated by Fagin, Oliver discovered in the silence of his "prison" the resounding power of the written word; while Fagin, in his cell, experienced the memorial-imaginative disruption of everyday time, as he explored the time of guilt. Time and language become highly visible when Dickens deals with imprisonment. "Time is very long, gentleman, within these four walls!" a prisoner told Dickens, during his visit to the solitary-confinement prison in Philadelphia.[18] When there is no imprisonment for David Copperfield, time flashes by, as for example when he gets on the right track at Salem House and at Dr. Strong's school. When the narrator collapses time during that part of the book, it is not for the same reason that Fielding does it in *Tom Jones,* that is, because "whole years ... pass without producing anything worthy [of the reader's] notice"; he is instead shown as being faithful to the temporal quality of the original experiences and, as well, to the way they are presumably remembered or forgotten. Compare, however, the slow, uncertain passage of time during imprisonment:

> The length of those five days [of childhood imprisonment by Murdstone] I can convey no idea of to any one. They occupy the place of years in my remembrance. The way in which I listened to all the incidents of the house that made themselves audible to me; the ringing of bells, the opening and shutting of doors, the murmuring of voices, the footsteps on the stairs; to any laughing, whistling, or singing, outside, which seemed more dismal than anything else to me in my solitude and disgrace—the uncertain pace of the hours, especially at night, when I would wake thinking it was morning, and find that the family were not yet gone to bed, and that all the length of night had yet to come—the depressed dreams and nightmares I had—the return of day, noon, afternoon, evening, when the boys played in the churchyard, and I watched them from a distance within the room, being ashamed to show myself at the window lest they should know I was a prisoner—the strange sensation of never hearing myself speak—the fleeting intervals of something like cheerfulness, which came with eating and drinking, and went away with it—the setting in of rain one evening, with a fresh smell, and its coming down faster and faster between me and the church, until it and gathering night seemed to quench me in gloom, and fear, and remorse—all this appears to have gone round and round for years instead of days, it is so vividly and strongly stamped on my remembrance. (4)

In this passage there is a time-sense of the narrator as well as of the hero, but the personal nature of time as it appears to a prisoner is clear. In this isolation, by means of a constant comparison between David's own rich imaginative world (including nightmares and dreams), with its wayward rhythms of sleep and waking, its unusually long nights, and the external world from which he has been shut out, Dickens creates a rich texture of subjective time.

But intensification of subjectivity, as Dickens's logic typically has it, produces new activity in the objective sphere. Prison-houses and language have an intimate connection, through the Promethean promises of the written word. The house has become a prison, but David, within that prison, finds a jolly corner in which he can brew a viable personality. Here he comes upon his only genuine inheritance from his "poetical" father, just as he is becoming "more and more shut out and alienated from" (4) his mother. The passage has been often quoted, and justly so:

> My father had left a small collection of books in a little room up-stairs,

The Aesthetics of Education

to which I had access (for it adjoined my own) and which nobody else in our house ever troubled. From that blessed little room, Roderick Random, Peregrine Pickle, Humphrey Clinker, Tom Jones, the Vicar of Wakefield, Don Quixote, Gil Blas, and Robinson Crusoe, came out, a glorious host, to keep me company. They kept alive my fancy, and my hope of something beyond that place and time,—they, and the Arabian Nights, and the Tales of the Genii.... It is curious to me how I could ever have consoled myself under my small troubles (which were great troubles to me), by impersonating my favourite characters in them—as I did—and by putting Mr. and Miss Murdstone into all the bad ones—which I did too. I have been Tom Jones (a child's Tom Jones, a harmless creature) for a week together. I have sustained my own idea of Roderick Random for a month at a stretch, I verily believe. I had a greedy relish for a few volumes of Voyages and Travels—I forget what, now—that were on those shelves; and for days and days I can remember to have gone about my region of our house, armed with the centre-piece out of an old set of boot-trees—the perfect realization of Captain Somebody, of the Royal British Navy, in danger of being beset by savages, and resolved to sell his life at a great price. The Captain never lost dignity, from having his ears boxed with the Latin Grammar. I did; but the Captain was a Captain and a hero, in despite of all the grammars of all the languages in the world, dead or alive.

This was my only and my constant comfort. When I think of it, the picture always rises in my mind, of a summer evening, the boys at play in the churchyard, and I sitting on my bed, reading as if for life. Every barn in the neighborhood, every stone in the church, and every foot of the churchyard, had some association of its own, in my mind, connected with these books, and stood for some locality made famous in them. I have seen Tom Pipes go climbing up the church-steeple; I have watched Strap, with the knapsack on his back, stopping to rest himself upon the wicket-gate; and I *know* that Commodore Trunnion held that club with Mr. Pickle, in the parlour of our little village alehouse. (4)

Thus, soon after Murdstone arrives, the boy learns ways of getting out of his own skin by using his imagination, as prompted by these fictions. "They kept alive my fancy, and my hope of something beyond that place and time." Earlier there had been no need for transcendence. Now this newly discovered ability to assume multiple roles has great pragmatic value in terms, paradoxically enough, of self-integrity. Like the young hero of Rilke's *Notebooks* David could say, "These disguises never, indeed, went so far as to make me feel a stranger to myself: on the contrary, the more varied my transformations, the more convinced did I become of myself."[19] And perhaps David could also add, following Rousseau, that "it is from my earliest reading that I date the unbroken consciousness of my own existence."[20] These fictions are life-affirming because transformative; thus David sits on his bed, "reading as if for life." Later David, drenched in fable, can say that "life was more like a great fairy story, which I was just about to begin to read, than anything else" (19).

Words make possible David's imaginative escape from stubborn reality, but words can be sinister, too, as the above passage suggests. Language (like the mirror image of the body) is from the first discovered as alien to consciousness, with a strangeness that enables it to be seen for itself. When Murdstone tortures him with the Latin grammar, David experiences the "tyranny of words"—words being the counters that the adult world handles for purposes of control. Words and numbers: a major indignity for a Dickensian child is to be asked a sum. Somehow neither Clara nor Dora Copperfield can survive in the adult world partly because they are constitutionally unable to do sums. In many of Dickens's works, children are bullied by adults in the name of the "appalling sum[s]" (4): in Salem House, Gradgrind's school, Pumblechook's seed shop, and elsewhere. We see bullying in behalf of words, in *Sketches by Boz* ("Astley's"):

> We never see any very large, staring, black Roman capitals, in a book, or shop-window, or placarded on a wall, without their immediately recalling to our mind an indistinct and confused recollection of the time when we were first initiated in the mysteries of the alphabet. We almost fancy we see the pin's point following the letter, to impress its form more strongly on our bewildered imagination; and wince involuntarily, as we remember the hard knuckles with which the reverend old lady who instilled into our mind the first principles of education ... was wont to poke our juvenile head occasionally, by way of adjusting the confusion of ideas in which we were generally involved.[21]

In the outer world, the word, detached from the true meanings that it ought to body forth, plays a dominant role in the relations not only of adult and child, but of master and man. The word separates men hierarchically, as unequals. Much of Dickens's works is satire on the phony language that society uses to conceal humbug and general emptiness:

> Mr. Micawber had a relish in this formal piling up of words, which, however ludicrously displayed in his case, was, I must say, not at all peculiar to him. I have observed it, in the course of my life, in numbers of men. It seems to me to be a general rule. In the taking of legal oaths, for instance, deponents seem to enjoy themselves mightily when they come to several good words in succession, for the expression of one idea; as, that they utterly detest, abominate, and abjure, or so forth; and the old anathemas were made relishing on the same principle. We talk about the tyranny of words, but we like to tyrannise over them too; we are fond of having a large superfluous establishment of words to wait upon us on great occasions; we think it looks important, and sounds well. As we are not particular about the meaning of our liveries on state occasions, if they be but fine and numerous enough, so the meaning or necessity of our words is a secondary consideration, if there be but a great parade of them. And as individuals get into trouble by making too great a show of liveries, or as slaves when they are too numerous rise against their masters, so I think I could mention a nation that has got into many great difficulties, and will get into many greater, from maintaining too large a retinue of words. (52)

Language, which it is so natural for man to enjoy for its own sake, is of course the most powerful instrument, whether used consciously or unconsciously for the purpose, of those who introduce into life the mystifications that conceal and propagate evil. The complaint that the word-wise adult David makes about language is similar to that of the little Jean-Paul Sartre, who protested that, when books were read to him, "rags were spoken of with magnificence; the words colored the things, transforming actions into rites and events into ceremonies."[22] But David and Sartre (and perhaps Dickens), move from being readers who make an imaginative fetish of fictions—David, in particular, is enmeshed in fables, myths, from the earliest moments of his danger— to being writers who dexterously manufacture them.

Not learning Latin grammar put David in the hands of Murdstone; learning shorthand puts him in the way of the parliamentary reporting that eventually leads to authorship. He began professional life by learning the mysteries of the law-courts and legal language; once his aunt loses her wealth he has to undergo new trial by disciplining himself in yet another secret language; he sets about gaining "a perfect and entire command of the mystery of short-hand writing" (36). (Dickens often uses the word *mystery* when talking about language.) He thus recapitulates the process which had begun his life, learning the alphabet at his mother's knee. Of the earlier experience he says, "To this day, when I look upon the fat black letters in the primer, the puzzling novelty of their shapes, and the easy good-nature of O and Q and S, seem to present themselves again before me as they used to do" (4). It is now necessary that he begin again, almost as a child learning the written language for the first time. This new language is appropriate to a new sphere of life, but to the neophyte it seems equally removed from reality (spoken language is after all closest to the real self at first), just as alien and yet ludicrously arbitrary, as the first language.

> I bought an approved scheme of the noble art and mystery of stenography ... and plunged into a sea of perplexity that brought me, in a few weeks, to the confines of distraction. The changes that were rung upon dots, which in such a position meant such a thing, and in such another position something else, entirely different; the wonderful vagaries that were played by circles; the unaccountable consequences that resulted from marks like flies' legs; the tremendous effects of a curve in a wrong place; not only troubled my waking hours, but reappeared before me in my sleep. When I had groped my way, blindly, through these difficulties, and had mastered the alphabet, which was an Egyptian Temple in itself, there then appeared a procession of new horrors, called arbitrary characters; the most despotic characters I have ever known; who insisted, for instance, that a thing like the beginning of a cobweb, meant expectation, and that a pen-and-ink sky-rocket stood for disadvantageous. When I had fixed these wretches in my mind, I found that they had driven everything else out of it; then, beginning again, I forgot them; while I was picking them up, I dropped the other fragments of the system; in short, it was almost heartbreaking. (38)

I quote all this partly because it is funny, but mainly to emphasize the fact that David grows by means of difficult encounters with words. At one point he says (in a passage Dickens deleted from the proof sheets) "I was so far from wanting words, that I had only too many of them. I didn't know what to do with them. I floundered among them as if they were water which I was splashing about."

The Aesthetics of Education

Maturation is in one respect the result of a verbal struggle, a process of learning the right language, one that is not alienated from the truth that is invisible to the "establishment": the lawyers, parliamentarians, schoolmasters, and others, who so often use language as a means of perpetuating the lies that are to Dickens the basis of the social system. But the right language, it turns out, is based on the false ones. The shibboleth of these priests becomes for the hero a complex truth, and because this can be so he transcends any mere contrast between the true and the fictive. In his verbal education David learns the languages of the legal and political cults and learns to manipulate them by becoming an author. If Copperfield's works could be supposed to resemble Dickens's, the process could be seen clearly, for Dickens himself used the false languages of lawyer and parliamentarian and, by mimicking them, was able to construct a language of integrity that could give the lie to its own sources. The son imitates the father and thus overthrows him. Like Hesiod's Muses, Dickens knew how to tell many falsehoods that seemed real, but also knew how to speak truth when he wanted to.

Micawber's verbal habits are worth mention in this connection. Micawber, as J. Hillis Miller notes, practices "transcendence through language," showing that "the manipulation of words is a fundamental expression of human freedom." "He throws forth a perpetual stream of metaphors, clichés, and hyperboles. He writes letters on every possible occasion, letters which, even if they assert his acceptance of the doom . . . effectually escape from reality by transcending it linguistically. 'Mr. Micawber's enjoyment of his epistolary powers,' as David says, '. . . really seemed to outweigh any pain or anxiety that the reality could have caused him.' "[23] He is a believer in the omnipotence of thought and the magical powers of words. David imitates him in one of his sillier letters to Dora's friend Miss Mills, which he writes "something in the style of Mr. Micawber" (38). But David sees the absurdity of Mr. Micawber's language, which helps him to see the absurdity of his own and that of the official cultists whom he has occasion to observe acting out their mummeries. Even as a boy he could appreciate the language of the Peggottys, which though it needed occasional translation from the Suffolk dialect, was always "written with a plain, unaffected, homely piety that [he] knew to be genuine" (38). The case of Micawber shows that one can try to do too much with words. The only useful thing Micawber accomplishes, the exposure of Heep, is done with a silence, internship, and cunning that imitates the silence and cunning of Heep himself. A vein of distrust runs through all of Dickens's writings for any excessively verbal persons (such as Skimpole, "Conversation Kenge," Honeythunder)—even though he is obviously fascinated by such men, perhaps because he was one of them. But even though the myth that the truth is silent, the myth of Cordelia, at times appeals to Dickens, he comes out in the end as a humanist who believes that words can be put to true uses, the main one being the showing up of lies. Language can police itself, and it can do this by directing attention to itself, as in the figured monologues of Dickens's famous talkers—and here Micawber has his paradoxical use—which let us see language in itself, and thus put us on our guard.

The growth of David's language consciousness parallels the growth of his self-consciousness and in fact is another phase of the latter, as analysis of the complex of events surrounding and issuing from the all-important first intrusion of evil into David's life shows. The act of imagination in which the hero discovers himself as at once alien and private (as in the mirror experience) is congruent to the act in which language is discovered as language, and is also perceived both as alien and as intimate to the self. In all phases of early crisis we see David living and growing in the midst of, and by means of, fictions—including the apparently fictive time of the incarcerated consciousness, the liberating fictions of literature, and the fictions inherent in language ritual.

III. *Plus Ça Change:* "The Virgin Page of the Future"

David's real growth is a process of acquiring and using self-consciousness and learning to manage such objective instruments as language. But David as hero—creature with strong inertial consciousness that he is—rarely goes questing for this history. While he tries to preserve whatever in his life can be preserved, if only in memory and the imagination, the stimulus of evil and error prods him into the future. John Henry Raleigh's description of the "temporal modes of

The Aesthetics of Education

the book" as "initiatory and forward looking in boyhood, reminiscent and retrospective in adulthood" needs considerable qualification.[24] David is obsessively retrospective from the first moment of childhood exile, and even in adolescence he is incapable of looking forward very much. We have little of the "young ego dreaming of the great universe and futurity."[25] For instance, like Richard Carstone in *Bleak House,* he has a great difficulty in envisaging a future vocation.

> My aunt and I held many grave deliberations on the calling to which I should be devoted. For a year or more I had endeavoured to find a satisfactory answer to her often-repeated question, "What I would like to be?" But I had no particular liking, that I could discover, for anything. (19)

He prefers the frozen certainty of the past to the supple and indeterminate future. The future is the one dimension where David's imagination fails him. This imagination occasionally helps him to transcend himself in the present, by identification, imitation, and fantasy, but it is not capable of figuring a future that is new, that offers an image of the self different from the present past-directed self. The future exists mainly as a negation of everything, when it exists at all. While at Murdstone's and Grinby's David feels that the future is closed to him: "My rescue from this kind of existence I considered quite hopeless" (11). Later in the story, after Dora's death, he feels the same way: "I came to think that the Future was walled up before me, that the energy and action of my life were at an end, that I never could find any refuge but in the grave" (54). David's fixation on the past and his consequent tendency to empty the present make the future appear blank. Imagination and memory have become too narrow, too specialized. As Micawber says, a few pages later, thinking about his own future in Australia, "the time is come when the past should be buried in oblivion" (54). This is, as one might expect, too extreme a statement of the need to get on the right terms with the past. Were the past to be simply buried, even as deep as David's father, it would keep digging itself up and returning phantomlike to oppress the present. David needs instead to accept his aunt's advice: " 'It's in vain, Trot, to recall the past, unless it works some influence upon the present' " (23). The heavyweight nostalgia, caused by the perpetual lure of the childhood he never wants to lose, has to be somehow overcome. Somehow he has to leave behind the relics and shrines of his "good" past, as well as the ghosts of that other past, the evil one. Otherwise the past will inhibit growth, as it did for the "haunted man" until he could lay the ghost of it with a fully imaginative and constructive kind of remembering. Unless this happens, the unpruned past strangles the present and future with its luxuriant foliage. As Nietzsche said in *The Use and Abuse of History,* "We must know the right time to forget as well as the right time to remember."[26] David evidently cannot fully grow up (integrate his personality, objectify himself) until the immediate and prospective elements of life become more powerful than what he drags behind him with an ever increasing weight. He must learn to forget. This forgetting must be the kind that leaves no gaps in the self, no discontinuities between child and adult.

The final crisis of the book, the importance of which we can judge by the passionate flow of the narrator's account, is a crisis of forgetting. Here David is faced with the whole paradox implied in the dual aim of his autobiography—the aim of seeing himself as continuous and yet as temporally self-transcending at the same time. He is also faced with the complex original question about his own heroism: whether he is what he is *sui generis* or whether he is what he is because of some agency other than himself. At the first of the book he brought up the question of destiny. In the course of his researches he finds that, if there is a destiny, it is operant through Agnes or not at all. At any rate, the question as to whether he is the hero of his own life becomes the question as to whether, in those final crucial episodes, Agnes makes him what he is.

Prior to the final crisis, what does David know about forgetting? Aunt Betsey, as we saw above, encourages him to forget. Her practical intelligence works mainly in the present; for the most part she is free of crippling emotional ties to the past—except as regards her estranged husband. When she pretends to lose her money she forces David to acquire a strength of motives he had not had before; he must try to forget the comfortably spectatorial and retrospective life and make a new start. A helper in another sense is Micawber: he exudes possibility and futurity. His effective sphere of operation is not in the present but in the future, as implied by his famous tag-phrase. His ability to transcend the present contrasts with David's feeling of hopelessness. He is the Old Man of the Sea who is never fully definable, the confidence-man and trickster for whom the past, "tinged by the prismatic hues of memory," barely exists, while the present is merely the time when one falls back "for a spring." He changes his name, profession, and home several times, disguises himself, alters as circumstances alter, and is always ready for a fresh start, as if he had never been known to fail. (His comic inflexibility lies in his habitual reliance on a future change of luck; there is not as much possibility in the world as he thinks.) The adaptable commercial traveler who makes the best of the city and remains elastic in spite of the pressures of reality, in spite of being victimized by the very city in which he feels at home, Micawber is a comic version of the traditional avuncular mentor, who guides the hero through "the arcana of the Modern Babylon" (11). He appears for the first time just when David is newly exposed to the infinite possibilities of what seems at first to be the urban chaos, and leads him to a new home, the floating sanctuary, the House of Generation, of the Micawbers. Having the same general role as Joyce's Leopold Bloom, Micawber, sometime "town traveller for a number of miscellaneous houses," is a truly metropolitan creation, a dealer in appearances, with his shabby-genteel dress and manners and his advertising rhetoric.

There is also Mrs. Gummidge, one of the original occupants of the boat-house, a person who temporarily opens David's eyes to the future. Given the chance, she quickly sheds her old grievances and old way of life, and, in advanced age, emigrates to Australia and a completely altered and daring existence. "I could not meditate enough upon the lesson that I read in Mrs. Gummidge, and the new experience she unfolded to me," says David (32).

The first stage of the final crisis consists of severances of all sorts, an emptying of David's life (as he sees it: actually several important people are still accessible), when many of the people from his early world are plucked away from him and thrust into the ever-growing memorial past. Ham, Steerforth, and Dora die; Micawber, Emily, Mr. Peggotty, and others leave for Australia. Each had affected him and contributed to his education at a different stage of his life and the trim of the novel is such that they must fall away. The hero leaves England for the first time to travel about in Europe for three years. This is a watershed period; he is "alone with [his] undisciplined heart," but still "haunted" by his past.

> It was a long and gloomy night that gathered on me, haunted by the ghosts of many hopes, of many dear remembrances, many errors, many unavailing sorrows and regrets.... I left all who were dear to me, and went away.... The desolate feeling with which I went abroad, deepened and widened hourly. At first it was a heavy sense of loss and sorrow, wherein I could distinguish little else. By imperceptible degrees, it became a hopeless consciousness of all that I had lost—love, friendship, interest; of all that had been shattered—my first trust, my first affection, the whole airy castle of my life; of all that remained—a ruined blank and waste, lying wide around me, unbroken, to the dark horizon.... I roamed from place to place, carrying my burden with me everywhere.... I had had no purpose, no sustaining soul within me, anywhere. (58)

A familiar stage of development: the wandering in the desert, the spiritual dryness, that precedes a new orientation, a new motivation. As Gwendolyn Needham pointed out, this is similar to Carlyle's "Everlasting No," in which the hero experiences life as negation, with the "loss of Hope" that precedes new affirmation, the "Everlasting Yea."[27] Until David can get on the right terms with his past it will torment him as a ghostly burden, and there will only be a "dark horizon" where the future should be.

The "Redlaw"-past is troublesome, the present is depleted, a "ruined blank and waste," and the future needs to be born. Now, after a number of years during which he had developed something of an objectified self, David is thrown back on inner resources, and the novel becomes more psychological than ever before. The ensuing crisis centers on redefining the relationship with Agnes. For her to change from "sister" to wife would presumably involve a recognition of adult sexuality—the sexuality that Emily had come to represent in its negative aspect. The Agnes who is a gift from the past is not the Agnes he now needs. But to take her on a new basis is to shatter that precious image from the past, which would be for him a break in continuity too great to bear, since she is represented as being one of the few living relics of his past. With so many severances, this additional one would seriously threaten the identity that he has based so

The Aesthetics of Education

firmly on the past. "I made no effort to conceal from myself, now, that I loved her, that I was devoted to her; but I brought the assurance home to myself, that it was now too late, and that our long-subsisting relation must be undisturbed" (58). He does not think it possible to begin life anew.

Entering the valley in Switzerland, David, so caught up in the inner struggle with his burden, suddenly finds release from his self-absorption. All that is locked up within him can be jettisoned. He can lay his burden down.

> I came, one evening before sunset, down into a valley, where I was to rest. In the course of my descent to it, by the winding track along the mountain-side, from which I saw it shining far below, I think some long-unwonted sense of beauty and tranquility, some softening influence awakened by its peace, moved faintly in my breast. I remember pausing once, with a kind of sorrow that was not all oppressive, not quite despairing. I remember almost hoping that some better change was possible within me.... All at once, in this serenity, great Nature spoke to me; and soothed me to lay down my weary head upon the grass, and weep as I had not wept yet, since Dora died! (58)

These tears, signifying the end of the dryness, also signify release from the bulk of the oppressive past. This is made possible by the (disturbingly unconvincing) intrusion of Nature into David's egotistical world. By means of a kind of grace, he makes imaginative contact with what had before seemed an alien waste. This is one of the most profound moments (no matter how rhetorical and overdone) of engagement with a present reality that David experiences as an adult. In *Oliver Twist* something like Providence managed events throughout their course; in *Copperfield* the continuous action of Providence is replaced by the momentary operation of grace, though the decisive event is the ensuing self-cure through memory: David attempts to write something like an indirect, though perhaps confessional, autobiography. "I wrote a story, with a purpose growing, not remotely, out of my experience." And this project of verbalizing the now at least temporarily controllable past is later "continued" in the book *David Copperfield* as well.

Let it be noted that Nature does not speak to him until Agnes does first. "I had found a packet of letters awaiting me but a few minutes before." She represents, instead of David's destiny, a form of grace operating through human beings, and she works in parallel with Nature.

> She gave me no advice; she urged no duty on me; she only told me, in her fervent manner, what her trust in me was. She knew (she said) how such a nature as mine would turn affliction to good. She knew how trial and emotion would exalt and strengthen it. She was sure that in my every purpose I should gain a firmer and a higher tendency, through the grief I had undergone. She, who so gloried in my fame, and so looked forward to its augmentation, well knew that I would labour on. She knew that in me, sorrow could not be weakness, but must be strength. As the endurance of my childish days had done its part to make me what I was, so great calamities would nerve me on, to be yet better than I was; and so, as they had taught me, would I teach others. She commended me to God, who had taken my innocent darling to His rest; and in her sisterly affection cherished me always, and was always at my side go where I would; proud of what I had done, but infinitely prouder yet of what I was reserved to do. (58)

Not only does Agnes suggest to David that he has a future, she also reminds him of the time-honored notion, so often encountered in developmental literature, that affliction can be turned to good. The errors of the past that he had been flagellating himself in the remembrance of can now be understood as positive contributions to his identity. This is a characteristically developmental view of experience, which does not judge each event in and for itself, but as part of a total structure in which the meaning of past events changes as time passes. By contrast, where there is a notion that evil is simply and absolutely evil, there can be no idea of the self's development through checks and trials. Evil remains in static, eternal opposition to good. Agnes in effect awakens David to a sense of the temporal structure of his life. He should perpetually be able to transvalue his hard times while making them a part of an ongoing identity.

After this point David acquires a time sense that is not as bewildering as before. Because his past is temporarily in order, the future can open up, for the two are dependent on one another, reciprocally, for their existence. "I could think of the past now, gravely, but not bitterly; and could contemplate the future in a brave spirit" (59). This

The Aesthetics of Education

future, however, as he sees it on his return to England, is still a future without Agnes in the way he would have it include her—as wife. Returning to England after the *Wanderjahre,* he knows he is unable to tell her about his "other love" for her, because he "could not have borne to lose the smallest portion of her sisterly affection" (58). It is now, he thinks, the discipline of his heart that he must renounce Agnes and accept his past mistake as one that cannot be remedied. He had "thrown away the treasure of her love" when he had had the freedom to accept it, and he must abide by that decision to renounce. It is rather like Isabel Archer's decision, in *The Portrait of a Lady,* to remain with Gilbert Osmond, her unsatisfactory husband, apparently in order to verify the freedom with which she had chosen him.

David can say for the time being, "I had faithfully set the seal upon the Past" (55). And what is more, he is able to say, again for the time being, "I . . . had worked out my own destiny" (62), for he has bound himself to his own decision.

So even though the future has opened up before him, it exists mainly as a time when he will enshrine the memory of what Agnes had once been to him, as well as his regrets that she could not be more. He is bound to his past in this one important respect. A final act of transcendence is called for, in which a new feeling for Agnes will replace the old. In these final scenes we look for another beginning in which the mistaken past will indeed be forgotten—that is, displaced so as to take its subordinate role in the total system of time. And if David takes this step on his own, he deserves to think of himself as the author, or hero, of his own life.

But although David comes to understand the possibility of having Agnes for a wife, he can do nothing about it, thanks to his fear of disturbing the past. If any step is taken, it is taken by Agnes (with the help of Aunt Betsey), who shows David he can have things both ways, that he need not give up the sister associated with his sacred past in order to gain a wife. We are thus shown a change in relationship that is not a change at all. Agnes herself does not need to change: "She did not once show me any change in herself. What she always had been to me, she still was; wholly unaltered" (62). And David does not have to change and leave behind any more of his past. As he returns to her home he sees that the old rooms, the old objects, have been religiously kept intact by her fidelity. He finds "everything as it used to be when we were children."

> The staid old house was, as to its cleanliness and order, still just as it had been when I first saw it.... I was shown up the grave old staircase (cautioned of the steps I knew so well), into the unchanged drawing-room. The books that Agnes and I had read together, were on their shelves; and the desk where I had laboured at my lessons, many a night, stood yet at the same old corner of the table. All the little changes that crept in when the Heeps were there, were changed again. Everything was as it used to be, in the happy time. (60)

The step from sister to wife will not be a step away from the "happy time." It will be fully in keeping with the past. We look in vain for signs of a new life; in fact everything suggests that the marriage of these two will be a consecration of the past and a denial that the future contains anything new. This is so in spite of the fact that David says, after her hint to him about her long hidden love, "New thoughts and hopes were whirling through my mind, and all the colours of my life were changing" (62). For one cannot deny the backward-looking quality of these final scenes with Agnes. She is still the priestess of the childhood shrines, and David gives up little of his past to have her. They are both, in this respect, constants and not variables. If they discover anything about each other, it is something that had been present but merely concealed all along. But in any case it is Agnes who guides the final crisis to its conclusion. David can now say to her, contradicting his earlier statement that he had worked out his own destiny, " 'What I am, you have made me, Agnes' " (60). That the narrator, at least, concurs in this judgment can be divined from the apostrophe that ends the novel:

> One face, shining on me like a Heavenly light by which I see all other objects, is above them and beyond them all.... The dear presence, without which I were nothing, bears me company. Oh Agnes, Oh my soul, so may thy face be by me when I close my life indeed; so may I, when realities are melting from me like the shadows which I now dismiss, still find thee near me, pointing upward! (64)

Rhetoric not far from the Micawberesque. David, who has grown in the respects mentioned, who has risen above most of the false language of the world, has not found an authentic language—and we confirm this by looking at *Great Expectations* — to express the love of a grown man for a grown woman. The Angel in the House with the aura of "stained glass windows," supports the existence of the hero. A stable motherly-sisterly (but perhaps not wifely) presence stands beside an incomplete man. This novel confirms our suspicion that, if the hero of a novel of sentimental education cannot get past the stage of such sexless idealism, he is an apprentice who can never become a master. The only promising sign of achievement visible in these last words is that the past is now dismissed (as a shadow), while the present becomes for once the reality; but this dismissal of the remembered past seems to be possible mainly because so much of David's past is with him, in the flesh, in the form of Agnes, Aunt Betsey, and Peggotty.

Copperfield ends with a strong sense of the indoors (as at the beginning), of the hearth, of unassailable occupancy, which is intensified by the fact that the final home contains so much in it of the original home, as well as of the other early homes which were versions of that first one. The hero's exile has definitely ended, for Dickens incarnates a dream of return perfectly suited to a mind like David's, absorbed in origins as it is. The beginning of David's life and the end of his trials meet and close a mythic circle. Time's arrow is really a boomerang after all. The end is a repetition on a higher and even more stable level of the situation at the beginning. The sense of reacquisition, thanks partly to the narrator's exertions in researching his life, overcomes the sense of loss. And David might say, as one of Kafka's curious narrators says, "How much my life has changed, and yet how unchanged it has remained at bottom."[28]

In constructing the famous pattern of the "Circuitous Journey," Dickens of course recreates an experience offered by so many stories that it is almost pointless to give examples. The undisplaced pattern has essentially three stages: (1) Life begins in a static (but vaguely incomplete) state of being at home, into which there intrudes a stimulus from beyond. This leads the hero into (2) another world to which he must accommodate himself as best he can, the accommodation being, sometimes obscurely, a condition for (3) the return to a home which has many of the characteristics of the original one, but where there is a static harmony and completeness that expresses the hero's experience of both (1) and (2) and his transcendence of them. This completeness is often expressed in the form of marriage—obviously the best image for union, for resolution of life's contradictions, in purely human terms. Time comes to an end, as does the myth (that is, the old story) with the usual suggestions of bliss eternally perpetuated. The pattern gratifies the need for a sense of closure of all experience that is feared to be linear, by affirming, as a new structure, a meaningful concord between beginning and end.[29] Development, becoming, takes place during (2), and the myth seems thus designed for the containment of time. The pattern exists in *The Odyssey,* in the Bible, and in many other great literary works. M. H. Abrams has shown something like it to be central to Western literature, especially Romantic mythology.[30] The story of the prodigal son, with its many variations from the Bible to Gide, Rilke's *Notebooks,* and after, is the one expression of the pattern that is perhaps most clearly linked to confessional literature. One finds the pattern often in the Romantics (E. D. Hirsch writes about "Tintern Abbey" in much these terms),[31] but perhaps nowhere in such a pure form as in Novalis, who created it again and again in *Die Lehrlinge zu Sais, Hymnen an die Nacht,* and *Heinrich von Ofterdingen.* T. S. Eliot gave the pattern a consolidated expression in "East Coker."[32]

In *Copperfield* Dickens used this ancient structure with two important personal emphases. First of all, the hero's setting out is not done out of curiosity and thirst for experience of things that the tame home life does not offer (as in most versions of the story). Secondly, the return is to conditions that speak more of beginnings than would seem appropriate for a hero who has developed during the temporal phase of the quest. In Novalis, for instance, return is usually to a home that is definitely more a transfiguration of the original than a reestablishment of it.[33] An even more radical pattern of departure (thus suggesting a more radical change) would show the hero making the other world of exile itself into a new home, as in the literature the French call, after Defoe's hero, *"robinsonnades."* And a yet more truly open form would show the hero, to use W. H. Auden's polar terms, as perpetual "pilgrim" rather than ever again as "citizen."[34] D. H. Lawrence's characters in *Women in Love* are such pilgrims; the circle has become a straight line, as also in *Jude the Obscure, What Maisie Knew, Ernest Pontifex,* and *Lord Jim.* These are all spatial terms, of course, for talking about what can be emphasized in the various accounts as temporal experiences. The stage of exile is the temporal, developmental phase; the open form of life-myth (so especially appealing in the late nineteenth century and after), were it translated into purely temporal terms, would have for hero someone whose character and consciousness are perpetually changing. The two opposite ways of depicting this linear change represent definitely opposed conceptions of time. To borrow W. J. Harvey's distinction, one could say that there is (1) "Time viewed pessimistically as linear" and (2) "Time viewed optimistically as linear."[35] Both of these patterns are explored in *Great Expectations*.

By presenting David's experience as ultimately circular, Dickens does not merely give us a happy ending: He shows us, besides an earlier process of linear development in time, the circularities of consciousness itself, an imprisoning psychological pattern made explicit. Whatever might be objected to, by those who prefer "realism" in the novel, in the purely mythic consolation that the ending of the novel offers—for in effect, here, according to the Miltonic-Keatsian formula, Adam awakens from his dream and finds it truth—we are able to see in the ending a truth that many of the other happy endings available to Dickens could not have shown. It is in his selection of a particular happy ending that Dickens shows his integrity. Had there been an ending that emphasized David's ability to grow and change happily in all respects, so that he could really be free of his past, it simply would not have corresponded to what Dickens was as yet willing to imagine possible; in this he reaffirms a pervasive interest in retrograde tendencies of the psyche.

In spite of the narrator's attempt to recreate himself in a verbalization of his life, a recreation which succeeds up to a point, the hold of the past remains persistent. It is not easy to see just why liberation through constructive memory does not succeed entirely, for the theory of memory holds out the hope of success, at least. There are two possible explanations, both of which suggest imaginative steps that David supposedly might take before his attempt can succeed. For one thing, David is inclined to see evil as something that he can put away from himself and onto other people, who then are seen as different in kind from himself. Once their guilt has become clear,

Steerforth, Emily, and Martha remain at a psychic distance from David, a distance which we can best see in the scene where Rosa Dartle confronts Emily and abuses her while David eavesdrops without interfering. This eavesdropping is not just a narrative device to make it possible for David to report on an interesting confrontation; it reveals subterranean fears of contamination and shows how the evil person must be kept in quarantine. We observe this later when David sees Emily and the rest off to real quarantine in Australia: there is a definite "touch me not" feeling conveyed by David's behavior. He cannot confront sexual evil and thus cannot admit to himself a serious connection with adult sexuality. Indeed, his fear of contamination reveals that David is still treating others narcissistically—a narcissism which itself shows immature sexuality. The theory of memory is based on the premise that the encounter with evil is inevitable and that a character must embrace it imaginatively (though not literally), bring it into himself, so that it no longer exists as a mystery with lurid appeal, separating him from others.

A second limitation in David is suggested in his attempt to write his autobiography for himself. I think it is a significant sign, if we interpret it in the light of the later works, that David never succeeds in getting beyond his past by constructively remembering it. David is not as free of other people, or of himself, as he might think. His real development is always in an exchange with the world, and the exchange evidently must continue perpetually. As the theory of memory asserts, David has a psychic structure he can rise above only by being conscious enough of it to allow himself to follow its guidance willingly. It is unfortunately that very self-consciousness which makes it possible for him to go against his own nature, though never totally, as Dickens sees it. Evil awakens self-consciousness. But the Utopian clause of the theory of memory suggests that self-consciousness can be used positively, so that eventually the division of outer self from inner self can be healed by what becomes for Dickens the ultimate human act—confession—which transposes everything that is inside and secret to the outside, strips away all the masks (but not genuine differences) that for so long are admittedly a necessary protection, and makes possible genuine imaginative human community. Confessions are not directed to God, as Augustine's supposedly were, but to other people, and the act is an expression both of a character's willingness to recognize the difference and reality of others and of his or her partial dependence on them for his or her own reality. There is thus a complex dialectic of difference and similarity, freedom and dependence in all this, and there are no doubt many problems and inconsistencies, naturally, in Dickens's notions, the general drift of which I have been attempting to rationalize.

Dickens was indeed working toward a vision of communion as opposed to individualistic separation. This explains the considerable passivity of his heroes, who, to be active in any obviously manipulative way, would have to be secret, opaque, and unable to participate in the exchange with others, which involves as the central restorative action nothing more dramatic than confession. Dickens's children sometimes act violently in imitation of hardened adults, but this act is a necessary transgression which they must balance with a more peaceable exchange with others in adulthood.

At the end of *Copperfield,* Dr. Strong is, like Mr. Dick, still at work on his allegorical verbalization of himself, the Dictionary. He has not, however, got past the letter *D* in this endless project. David, and perhaps Dickens himself, are also unable, by the end of the novel, to get past the self, the letter *D.* The apotheosis of Agnes, which is meant to suggest that others make us what we are, seems rather more convincingly to represent a denial of the inner reality of another person in order that she might correspond to one's own invention of her. Agnes certainly seems to be an anima-figure, an "inner maiden," so that we would not be surprised if, following Novalis's hero, David were to "lift the veil of the goddess" and see, as in a mirror, "wonder of wonders—himself."[36]

Notes

1. Needham, "The Undisciplined Heart."
2. Barbara Hardy, "The Change of Heart in Dickens' Novels," in *Dickens: A Collection of Critical Essays,* ed. Martin Price (Englewood Cliffs, N.J.: Prentice-Hall, 1967), p. 48.
3. Chap. 2. Q. D. Leavis, in *Dickens the Novelist* (Harmondsworth, Middlesex: Pelican Books, 1972), pp. 152-56, discusses the important fact that *Jane Eyre* appeared before the writing of *Copperfield* and that Dickens was probably influenced by Brontë's book. But, in not mentioning this scene, she leaves out one important piece of evidence.
4. *Écrits* (Paris: Éditions du Seuil, 1966), p. 90.
5. Ibid., p. 91.
6. See J. Hillis Miller, *The Form of Victorian Fiction* (Notre Dame, Ind.: Notre Dame University Press, 1968), pp. 35-39.
7. In *The Primacy of Perception and Other Essays,* ed. James M. Edie (Evanston, Ill.: Northwestern University Press, 1964), p. 125 n.
8. Ibid., p. 127.
9. Consider Poe's "William Wilson," Mallarmé's *Igitur* and *Hérodiade*, and Sartre's *Les Mots,* for a few examples out of many that could be cited. A very interesting Dickens example is in "The Ghost in Master B.'s Room," a section of the Christmas story of 1859, *The Haunted House.* Again we might speculate about Dickens's punning propensities: "Master B" the narcissist.
10. For a summary of Rank's views and a commentary on this point, see Lawrence Kohlberg, "Psychological Analysis and Literary Forms: A Study of Doubles in Dostoyevsky," *Daedalus* 92 (Spring 1963): 358-59.
11. *Search for a Method,* trans. Hazel E. Barnes (New York: Vintage Books, 1968), p. 149.
12. Ibid., p. 97.
13. *The Poetry of Experience: The Dramatic Monologue in Modern Literary Tradition* (New York: W. W. Norton, 1963), p. 29.
14. Merleau-Ponty, *Primacy of Perception,* pp. 154-55.
15. Ibid., p. 125.
16. Ibid., p. 110.
17. [John Butt], "Shavings from Dickens's Workshop. Unpublished Fragments of the Novels," *The Dickensian* 48 (1952): 159.
18. "Philadelphia and Its Solitary Prison," *American Notes* (1842).
19. *Notebooks,* p. 92.
20. *Confessions,* trans. J. M. Cohen (Baltimore: Penguin Books, 1954), p. 19.
21. (New York: Macmillan, 1958), pp. 95-96.
22. *The Words,* trans. Bernard Frechtman (New York: Fawcett Books, 1966), p. 29.

23. *Charles Dickens: The World of His Novels,* p. 151.
24. Raleigh, "Dickens and the Sense of Time," p. 136.
25. Ibid., p. 135.
26. Trans. Adrian Collins (Indianapolis: Bobbs-Merrill, 1957), p. 8.
27. Needham, "The Undisciplined Heart," p. 103.
28. "Investigations of a Dog," in *Selected Short Stories of Franz Kafka,* trans. Willa and Edwin Muir (New York: Modern Library, 1952), p. 202.
29. Here I am indebted to Frank Kermode's *The Sense of an Ending: Studies in the Theory of Fiction* (New York: Oxford University Press, 1966).
30. *Natural Supernaturalism;* see especially pp. 32-37, "The Design of Biblical History."
31. E. D. Hirsch, *Wordsworth and Schelling: A Typological Study of Romanticism* (New Haven: Yale University Press, 1960), p. 75. The change is "from immediacy to mediation. In youth, the forms of nature evoked a direct, immediate feeling of joy. In maturity, these same forms, coupled with a remembrance of immediate joy, evoke a quieter joy which is mediated by thought and human experience." I take this to be essentially a restatement of the pattern Abrams isolates for study.
32. In *The Complete Poems and Plays: 1909-1950* (New York: Harcourt, Brace and Co., 1952), p. 123, the famous concluding lines:

> Home is where one starts from. As we grow older
> The world becomes stranger, the pattern more complicated
> Of dead and living. . . .
> We must be still and still moving
> Into another intensity
> For a further union, a deeper communion
> Through the dark cold and the empty desolation,
> The wave cry, the wind cry, the vast waters
> Of the petrel and the porpoise. In my end is my beginning.

33. As in the fable of Hyazinth and Rosenblüte in *Die Lehrlinge zu Sais.*
34. *The Dyer's Hand and Other Essays* (New York: Random House, 1962), p. 279.
35. *Character and the Novel* (Ithaca, N.Y.: Cornell University Press, 1965), p. 103.
36. *Schriften,* ed. Paul Kluckhohn and Richard Samuel (Stuttgart: W. Kohlhammer Verlag, 1960)1:110. "Einem gelang es—er hob den Schleier der Göttin zu Sais—/ Aber was sah er?—Wunder des Wunders—Sich Selbst."

FOUR

Great Expectations and the Fictions of the Future

In *Oliver Twist* Dickens defines the hero by an appeal outside of and antecedent to time, beyond his existential condition. In *Copperfield* an individual can be defined by his experience, but the essential experience is of childhood. The locus of identity for an adult is in the past, and the essential mode of consciousness is memory. Experience is important in defining David, but he cannot resist the impulse to mythify his past as he attempts to establish an essential self that is independent of the moment-to-moment experiencing self. This self does not significantly change after the early years of radical crisis. David, having been born once, cannot be born again.

In *Great Expectations* Dickens creates what William James would call a "twice-born" hero.[1] Pip is a creature of passage in a much fuller sense than David is, much more supple in change. He is an individual whose history genuinely encompasses both childhood and adulthood. The mode of consciousness that defines him is "expectation"—his mind is typically directed toward the future rather than toward the past. Pip transcends the identity he starts out with and attempts to define himself in accord with a dreamed-of future identity. Because it is in time that this new identity will come into existence, Pip is committed to life in time in a way that Oliver and David are not. Time is the medium in which the desired transformation of the ugly duckling into the proud swan will presumably take place. In *Copperfield* the controlling fiction was that of the Noble Child, and the plot was a circular track that enabled the hero to find his end in his beginnings.

In *Great Expectations* the hero's version of the informing fiction is essentially linear, and the pattern appears to be the straight way into the infinite distance—infinite because the desired end cannot be seen at all clearly; it does not resemble anything the hero has with him at the beginning. Like the narrator of *Epipsychidion,* Pip lives "feeding [his] course with expectation's breath." The infinite postponement of completeness generates more hope and belief in the possibilities of time than the primitivistic myth lived by David. For David time is negative because every moment threatens to open an impassable gap between himself and his origins; he is constantly being hurried away from what he wants. For Pip time is positive, because every moment brings nearer the expected fulfillment; he is constantly becoming more than he was at first; time is not diminishment but growth. And yet time is also a great danger.

I. In the Graveyard

"To be quite sure I had fallen into no unconscious repetitions, I read David Copperfield the other day, and was affected by it to a degree you would hardly believe," Dickens wrote to his friend Forster, when just beginning *Great Expectations.*[2] The connection between the two books is, at the outset, negative, or rather reciprocal: Dickens of course did not want to repeat himself, to write the same book twice. True, this new book was seemingly based on the same life as *Copperfield* and *Oliver Twist,* but the author needed to go beyond his earlier views of that life, even to transcend it as a source of material for a novel. According to Johnson, "The impulse that sent Dickens back to this world of his childhood, now the landscape of his daily walks, was more ... than the desire to have an appropriate setting for his story. It rose from some deeper need to explore, once again, more profoundly even than he had been able to do in *David Copperfield,* his formative years and the bent they had given him. ... There were crucial ways in which he had developed tremendously beyond the man he had been."[3] Although Johnson is correct in stressing autobiographical considerations as the source and origin of the novel, it is most visibly Dickens's growth as an artist that prompted him to return less to his childhood world than to the novel that ostensibly grew out of it; for his explorations at the time of *Copperfield* made it evident that, if he could not write about his life, he could write his way out of it. *Great Expectations* is confessional partly in that it dramatizes its author's imaginative development as a writer of narrative, not his earlier life as such.

We are fortunate to have two fictional autobiographies, written a decade apart, by a writer as important as Dickens. This gives us a rare chance to study changes in perspective, as well as significant continuities. We have considered the opening passages of the other two novels; here, at some length, is the beginning of *Great Expectations:*

> My father's family name being Pirrip, and my Christian name Philip, my infant tongue could make of both names nothing longer or more explicit than Pip. So I called myself Pip, and came to be called Pip.
>
> I give Pirrip as my father's family name, on the authority of his tombstone and my sister—Mrs. Joe Gargery, who married the blacksmith. As I never saw my father or my mother, and never saw any likeness of either of them (for their days were long before the days of photographs), my first fancies regarding what they were like were unreasonably derived from their tombstones....
>
> My first most vivid and broad impression of the identity of things seems to me to have been gained on a memorable raw afternoon towards evening. At such a time I found out for certain that this bleak place overgrown with nettles was the churchyard; and that Philip Pirrip, late of this parish, and also Georgiana wife of the above, were dead and buried; and that Alexander, Bartholomew, Abraham, Tobias, and Roger, infant children of the aforesaid, were also dead and buried; and that dark flat wilderness beyond the churchyard, intersected with dykes and mounds and gates, with scattered cattle feeding on it, was the marshes; and that the low leaden line beyond was the river; and that the distant savage lair from which the wind was rushing was the sea; and that the small bundle of shivers growing afraid of it all and beginning to cry was Pip.
>
> "Hold your noise!" cried a terrible voice, as a man started up from among the graves at the side of the church porch. "Keep still, you little devil, or I'll cut your throat!"
>
> A fearful man, all in coarse grey, with a great iron on his leg. A man with no hat, and with broken shoes, and with an old rag tied round his head. A man who had been soaked in water, and smothered in mud, and lamed by stones, and cut by flints, and stung by nettles, and torn by briars; who limped, and shivered, and glared and growled;

and whose teeth chattered in his head as he seized me by the chin.

"O! Don't cut my throat, sir," I pleaded in terror. "Pray don't do it, sir."

"Tell us your name!" said the man. "Quick!"

"Pip, sir."

"Once more," said the man, staring at me. "Give it mouth!"

"Pip. Pip, sir."

"Show us where you live," said the man. "Pint out the place!"

I pointed to where our village lay, on the flat in-shore among the alder-trees and pollards, a mile or more from the church.

"Now lookee here!" said the man. "Where's your mother?"

"There, sir!" said I.

He started, made a short run, and stopped and looked over his shoulder.

"There, sir!" I timidly explained. "Also Georgiana. That's my mother."

"Oh!" said he, coming back. "And is that your father alonger your mother?"

"Yes, sir," said I; "him too; late of this parish."

"Ha!" he muttered then, considering. "Who d'ye live with—supposin' you're kindly let to live, which I han't made up my mind about?"

"My sister, sir—Mrs. Joe Gargery—wife of Joe Gargery, the blacksmith, sir."[4]

In this much-discussed scene the narration—including the relation of the narrator to the hero—is different from that in *Oliver Twist* and *Copperfield,* and in this difference one glimpses some small but significant changes in the author's way of representing childhood in its relation to adulthood. This scene, which begins the carefully articulated series of events forming the first prolonged identity-crisis for Pip, is, to start with, certainly much more present, more "dramatically" realized than the earliest moments of Oliver's and David's stories. After all, an event relatively late in childhood (Pip is about seven years old) has been selected to begin the novel, an event that would be vividly accessible to memory, for here there is no dependence on second-hand information as in the first chapter of *David Copperfield.* There is no longer any dwelling on mysteries of birth; birth is not a resonant event in itself, perhaps because it is not here viewed as an experience. And childhood is not dwelt upon for its own sake, as it often was during the earliest scenes of *Copperfield*. As the narration continues through and beyond this first scene, there is no lingering, no aimless sampling or tasting of childhood, no evocations of a state of being. Childhood has urgencies that link it immediately to the crimes and passions of adults. From the first important moments of self-consciousness, childhood is a period of change, of becoming.

Although he presumably bases his account on memories of his own childhood, the narrator is objective about the child he describes. Robert B. Partlow, in his discussion of point of view in this novel, emphasizes this objectivity and asserts that "the narrator, in fact, feels a kind of alienation from Pip," so much so that there is a "gap between the present telling and past events."[5] Partlow suggests that, in places, the child Pip is virtually a different person from the adult narrator, so great is this gap. Actually, the objectivity of this narrator is a fortunate compromise between the objectivity of the omniscient narrator of *Oliver Twist* and the subjectivity of the narrator of *Copperfield*. This first-person objectivity (though we catch glimpses of it in Esther's narrative in *Bleak House*) is an innovation for Dickens. It is the objectivity of a man (Mr. Pirrip) who has earned the right to it because he has lived through and come to understand the events he recounts. The narrator, were he anybody else than Mr. Pirrip, who so often exposes to ridicule a child's suffering and error, would often seem either heartless or impertinent, and that would be a terrible strategical error. Who the narrator is makes all the difference; nevertheless this narrator is less obtrusive with his own personality than the speakers in the other two novels. The narrative does not often—as in *Copperfield*—call attention directly either to the act of narration or to the existence of the speaker, who might well be situated almost anywhere in time. We eventually come to know that he is a middle-aged bourgeois looking backward from some unknown place in time (supposedly the "now" of narration)—a place which we were usually kept aware of in *Copperfield*, because part of the narrator's consciousness would often ricochet off that place as his past impetuously came forward. But for Mr. Pirrip this place does not seem to exist. Indeed, the narrator rarely indicates his position in time in relation to the hero. If this place exists it is only at a theoretical, indefinite distance from Pip; no triangulation the reader performs can quite locate it. But as one actually experiences the novel, one feels that the narrator typically seems to be with Pip in time, as a subtle, ironic observer poised, for all one knows, directly overhead, almost where one would expect to find an omniscient narrator. Seldom is one made aware of the density, of the duration, of time (which Partlow sees as separating the narrator and hero), as one was in *Copperfield*. Two emotional lives, attributable to two distinct phases of identity, do not interact much in *Great Expectations;* the narrator for the most part refrains from directly speaking of his own feelings, though he does not conceal his identity. And yet his analyses and judgments are pervasive. The irony that was only intermittent in *Copperfield*, as when David was wooing young ladies and posturing before mirrors, sustains itself over much longer periods in this novel.[6] Pip is always being exposed and judged, but this judgment often is managed by a slight displacement of the boy's own language: " 'Now, Biddy,' said I, 'I am very sorry to see this in you. I did not expect to see this in you. You are envious, Biddy, and grudging. You are dissatisfied on account of my rise in fortune, and you can't help showing it.' " (19). The narrator enters Pip's own language and seems to dwell in it unobtrusively. He is not looking back saying "What a cad I was," and so forth, as Copperfield often was. The narrator seems to reconstruct the boy's language so that it unconsciously reveals a state of mind that everyday speech does not often so clearly reveal. This state of mind, disclosed here in Pip's patronizing repetitions, is something Dickens evidently wishes us to think of as revealed for us by a narrator whose intimate knowledge of the boy allows him to "adjust" the boy's speeches (the narrator does not even pretend to remember and record speeches verbatim) in the interest of a truth that could not emerge in a literal, autobiographical record. Dickens enables us to adopt the illusion that the narrator knows Pip's mind so well, and yet is also so completely able to keep his distance from it, that we can assume the narrator once was that very boy. This assumption helps us to accredit the narrator's wisdom as well as to recognize his distance from Dickens himself—Dickens, who remains almost entirely invisible, concealed behind a narrator whom casual readers might tend to think of as speaking with Dickens's authentic voice.[7]

Fictions of the Future

The objectivity, the amused yet tolerant irony of this narrator, shows him to be more complete, more a total adult than the narrator of *Copperfield*. For this grownup narrator, many of the things that were sacred in *Copperfield* have lost their magic. Anyone who reads the Christmas dinner scene in *Great Expectations* can easily see how much control the narrator has over any tendency to sympathize unconditionally with childhood. No longer is childhood sacred simply because it is childhood; no longer is there an overflow of sympathy for children as such. The narrator seems to have got beyond his past, as if to say it is only the child in us that worships childhood. This novel seems primarily to be written neither for recapture of the past nor for enough knowledge of it to change the narrator's present identity (the two motives behind *Copperfield*). If, as Robert Garis has asserted,[8] Pip's life story is an exemplum, it is a modern exemplum written by a wise narrator to illustrate, for one thing, the necessity for getting on the right terms with one's past and one's friends. *Copperfield* was ostensibly written by and for the narrator; *Great Expectations* can be seen as written by the narrator for other people. Its concern is not with an individual as such, or it would have been named, perhaps, *The Personal History of Philip Pirrip;* the real concern (as the title does suggest) is thematic and, in a way, impersonal. Thus we glimpse higher, more adult intentions in Pirrip's autobiography: it is truly the narrator's confession (in the sense of speaking about oneself to another person). What is truly remarkable is Dickens's ability now to treat a theme by using his hero dramatically and concretely; in *Copperfield,* which dealt with one concrete individual, the hero often vanished, either lost somewhere between the past and the present, or (like Fagin in prison) distributed bewilderingly throughout time, fragmented.

We are given so much of the novel by implication in the first few pages that it is valuable to pursue what we find there. Considerable attention is paid to names: the name of the hero, the names of his family. Oliver and David were of course assigned names at birth—and David was given several new names by his friends in the course of his life, a fact which, according to Sylvére Monod, "emphasizes the differences in the nature of the relationships involved,"[9] but which also suggests David's amorphous character. His names, in several cases, imply that others appropriated the passive David for their own, however innocuous, purposes. It is a departure, in terms of independence, for Pip to name himself. As far as names go, he is given much more of a fresh start than either Oliver or David.

The inability of Pip's "infant tongue" to pronounce his given name shows once again the alien quality of language as the child encounters it. But the acquisition of a name is the first step in becoming committed to language. It is appropriate that this pseudo-autobiography begins with repetitions of this most significant of all words for the self, the acceptance and use of which must be among the first acts whereby one understands that he is conventionally differentiated from other people.[10] To feel that one truly has a name, to use that name, and to encounter it in the speech of other people must be one of the ways in which a person recognizes the possibility of finding his truth in words, the final and most developed form of this personal truth being, with all its limitations, written confession. This confession is, in a way, an extended naming of oneself. It is a fine piece of psychology for Dickens to show Pip being forced to utter his name over and over to Magwitch, for Pip's identity and existence are being challenged at the very moment they are first firmly established. His name is the sound that *is* Pip, the sound that—on this occasion of his "first most vivid and broad impression of the identity of things," when Pip learns what he is partly by learning he is not what is outside him—expresses the sense of an identity even intensified by terror. Pip gives himself away by speaking his most precious word, and thus receives himself back again, for the name saves him from immediate harm. This primitive structure of giving and receiving is a major motif in the novel's general pattern. Pip is nothing but a pure, unelaborated self at the beginning, but in finding himself he finds a speck (a pip) of identity that is somehow viable, and this viability is partly a function of his being identifiable in his name.

The questions that the convict goes on to ask the boy are primitive orientation questions like those that well-meaning adults often politely ask a child, when they want to encourage him by seeming to test his verbal awareness of who he is, where he lives, and who his parents are. The child signifies his trust in the adult world by his willingness to answer questions that locate him so inexorably as a person set off from strangers. It must always be with a certain *frisson* that a child answers these questions, for instinct must, in however faint a way, whisper that there is safety as well as danger in being indefinable. To be located, to exist in a language, defined for another person, especially when one is as full of potentiality as a growing child, this must at times be burdensome and imprisoning. When Pip meets Estella he suffers from being defined as a blacksmith's boy. He is allowed no appeal to his potentiality, his indeterminateness.

A garbled name, threatening questions: "language games" confront the child with both a strangeness and a curious intimacy, for the very self is located in time and space (with all the danger that implies) by means of words. But much of the verbal information that Pip needs to define himself with is scrambled or absent. What ought to point the way to the ancestral past is only a collection of half-understood words. As Pip says later on, "At the time when I stood in the churchyard, reading the family tombstones, I had just enough learning to be able to spell them out. My construction even of their simple meaning was not very correct, for I read 'Wife of the Above' as a complimentary reference to my father's exaltation to a better world; and if any one of my deceased relations had been referred to as 'Below,' I have no doubt I should have formed the worst opinions of that member of the family" (7).

There is no verbal tradition for the boy, no lore that even his sister will pass on, no communication with the identities of his parents, as there was even for Oliver and David. By eliminating the givens and supplying us with a true orphan, Dickens necessarily intensifies the concern with what education and the passage of time will make of the boy. The "like father like son" formula does not figure at all—or rather it is tested implicitly in a new way, because this child who has named himself will also try out new parents for himself. But it is his act of acknowledgment that defines them as parents, no biological event. It is appropriate that Pip gains his sense of himself at the same time that he discovers "for certain" that his parents are "dead and buried."

The absence of a father is an important fact to notice in a developmental account because of the freedom and danger this absence opens up. But in the first scene of *Great Expectations,* Dickens repeats a rather strange notion he had employed in *Copperfield.* Both David and Pip are fascinated by the tombstones of their fathers (which are among the first things mentioned in both books), as if they contained some partly legible meaning for their lives. For both children the awakening of self-consciousness is associated with the advent of a man of threatening aspect who appears "like Lazarus raised from the dead" in *Copperfield* and "like a pirate come to life" in *Great Expectations.* And they appear in the immediate vicinity of the fathers' graves. It is the manifestation of the spectral anti-father, paternity under a negative sign, that jolts these children out of the anonymity of infantile innocence.

Two features of these episodes should be singled out: First of all, in them the notions of life and death are, structurally speaking, synthesized by Dickens's rather insistent device of making the tombstone a theme of the earliest moment of significant psychic activity; so one gets the impression that life must issue from not-life, that death is necessary to life. Death is shown as a reciprocal, as a frame for life as it is in the Venerable Bede's famous allegory of the sparrow flying from outer darkness into a lighted hall and then back into darkness. But the accommodation, the placement of (parental) death in the consciousness of Dickens's characters is problematical, as we can see when such strange, anomalous figures vengefully rise up as if out of the grave, just when life has simultaneously been discriminated from death and linked to it.

These figures symbolize the fact that death cannot be comfortably relegated to the horizons of life, the beginning and the end; with their deathly aspect and deathly threats they reveal the death that is in life, especially the kind of fatality implicit in the process of radical change (as from childhood to adulthood). Their "resurrection" is a dark parody of the genuine rebirth that offers, as a justification for the death of the old self, a new and different self that is the more alive for having emerged from a death. Here we glimpse more of the meaning of Dickens's passion for the motif of "the surfacing of what was hidden underground," and the allied motif of haunting. Murdstone and Magwitch, when they first appear, lacking what Coleridge with nice discrimination called "living life," are proleptic images of the danger that passage of time holds for these children who will have to grow up (thanks to these men), perhaps to die to their childhood and to assume the mortifying role of adults. By bringing deathly, guilty adult and awakening child together in violent encounters, Dickens establishes, for the most part subliminally, initial negative predictions about the future development of David and Pip; a course of defeat is hypothesized, and testing the hypothesis will produce an understanding of time and change.

A second thing to notice in these episodes is that Murdstone and Magwitch "come out of the earth"—the consecreated ground of the graveyard—in another sense than that of resurrection. Even in their pallor they seem to represent sources of a kind of terrible and alien chthonic energy that will have to be dealt with by David and Pip, who must in some way absorb and utilize it or else repudiate it. Claude Lévi-Strauss has stressed the importance for primitives of asking the question whether they are "born from different or born from same," whether they are of autochthonous origin or born of two human beings.[11] This problem did not escape Dickens, who often was able to see human issues reduced to primitive essentials. He works it out in *Great Expectations* in terms of the derivative problem (this phrasing is after that of Edmund Leach[12]): "How is it that I am on the one hand an animal (natural) and on the other hand a human being (cultural)?" To the extent that he imagines he is Magwitch's son Pip feels he is not only a criminal but virtually an animal; to the extent that he imagines he is Miss Havisham's son he feels he is a fully acknowledged human being. But Dickens is not about to be simplistic in defining his central figure. Oliver could repudiate all that was both criminal and chthonic (Fagin and the workhouse origins), and Dickens's story remained polarized into static oppositions. But the possibility of character change makes for more complex representations in which the supposed dichotomies of life (good and evil, human and nonhuman, etc.) can be treated synthetically.

In the first scene of the novel we can already see connections being made between seeming opposites. Just as Pip's childhood is more complex than David's (which had its period of unalloyed bliss followed by a period of misery), so Magwitch is more complex than Murdstone in the way he first affects the hero. Pip and Magwitch have something in common when they meet: they are both escapees. And Pip is a "small bundle of shivers growing afraid," while Magwitch is a frightened man "who limped and shivered." Pip admits to "pitying his desolation." In the encounter of these escapees the moral problems of growing up are thrust into the framework of criminality that is the superstructure of the novel. The terms that ordinarily define Magwitch and his sphere of life are analogically applied to Pip and his world, so that eventually it becomes pointless to speak of two separate worlds and two kinds of being in opposition, as there were in *Oliver Twist.* We come to see the convergence in one soul of the criminal and the innocent, and the product of this convergence is a condition we might call, after Blake, "experience."

Growing up in *Copperfield* meant assuming responsibility for some minor errors, but—except in the conflict with Murdstone, when David wondered if he were an "atrocious criminal"—the hero was not linked with criminality. He was often shown at a moral distance from criminals that entitled him to a certain smugness, as in his encounter with Heep and Littimer in prison. But even in that novel we could see the insistence of evil as a Dickensian concern, and immoral behavior was attributed to two of the more sympathetic characters of the book, Steerforth and Emily. Throughout the whole of *Great Expectations,* the privacies of moral evolution in the central character himself are linked in various ways with overtly criminal events. This is a form of extremism that indicates Dickens's desire fully to objectify, to find powerful, immediate images that express the problems of psychic development. This objectification affords a way of showing an individual vitally implicated in his own decisions and actions. No longer is there any dwelling on the texture of psychic life, no longer is reverie (for instance) there for its own sake as it had often been in *Copperfield;* now there must be a firmer connection than before between musings and actions.

Pip is "vitally implicated in his decisions and actions," but I do not mean to imply that he has powers of the sort possessed by those Balzacian figures who can make themselves great reservoirs of energy and then channel their passions into actions that are decisive even in their futility. In Pip there is nothing of the confident, though ill-fated, decisiveness of climbers like Lucien Chardon "de Rubempré" in *Illu-*

sions Perdues. One sees real potency only in Dickens's lesser characters, like Miss Havisham, who has all the virginal energy in her single-minded vindictiveness of a Cousin Bette; or like Magwitch, whose monomania is almost as powerful as that of a Baron Hulot or an Old Grandet.

II. The First Crisis: Deception and Growth

Examination of the first major crisis in the novel shows that Pip's development takes place in a complex net of interactions. It involves deception, which, far more than mere violence, implies a special relationship with other people, a certain tacit acknowledgment of their powers of perception. In general, Dickens establishes a close connection between inner life and external circumstances. As Barbara Hardy says, "Pip's progress in *Great Expectations* is probably the only instance of a moral action where the events precipitate change and growth as they do in George Eliot or Henry James."[13] Perhaps more precisely, Dickens might be aligned with the James of, say, *The Ambassadors,* rather than with Eliot, who throughout her novels respects, somewhat more than James, the pressure of environment. James and Dickens generally agree in suggesting that perception and imagination, and not so much environment and external events, are what bring about inner change, moral choices, new actions.

Dickens begins by establishing a chain of causality for Pip, but this chain is soon transformed, by the character himself, into a logic of behavior deriving immediately from his assessment of environmental complexities and the interaction of persons. For this to happen, the character confirms his sense of what might crudely be called the distinction between inner (subjective) and outer (objective) self. I examined such distinctions somewhat more elaborately in reference to *Copperfield,* but here I shall try to acknowledge Dickens's new emphasis on the interaction of persons in the developmental crises.

Pip, like Oliver, is not much more to begin with than an "item of mortality," a mere speck, "a small bundle of shivers." He has temporarily escaped from his sister's prison-house and has just stolen a few moments of meditative freedom. Suddenly he is "arrested" by a frightful stranger, Magwitch. This "arrest" is the true beginning of

Pip's subsequent separation from the disturbingly ambiguous world of his childhood society. The separation is both an enfranchisement and an alienation since that original world was both good (there is Joe) and bad (there is his sister). Murdstone had inverted David's simple world with his intrusion into it; Magwitch does the same for Pip's complex one. Many critics have noted that the familiar objects of orientation, the church, the tombstone, and so on, are literally inverted when Pip is jerked upside-down into the air, thus repeating no doubt the motion whereby newborn children are induced to "take upon [themselves] the office of respiration" (*OT*, 1). In effect, Magwitch administers a parody of the "First Office of Instruction" from the *Book of Common Prayer*:

Question: What is your Christian Name?
Answer: My Christian Name is ___.
Question: Who gave you this Name?
Answer: My Sponsors gave me this Name....[14]

The inversion shows Pip that things are not as monumental as he was led to believe, as unchallengeable in their permanence and authority. "I saw the steeple under my feet." "I was seated on a high tombstone." The psychology of this is close to that of the Biblical episode in which Satan sets Jesus on the temple. Jesus was not one to shift his perspective, however—Pip is. The "little devil" (as Magwitch calls him) is allied to his mentor, as the next scenes prove, when the boy violates the sacred usages of familial authority and of Christmas festival by stealing the forbidden pork pie. This particular theft is a gratuitous act, whereas stealing the other food might be justified as conditioned—done out of fear of the mythical "ferocious young man" who, Magwitch promises, will eat his heart and liver. Having been introduced to the sacrilege of sitting on tombstones, he can now scramble up into the forbidden places of his sister's household. He thus takes the first step toward disturbing the status quo of the adult world—as every child probably must in some way, even though he is inevitably blamed for it by those for whom every new presence in the world is merely intrusive.

After meeting Magwitch, Pip enters into a false relationship with his sister, which does happen to have its advantages. She has, after all, imprisoned him: she locks the front door, lets him out only for specified intervals, and feeds him a meagre diet of "mortifying and penitential character." In service to his new master, Pip acquires a certain mental freedom from his sister more significant than that enjoyed when secretly manufacturing "that intoxicating fluid, Spanish-liquorice-water" in his bedroom. His obligation to the convict clashes with his obligation to his sister, who, rather like Magwitch, makes it clear to Pip that she "lets him live" only by the most irksome restraint of violent tendencies. He cannot satisfy both people at once, but then neither can he refuse to satisfy them. Contradictory commands cannot be reconciled except by the invention of new techniques: secrecy, theft, and eventually lying. The theft has for Pip the amazing result of showing up the weakness of Mrs. Joe, whose omniscience had been so much respected, especially by Joe ("Your sister's a master-mind. A master-mind" [7]). Pip gets away with his secret act. Punishment, which had seemed to rain down for every slight deviation of his or Joe's, is revealingly absent in the case of the pork pie. So Pip discovers an inside which cannot be probed by the supposedly all-seeing sister; he is opaque.

Rousseau, in his *Confessions,* records a contrary but structurally similar incident, when he was accused of a misdemeanor he had not committed. After being beaten severely many times for his refusal to confess to the offense, he discovered a new freedom of thought for himself: "It was an entirely different kind of existence. No longer were we young people bound by ties of respect, intimacy, and confidence to our guardians; we no longer looked on them as gods who read our hearts; . . . we began to be secretive, to rebel, and to lie."[15] Thus was also planted the seed of Rousseau's desire to write his *Confession,* a confession that nobody could force him to produce. Thus the child forced to lie becomes the adult who feels free to confess.

> I have often thought that few people know what secrecy there is in the young, under terror.... I was in mortal terror of the young man who wanted my heart and liver; I was in mortal terror of my interlocutor with the iron leg; I was in mortal terror of myself, from whom an awful promise had been extracted; I had no hope of deliverance through my all-powerful sister, who repulsed me at every turn; I am

afraid to think of what I might have done on requirement, in the secrecy of my terror. (2)

This shows the arousal of self-consciousness in the presence of a terrifying dilemma. For Pip to be in terror of himself indicates that a dual structure has been created, in that part of him can ally itself to projects which the rest of him recoils from. There is a self within the self; there is the experience of a more or less objective identity (partly in that it has a "social" dimension—it is capable of "keeping promises"—and partly in that it is an object of knowledge for the other part of the self) and, split off from that, an identity that is somehow deeper, more immediate, more real (which simply feels terror). At the same time that he displays this duality of structure, Pip discovers more emphatically than ever before his separateness from others, his individuality—just as the criminals in *Oliver Twist,* and David Copperfield himself, did—in the isolation created by suffering. It is significant that, just at the time Pip discovers he has an inside, he fears so much the cannibalistic young man, who might, to Pip's horror, "get inside" of him.

> I do not recall that I felt any tenderness of conscience in reference to Mrs. Joe, when the fear of being found out was lifted off me. But I loved Joe ... and, as to him, my inner self was not so easily composed. It was much upon my mind ... that I ought to tell Joe the whole truth. Yet I did not.... The fear of losing Joe's confidence, and of thenceforth sitting in the chimney corner at night staring drearily at my for ever lost companion and friend, tied up my tongue. (6)

But the upshot of Pip's action is painful self-division, and separation from Joe as well. The discovery of new mental properties occurs in isolation and at first increases isolation from others as well as distance from an earlier self. Much of the novel deals with the problem of reestablishing companionship with Joe (that is, with the authentic human community); a further act of the imagination is needed, one which will allow Pip to transcend his narrow self in sympathy for others.

The first series of episodes comes to an end with Pip's discomposed state of mind which "lasted long after the subject [of the convict] had died out" (6). After discovering a problematic identity in his encounter with the underworld, Pip is next exposed to people who are above him, when he begins his visiting at Miss Havisham's. Exposure to criminals was the source of the first division in his life, and exposure to Miss Havisham and Estella widens this division into radical discontent with himself. For much of the rest of the novel, Pip's development is worked out in reference to one or the other of the two spheres that provide the alternatives to the one of his origins.

Pip's first visit to Miss Havisham leads to what is a more advanced transgression than the theft he had committed earlier. When he returns home and is bullied and subjected to a veritable *procès-verbal* by his sister and Pumblechook, he commits his first verbal sin by lying to them. He discovers how to use words inventively so as to insulate himself from the indignities his child's position exposes him to. But to tell lies, such fantastic arabesques of lies, is to move into a more definite zone of offense than that of the silent theft. The theft was covered up without any deliberate attempt of his to conceal it through lies. But it taught him something about his imperviousness to scrutiny by others, which in turn made lies possible. Certainly, to sift the ethics of the theft, it was committed under more extenuating circumstances (even though it had its gratuitous element) than the predominantly willful, marvelously sportive lies Pip indulges in. The lie is more complex than the theft; it implies a duplicity that is not a necessary adjunct of theft, which needs only secrecy. In fact, saying what one knows is false involves duplicity compounded, for one constructs for others a plausible self-image both with words and with accompanying gestures, and all of this is a negation of the "real" self. Lying involves hypocritically making a mask, one which cannot be contrived unless one assesses and manipulates the view that others will have while one is lying. That is to say, lying involves knowing oneself as an object for others, so that false words can issue plausibly from the mask. However, the taboo against verbal sin of this sort must acquire some of its force from the fact that, given an initial complexity of consciousness, it is one of the easiest sins to commit. It is generally so easy to lie that, were lies not the object of universal contempt, they would undermine all social life and communication (even though there are people, not necessarily cynics, who say that the lie is what makes personal life bearable and social life possible). But we despise the exposed liar more than the thief; and Satan comes to be known not as the Prince of Thieves, but as, according to Joe, "The father of lies" (9).

When he decides to lie to his sister and Pumblechook, Pip says, "I reflected for some time, and then answered *as if I had discovered a new idea*" (9, italics mine). He begins with a tiny preparatory lie, prompted by the usual Dickens child's animus against being "asked a sum." Then he moves on to more advanced lies, when he tells Mrs. Joe and Pumblechook, "with an obtrusive show of artlessness on my countenance" (9), his version of the sports at Satis House. (He is remembered by the narrator as not yet fully able to manipulate his exterior.) When these lies are passed on to Joe, and Pip realizes the contagiousness of deception, he says that "I considered myself a young monster" (9). Prior to lying there is usually nothing to confess. Thus self-defined as a monster, he steals into the forge and confesses to Joe, confessing as well that his lies are linked to the fact that he had that day learned about his "commonness" from Estella. "And then I told Joe . . . that I wished I was not common, and that the lies had come of it somehow, though I didn't know how" (9). To which Joe answers that "lies is lies" and that "if you can't get to be oncommon through going straight, you'll never get to do it through going crooked" (9). As he meditates that night in a "disturbed and unthankful state" (9), he realizes that a great change has come over him since going to Miss Havisham's. This change is shown in his willingness to deceive the people of his "common" world in order to protect his private knowledge of the people of the world he has just discovered. Lies and fictions in general are the result of his entrance into that new world. Later it will be confession that frees him from it.

III. Pip and Puberty: The Fictive "Distortion" of Developmental Time

I have been discussing crises that are essentially mental; does my emphasis on the growth of the mind mean to suggest that Dickens does not deal much with crises of physical growth as well? In the normal course of physical growth—for real people—puberty is the central event. Dickens's imaginary protagonists do not develop in a social void; but are they to grow up inhabiting a physical void? The fact is, Dickens does give us a fictive version of puberty crisis. Quite remarkably, unlike a contemporary novelist, perhaps unlike any novelist, Dickens creates a detour in time when dealing with puberty and superimposes early adolescence on early boyhood. In *Great Expectations,* at any rate, we discover a displacement backwards in time of an event that (if we were asking a novelist to be consistently anthropo-mimetic) ought to be considered in the context of adolescence.

Later nineteenth-century writers of personal history, André Gide perhaps supreme among them, emphasize adolescence as the significant time of mental, spiritual, and physical awakening. Dickens commands the poetry of adolescence to a certain extent, but his emphasis more often is on childhood (that is, when he is interested in development as such), the period of life which he almost alone made novelistically respectable. Only Charlotte Brontë (*Jane Eyre*) and George Eliot (*The Mill on the Floss*) had a comparable success. Dickens often shows physical and mental awakening as features of very early life, earlier than we would ordinarily expect. In the case of bodily awakening, this has little to do with a Victorian reticence about sexual behavior. What appears to be disguised or covert in Dickens's novels seems so only because Dickens's creative vision does not correspond to our humdrum expectations—he surprises us. He gives us, instead of an account, in sequence, of an adolescent's physical awakening, a polysemous moment, in which puberty-crisis seems translated into an episode revealing the supposedly more innocent awakening of a child to his own body. It is not a deception, but a double-exposure. Interpreting the double-event in *Great Expectations,* we should not think of it as a concealment of adolescent sexuality; rather, in this event, adolescent sexuality can be seen as an indirect device for revealing the importance of childhood sexuality. Childhood sexuality Freud tells us about, in the second of his *Three Contributions to the Theory of Sex* (1905); novelists like Dickens and Charlotte Brontë depicted it long before then.

How does Pip experience his body during and after his first identity crisis? Dickens is far from being a celebrant of Freudian "polymorphous perversity" or the Whitmanesque "body electric." We know that Pip has, at the time of this crisis, a lamentable history of corporal punishment—he was "brought up by hand" with "the Tickler." Dickens was fascinated by the "battered child" motif, which lies behind his pictures of numerous Jellyby and Pocket infants threatened by accidental bashings, stabbings, etc. Corporal punishment, we recall, was associated with David Copperfield's first awareness of his body. But bodily punishment for Pip is related to the sense of his body as an excrescence, an outward and visible sign of his superfluity. Joe tells him, with regard to his infancy, " 'If you could have been aware how small and flabby and mean you was, dear me, you'd have formed the most contemptible opinions of yourself!' " (7). At the Christmas dinner, as well as at the festivities in which he is bound apprentice to Joe, he feels he is "an excrescence on the entertainment" of the adults. Pip feels physically obtrusive, *de trop*, at the Christmas dinner table where he is "squeezed in at an acute angle of the tablecloth, with the table in my chest, and the Pumblechookian elbow in my eye ... I was not allowed to speak ... I was regaled with ... those obscure corners of pork of which the pig, when living, had had the least reason to be vain" (4).

As the famous Christmas dinner proceeds, the company go on to equate Pip and the pig in an exchange that insistently plays on the motif of cannibalism; so much so that when one remembers the stolen pork pie it becomes retroactively equated with Pip, too. Strange connections are made here that suggest a quite primitive notion. The people gather to "eat" Pip, but he has "saved" part of himself that instead Magwitch eats. If Pip "is" food in this scene, it is possible in an earlier scene to see that food is a part of Pip. A form of metaphorical thinking suggests the interchangeability of food and Pip's body. Food comes to stand for the body in its alienation from the self. In this earlier instance we see guilt feelings about the body that refer to the physical growth of the sexual organs at puberty, at which time a growing child can become, in his own mind, more of an excrescence than ever. I should imagine that most readers of that comic episode in which Pip and Joe share part of a loaf of bread sense that there is some sexual business in the apparently innocent scene. Pip does not join in the usual ritual with Joe (which includes a comparison of bread slices) and, instead, in order to have some bread to give to the convict, hides the half slice of bread down his trouser leg. "The effort of resolution necessary to the achievement of this purpose, I found to be quite awful. It was as if I had to make up my mind to leap from the top of a high house, or plunge into a great depth of water" (2). Pip's subsequent thoughts seem only too revealing: "Conscience is a dreadful thing when it accuses man or boy; but when, in the case of a boy, that secret burden co-operates with another secret burden down the leg of his trousers, it is (as I can testify) a great punishment" (2). Then this "load upon my leg" is associated more definitely with "the load upon *his* [the convict's] leg" (2), so that the sexual implications are obscured, somewhat. But the fact that the above passage generalizes in an amazing way about a very specific act of Pip's is a sign that it applies to a growth and presumably a guilt that happens in all boys. I suspect even Dickens was not fully aware of what he was doing here.

After meeting Estella, Pip becomes more conscious and ashamed of his body than ever before: "I took the opportunity . . . to look at my coarse hands and my common boots. My opinion of those accessories was not favourable. They had never troubled me before, but they troubled me now, as vulgar appendages" (8). And again, "I had never thought of being ashamed of my hands before, but I began to consider them a very indifferent pair" (8). And further:

> Miss Havisham stopped short as she and I were walking, she leaning on my shoulder, and said with some displeasure:
> "You are growing tall, Pip!"
> I thought it best to hint, through the medium of a meditative look, that this might be occasioned by circumstances over which I had no control. (12)

Estella inspires in Pip a bodily *pudeur,* but also more generally a contempt for his animality, an animality that, in turn, is associated with Magwitch and all that he stands for, including the violent (as opposed to the cunning) aspect of criminality. Thus the body becomes a pawn in the conflict between nature and culture so important in Pip's life.

IV. The Fiction of Decline and Fall: Becoming a Criminal

In *Oliver Twist* we saw the juxtaposition of two alien worlds: Innocence and Evil. They were in tangential contact but could not interact dialectically. *Great Expectations* proposes two life-patterns, two myths of development: one a pattern of degeneration in time, the other a pattern of regeneration. These fictive patterns are not juxtaposed; they are superimposed upon one another, and together create the "doubleness" that characterizes Dickens's late style. The stylistic progression has been: (1) juxtaposition of alien entities in *Oliver Twist;* (2) serial deployment of them in *Copperfield,* with the aliens supplanting the "familiars," followed by a victory for the familiars, so as to form a "Circuitous Journey," a plot of departure and return ostensibly on a "higher level" of humanity; (3) simultaneous projection of degenerative and regenerative patterns in *Great Expectations.* In this section I shall try to separate out the pattern of degeneration; in the next, the counter-fiction of regeneration.

At the beginnings of *Oliver Twist* and *Copperfield,* predictions were made about the lives of the eponymous heroes. Oliver was "born to be hung"; David was "destined to be unlucky in life." Both of these were, with some qualification in David's case, proven wrong. The adults who surround Pip, arrogating to themselves the time-honored functions of the choral community in English literature, contrive for Pip, too, a destiny of the "born to be hung" variety. Their initial assumption exceeds even the doctrine of original sin. "Naterally wicious!" is Mr. Hubble's verdict on Pip, issued before the evidence has begun to accumulate.

> I think my sister must have had some general idea that I was a young offender whom an accoucheur policeman had taken up (on my birthday) and delivered over to her to be dealt with according to the outraged majesty of the law. I was always treated as if I had insisted on being born in opposition to the dictates of reason, religion, and morality, and against the dissuading arguments of my best friends. Even when I was taken to have a new suit of clothes, the tailor had orders to make them like a kind of reformatory, and on no account to let me have the free use of my limbs. (4)

> [My sister] entered on a fearful catalogue of all the illnesses I had been guilty of, and all the acts of sleeplessness I had committed, and all the high places I had tumbled from ... and all the times she had wished me in my grave and I had contumaciously refused to go there. (4)

When Pip actually does resort to theft he simply brings his behavior into accord with the adults' expectations, which implies that there will be no simple subversion of the original prediction, as in *Oliver Twist*. Pip, to a certain extent by his own actions, validates the definition that adults (obviously unfairly—Dickens did not hold much with notions of original sin) try to impose on him. For a time he internalizes, as David did, a false and unfair label. The pattern has been acknowledged by both Rousseau and Sartre. Rousseau described as follows the process of an actual child's adjustment of his self-image in the face of punishment.

> Soon I had received so many beatings that I grew less sensitive to them; in the end they seemed to me a sort of retribution for my thefts, which authorized me to go on stealing.... I reckoned that to be beaten like a rogue justified my being one. I found that the thieving and the beating belonged together and were in a sense a single state.[16]

Sartre claims that Jean Gênet became a chronic thief because, at the age of ten, someone said to him, "You're a thief." The child, who did not know before that he was anything in the eyes of the adult authorities, immediately accepted their startling words as definitive and proceeded to confirm them in his behavior.[17]

With Pip it seems likely that the judgment of the adults who pester him will be equally self-justifying. Lillo's play (*The London Merchant, or the History of George Barnwell,* 1731) is read to him, and the adults claim to see in it a chart of Pip's future career. Consequently, this fiction within a fiction acts as a negative prediction of Pip's fall, a story of "running to seed, leaf after leaf."

> What stung me was the identification of the whole affair with my unoffending self. When Barnwell began to go wrong, I declare I felt positively apologetic, Pumblechook's indignant stare so taxed me with it.... Even after I was happily hanged and Wopsle had closed the book, Pumblechook sat staring at me ... and saying, "take warning, boy, take warning!" as if it were a well-known fact that I contemplated murdering a near relation.... (16)

This prediction, as many critics have claimed,[18] is symbolically verified a short time later when Pip returns home from the "Pumblechookian parlour" to discover that his sister has been nearly murdered by the convict's leg-iron, an event prompting a guilty thought: "With my head full of George Barnwell, I was at first disposed to believe that *I* must have had some hand in the attack upon my sister" (16). But he adds, "I [later] took another view of the case, which was more reasonable." As much as Pip wants to dissociate himself from surrounding evil he cannot completely do it, however.

> It was horrible to think that I had provided the weapon, however undesignedly, but I could hardly think otherwise. I suffered unspeakable trouble while I considered and reconsidered whether I should at last dissolve that spell of my childhood and tell Joe all the story [about the convict]. For months afterwards, I every day settled the question finally in the negative, and reopened and reargued it next morning. The contention came, after all, to this:—the secret was such an old one now, had so grown into me and become a part of myself, that I could not tear it away. In addition to the dread that, having led up to so much mischief, it would be now more likely than ever to alienate Joe from me if he believed it, I had a further restraining dread that he would not believe it, but would assert it with the fabulous dogs and veal-cutlets as a monstrous invention. However, I temporised with myself, of course—for, was I not wavering between right and wrong ... ? (16)

By deciding not to tell, Pip insures his isolation from Joe; for having a secret does not make possible better communication, as he mistakenly thinks. Dickens emphasizes, in this novel, the need for confession, the need for destroying the secrecies existing among its characters, which intensify their sense of egoistic individuality. When confession becomes possible, one enters upon life with others, an open—perhaps it could be called a more objective—life, with secrecies abolished and the heart no longer a fortified citadel.

The self-righteous adults who contrive a destiny for Pip are closer to the mark than perhaps they would ever think, even though events prove them to be literally wrong in their predictions. "A near relation" is almost killed, and Pip participates imaginatively in the act, feels himself associated with it, and benefits from it. One might go so far as to say, with Julian Moynahan in his influential article, that "Orlick acts merely as Pip's punitive instrument or weapon."[19] And further, Pip is "hanged" by Orlick, when the latter captures him in the shack on the marshes. "Bound tightly to a perpendicular ladder after being caught in a strong running noose, he suffers symbolically the hanging for which he had, in the eyes of his tormentors, been destined since boyhood."[20]

Not only does Orlick imprison and "hang" Pip, he first subjects him to a "trial" in which the ancient crimes of Pip against Orlick are recited. It seems that Pip is indeed not a person with totally clean hands. It seems that almost by the very act of breathing Pip has become involved in Orlick's evil. " 'You cost me that place.... You come betwixt me and a young woman I liked.... You was always in Old Orlick's way since ever you was a child.... It was you as did for your shrew sister' " (53). Orlick demonstrates in effect how a person can heap up guilt just by involving himself with others in the process of living. Almost everything that Orlick says is true in a certain sense, even the last charge, preposterous as it sounds. But Orlick draws the circle of guilt with a much larger radius than Pip would choose to do.

> "I tell you it was your doing—I tell you it was done through you," he retorted, catching up the gun.... "I come upon her from behind, as I come upon you to-night. I giv' it her! I left her for dead.... But it warn't Old Orlick as did it; it was you. You was favoured, and he was bullied and beat. Old Orlick bullied and beat, eh? Now you pays for it. You done it; now you pays for it." (53)

Imprisonment by Orlick is merely one of several imprisonments for Pip. So thoroughly does Dickens view Pip's life in relation to criminality that often Dickens's personal shorthand for the rite of passage, the process of initiation, is the pattern defined by the terms *arrest, imprisonment,* and *escape.* This is a modification of the endlessly repetitious, cyclical pattern that Magwitch lives. Pip's life, like Magwitch's, is a story of " 'In jail and out of jail, in jail and out of jail, in jail and out of jail' " (42). The difference between the two lives is that Pip is able to break the cycle of repetition and survive, while Magwitch dies "in jail" at last.

Time-present for Pip is often only a time to be endured. When it is not a vacuum drained of its reality by an insistent, alluring future, it appears as a succession of concentric imprisoning spheres: for each escape leads to new spaces, which soon become transformed into prisons—the home, the marsh, Pumblechook's shop, Satis House—and later London chambers and London itself. But it is essential to

Dicken's logic of growth that imprisonment be the prelude to transformation and escape into a new freedom gained after "doing time," while evolving new ways of response to life. Magwitch, in his moving confession in Chapter 42, says that he " 'reg'larly grow'd up took up' "; this is indeed also the pattern for Pip, as shown in almost every one of the critical experiences from the outset of the book (when he was "took up" by Magwitch) onward.

For instance, when Pip leaves home to begin his visits to Satis House, he is "arrested" and manhandled by his sister, who, in accord with an unconscious sense of fitness, scrubs the boy free of his old dirt and dresses him in fresh clothes. "When my ablutions were completed, I was put into clean linen of the stiffest character, like a young penitent into sackcloth, and was trussed up in my tightest and fearfullest suit. I was then delivered over to Mr. Pumblechook, who formally received me as if he were the sheriff" (7). This bodily feeling of crampedness is often experienced by initiates in developmental fictions, along with the additional feeling of spiritual confinement. But the seed has to be buried, confined, before it can sprout, and Pip is here temporarily in the hands of the seedsman. In Pumblechook's shop, the boy sees what could be an image of his own development. "I wondered when I peeped into one or two [drawers] on the lower tiers, and saw the tied-up brown paper packets inside, whether the flower-seeds and bulbs ever wanted of a fine day to break out of those jails, and bloom" (8).

V. The Fiction of Fortunate Rise: Becoming a Gentleman

Symbolically, Pip fulfills the destiny that others imagine for him in their hostility or self-righteousness; literally, he evades that destiny. Dickens had been hankering for years, since the time of *Dombey and Son,* for an opportunity to show unequivocally the degeneration of a central sympathetic male character, but he could not go that far with Pip, at least on the literal level of the novel. The second destiny that this novel projects for its hero, however, Pip contrives for himself (with only the occasional help of others), and it is the exact opposite of the "born to be hung" prediction. He is only too willing to think that life for him will be a fairy tale with a happy ending (the ending

Fictions of the Future

to be marriage, rather than death, as the other destiny had it). Aspirations awakened by Estella and furthered by his sense of alienation from his origins are only too readily converted by Pip into expectations. This is the way his imagination works:

> In her hand she had a crutch-headed stick on which she leaned, and she looked like the witch of the place. (11)
>
> "This is a gay figure, Pip," said she, making her crutch stick play round me, as if she, the fairy godmother who had changed me, were bestowing the finishing gift. (19)
>
> She had adopted Estella, she had as good as adopted me, and it could not fail to be her intention to bring us together. She reserved it for me to restore the desolate house, admit the sunshine into the dark rooms, set the clocks a-going and the cold hearths a-blazing, tear down the cobwebs, destroy the vermin—in short, do all the shining deeds of the young knight of romance, and marry the princess. [It was all] a rich attractive mystery, of which I was the hero. (29)

We can take this last statement as an enthusiastically figured form of the second chart that applies to the hero's life, which is, like the first one, a fiction of personal transformation, though the transformation is positive, not negative—a rise, not a decline. One might argue that if this destiny were actually guaranteed to Pip, as he often assumes it to be, then Dickens's novel would be merely a demonstration of its premises, an expansion of a preliminarily revealed formula, and time-passing would be virtually irrelevant, because the end would have been assured in advance, as in *Oliver Twist*. Essentially, Pip's dream is translated into the desire to become a gentleman and marry Estella. (I follow what appears to be Dickens's emphasis and consider "the money" as secondary, as a means and not an end.) Both of these things do actually happen in the novel, but they happen in such a way as to prevent the novel from degenerating into a mere atemporal demonstration of a preordained fate, as in a fairy tale. Even though Pip projects a fairy tale existence, this novel is not a fairy tale. Partly by fulfilling both the positive and the negative prophecies about the hero, Dickens makes the notion of prophecy superfluous, while at the same time demonstrating the function of prophetic fictions in the process of becoming.

The most important aspect of Pip's destiny-myth for our purposes is the transformational element, which involves becoming a gentleman. Once Pip is a gentleman the rest will follow, he thinks, as the night the day. Like many people who envisage a happy future, he thinks in terms of a goal and a state of being to be achieved at the end of a process of radical change. As committed as he is to time—he wants to "set the clocks agoing" at Satis House—his whole project is dedicated to an end of transformation. The actual process of transformation is not something he relishes for its own sake, even though he must undergo it if he wishes to become a gentleman.

While his criminal destiny is such that, if he really believed in it, Pip would fear the passage of time, the consequence of having great expectations is of course quite different. Time-passing is in a way a comfort, and loving the future replaces Copperfieldian love for the past. Pip's consciousness is concerned to digest each present experience only in order to clear the way for the next one, which will be even closer to the goal: everything becomes provisional, with reality off in the future. Often too the pressure of expectation makes the present seem intolerable, especially at those times when the fortunate future seems less guaranteed than usually. A malaise characteristically Dickensian: Pip feels it first during the early stages of his life, before he acquires definite expectations, when he still has aspirations even more vague than his expectations prove to be. "What I wanted, who can say? How can *I* say, when I never knew?" (14). And later: "Dissatisfied with my fortune, of course, I could not be; but it is possible that I may have been, without quite knowing it, dissatisfied with myself" (18). This resembles the Faustian position, where the present can never be "enough" (Satis House is the major source of *dis*satisfaction) and the self must imagine a continual growth, perpetual transition, thanks to the oppressive sense of finitude so often created by one's ability to imagine other (however indefinite) selves, other places, other times. This is a disease not of memory but of the imagination—the artist's malady. Dickens himself may have felt like this; he wrote to Forster in 1851 that "such a torment of desire to be anywhere but where I am: to be going I don't know where, I don't know why; takes hold of me, that it is like being driven *away*."[21]

While Copperfield, another of Dickens's many characters who

cannot live in the present, always tended to fill the empty present with precious matter from the past, Pip yearns for a future which, unlike the past, can offer no definite images. The mystery of origins behind David's fetishism is replaced in Pip's mind by the mystery of the future, which contains a vague gentlemanly image and an equally vague (because changed) Estella. Easily enough the future can sometimes be everything, sometimes nothing. Sometimes this indeterminateness of the future, which is opposed to the familiarity of the present and the banality of the past, leads Pip into mental confusions and self-division characteristic of growth-situations.

> When I got into my little room I sat down and took a long look at it, as a mean little room that I should soon be parted from and raised above, for ever. It was furnished with fresh young remembrances too, and even at the same moment I fell into much the same confused division of mind between it and the better rooms to which I was going, as I had been in so often between the forge and Miss Havisham's and Biddy and Estella. (18)

David had particularly loved his bedroom and left it most unwillingly; Pip is confused, but feels little nostalgia. At this point in the novel he reveals, compared to David, an underdeveloped sense of the past. When he leaves his native village he feels sorry for the benighted provincials who remain content with a settled, repetitive life. "As I passed the church, I felt ... a sublime compassion for the poor creatures who were destined to go there, Sunday after Sunday, all their lives through" (19). "Farewell, monotonous acquaintances of my childhood, henceforth I was for London and greatness" (19). (An ironic echo of Crashaw's lines on St. Teresa: "Farewell house and farewell home,/ She's for the moors and martyrdom.") Pip repudiates almost everything associated with the seemingly static world of childhood—the original village, the old relationships, and of course the old crimes. But such a repudiation is fraught with consequences, as we discover later.

Let us look more closely at the process of becoming a gentleman. Progress through time (from childhood to adulthood) will also be movement upwards through social strata, as well as passage from the country with its simple, more natural lifestyle, to the city with its complexities and culture, this last being a passage common to all three of the novels I have been discussing. In all of this becoming we see Pip surpassing himself, surpassing the objective environment of his early life, as well as the contradictions that appeared in the awakening of his subjectivity. He ostensibly moves out of self-alienation into a more or less final wholeness of identity. But, as I shall show, this surpassing takes a different form from what Pip expects; he acquires a different identity from the one he bargained for—even in achieving the major objects (significantly transformed themselves) of his expectations. For this surpassing mysteriously contains within its process, and fosters forward, all that Pip thinks he leaves behind; all that was lived previously will be included in the total identity—even the myths, fictions, dreams, which would in a *non* developmental perspective be seen as mere appearances. This total identity will be the sum of, and yet also the transfiguration of, all his experience, and thus will exceed anything he could have projected for himself in his simplistic dreams. The novel postulates the connectedness (for consciousness) of past, present, and future. The hero comes to recognize this himself, but only after he bases the most important years of his life on a conception of transcendence of earlier selves.

Estella's treatment of him as an animal and especially as an unnecessary person, a superfluity, an uninvited nobody, works with his childhood sense of exposure to similar injustice to create Pip's desire to be a gentleman. "She . . . gave me the bread without looking at me, as insolently as if I were a dog in disgrace" (8). Pip, the unwanted child, the spurned boy, comes to think that the gentleman is a necessary person and that his worth is a function of his ability to satisfy external criteria of dress and language. Dress: Pip suddenly sees his own clothes (His "tightest and fearfullest suit") and body as objects that are patently absurd. "I took the opportunity . . . to look at my coarse hands and my common boots. My opinion of those accessories was not favourable. They had never troubled me before, but they troubled me now, as vulgar appendages" (8). And language: "I determined to ask Joe why he had ever taught me to call those picture-cards jacks, which ought to be called knaves" (8). So later he begins a stage of life, once he has acquired the cash advances on his expectations, that is similar to the foppish stage of David's life. Pip goes in for surfaces, comes to worship what Samuel Butler called "the husk," the shell that presumably separates the gentleman from the savage. The gentlemanly exterior is Pip's deceptive pattern of mature manhood.

Pip's first exposure to the gentlemanly side of life comes when, at Satis House, he meets the "pale young gentleman." Had he not been so full of illusions about his own worthlessness and the intrinsic value of the gentlemanly identity, he would have been able to read this incident as clearly as the reader can. For the fight with Herbert Pocket satirizes phony images and rituals. The code that Herbert teaches Pip shows this. There was no reason for the fight: it occurred mainly to provide an occasion for the rules to be observed. Thus "laws of the game," "regular rules," for ritualizing conflict have about as much relation to reality as do the criminal laws of England that protect gentlemen and punish "dunghill dogs" like Magwitch. But in spite of the ridiculousness of certain codes when they control the relations of adult life, Dickens shows that there is something inevitable about them at earlier stages of growth, when boys first learn these social usages. There is a phase of life—sketched out brilliantly and economically by Dickens in this scene, and in a comparable one later on, when Pip quarrels with Bently Drummle at the gathering of "Finches of the Grove"—in which these hollow games have to be played before they can be ultimately recognized for what they are. But if Pip was studying to be a gentleman, the impressive surface of Herbert Pocket's "dreadful preparations," which are all promise followed by no performance, ought to have aroused some misgivings. "He had a way of spinning himself about that was full of appearance," Pip says, his perceptions adjusted by the hindsight of the adult narrator of the story.

Because, in trouncing Herbert, he has tampered with this "pale young gentleman's" well being, Pip feels that the law that never protected *him* will nevertheless come to the aid of one of these creatures so necessary to the world's operation. Thus ensues additional guilt for Pip, which again cuts him off, in his own view of things, from the rest of mankind.

> I felt that the pale young gentleman's blood was on my head, and that the Law would avenge it. Without having any definite idea of the penalties I had incurred, it was clear to me that village boys could not

go stalking about the country, ravaging the houses of gentlefolks and pitching into the studious youth of England, without laying themselves open to severe punishment. For some days, I even kept close at home, and looked out at the kitchen door with the greatest caution and trepidation ... lest the officers of the county jail should pounce upon me. The pale young gentleman's nose had stained my trousers, and I tried to wash out that evidence of my guilt in the dead of the night. I had cut my knuckles against the pale young gentleman's teeth, and I twisted my imagination into a thousand tangles as I devised incredible ways of accounting for that damnatory circumstance when I should be haled before the judges. (12)

In passing we might note the twists of the imagination as Pip tries to devise lies suitable for "the judges." But also, by thus humorously identifying himself as the hunted object in some retributive scheme, Pip pays himself the compliment of being necessary to "the Law"—a truly Kafkaesque meditation.[22] Just as Rousseau felt justified when punished and saw punishment come as an integral part of an objective relationship between himself and the lawful punisher, whose rights were never called seriously into question, so Pip here reveals a psychically quite similar and logical tendency. Had the "myrmidons of Justice" awaited him on his next visit to Miss Havisham's, Pip's guilt (as it does later in court) would have become public and therefore real to him as a definition of himself supplied by others.

Let me pursue this notion of the gentlemanly image further. The first thing Pip does when he hears of his good fortune is to get measured for a new suit. Dickens, with his thoroughgoing Carlylean sense of the symbolic values of haberdashery, appreciates the ritual meaning of changing clothes. This can be seen in *Oliver Twist* and *Copperfield,* too, where dramatic changes in the circumstances of the heroes' lives are attested to by new vestments, appropriate to the new circumstances. But as with "Doady" the flâneur, whose boots bit him painfully, Pip's costume betokens the inadequacy of his notions about it and about everything associated with it. "My clothes were rather a disappointment, of course. Probably every new and eagerly expected garment ever put on since clothes came in fell a trifle short of the wearer's expectations" (19). In a small way this statement points out the falsity of "great expectations."

As did David, Pip now uses the mirror for reassurance about his existence in a world of apparently solid identities: "But after I had had my new suit on some half an hour, and had gone through an immensity of posturing with Mr. Pumblechook's very limited dressing-glass, in the futile endeavour to see my legs, it seemed to fit me better" (19). Another mirror for Pip, one which he had as lief not look into, is the one provided by the mimicking gestures of Trabb's boy. "He wore the blue bag in the manner of my great-coat, and was strutting along the pavement towards me on the opposite side of the street.... Passing abreast of me, he pulled up his shirt-collar, twined his side-hair, stuck an arm akimbo, and smirked extravagantly by, wriggling his elbows and body, and drawling to his attendants, 'Don't know yah, don't know yah, 'pon my soul don't know yah!'" (30).

The way other characters serve as mirrors for Pip has been treated fully by other commentators on this book.[23] I need mention only an example connected with issues I have been raising. Wopsle, who is also a country man who tries to make good in the city, is an ironic parallel to Pip. Dickens's presentation of Wopsle's theatre performances as witnessed by Pip emphasizes their absurdity by concentrating on the sartorial shortcomings. The *Hamlet* scene might seem to be a digression, but there is much in it that relates to Pip's own life. Is Wopsle, parading in the leggings and cloak of the Prince of Denmark, and looking absurd in his impersonation, at all a reflection of Pip's setting up as a gentleman? Pip dreams, right after seeing the play, that his "expectations were all cancelled, and that [he] had to give [his] hand in marriage to Herbert's Clara, or play Hamlet to Miss Havisham's Ghost, before twenty thousand people, without knowing twenty words of it" (31). Pip has anxieties about his image and about his playing well the part he has assumed.[24]

Wopsle, with his multiple identities ("He had been ominously heard of ... as a faithful black, in connexion with a little girl of noble birth, and a monkey. And Herbert had seen him as a predatory Tartar, of comic propensities" [47]), is the protean man who, as I mentioned earlier, so often appears in stories of growing up, as a sign both of the fluid possibilities of being and, here, of the comic futility of attempts to carry role-playing and imitation too far. A Master of Disguises mirrors the problems of identity. In this book, Wopsle is a warning against moving too readily into fictitious roles instead of into well-founded identities. There is something of Micawber in this character.

Pip's notion of gentlemanliness is based on exterior benchmarks, and the mirrors that help him to cultivate this exterior also provide its critique. The figure of the gentleman was, of course, in some trouble in the nineteenth century, where it often appeared in literature as a kind of stuffed shirt, lacking the proper filling, the humanity and intellect, that were once assumed to be gentlemanly characteristics. Newman, when discussing the typical product of the contemporary English universities, spoke of "that antiquated variety of human nature and remnant of feudalism, as they consider it, called 'a gentleman.' "[25] Pip's childhood friend Biddy is able to see that the notion of the gentleman, as understood by Pip, is based only on words:

> "Do you want to be a gentleman to spite [Estella] or to gain her over?" Biddy quietly asked me....
> "I don't know," I moodily answered.
> "Because, if it is to spite her," Biddy pursued, "I should think—but you know best—that might be better and more independently done by caring nothing for her words." (17).

Consider further (to focus still on earlier stages of Pip's development) the sort of education Pip acquires. There are at least two kinds of formal education in this book: apprenticeship—which is the provincial form of it—and "book learning." Apprenticeship is training for a specific job. The duties of the forge are obvious and clear-cut, and the blacksmith occupies a definite place in the rural economy—near the bottom. This is work of the body, work done to the monotonous chant of "Old Clem." Earlier it had been Pip's only expectation to have such a job at Joe's side. "Once, it had seemed to me that when I should at last roll up my shirtsleeves and go into the forge, Joe's 'prentice, I should be distinguished and happy. Now the reality was in my hold, I only felt that I was dusty with the dust of the small coal" (14).

During his apprenticeship, Pip continues his "dame-school" education. This is the beginning of his verbal learning. One of the causes of his severance from Joe is his attempt to get such an education. "Joe's education, like Steam, was yet in its infancy" (7). Pip,

Fictions of the Future

though, at about age eight, before he is bound as an apprentice, manages to acquire some of the rudiments of reading, writing, and "ciphering." As it is for Charley Hexam in *Our Mutual Friend,* there is something furtive and Promethean about this learning. It is presumably one means for getting free from adult control. It is an affront to Pip's sister, apparently, for Pip to acquire tools that might set him above her supreme authority, which is based upon the ignorance, passivity, and innocence of her two charges. " 'She ain't over partial to having scholars on the premises . . . and in partickler would not be over partial to my being a scholar, for fear as I might rise'," says Joe. " 'Like a sort of rebel, don't you see?' " (7). Language learning, like lying, is a source of guilt, and that is perhaps why Pip can say, as regards his arithmetic, "I fell among those thieves, the nine figures; who seemed every evening to do something new to disguise themselves and baffle recognition" (7). This is Pip's way of expressing the alien quality of language and numbers, the tools that the adults use and which he is trying to take over for himself. His sister is always dead set against any intellectual inquisitiveness. When Pip wants to know what a "convict" is, she attempts to silence his questions. " 'Drat that boy,' interposed my sister, frowning at me over her work, 'what a questioner he is. Ask no questions, and you'll be told no lies.' It was not very polite to herself, I thought, to imply that I should be told lies by her, even if I did ask questions" (2). Compare Pip's attitude toward the "nine figures" with the passage I cited earlier in which David Copperfield appreciates the "easy good nature" of certain letters of the alphabet, while suffering from the strangeness, the "puzzling novelty," of the others. Pip, like David, leaves childhood innocence behind partly because he becomes exposed to the mysteries of written symbols.

Pip "gets too big" for the dame-school, but not before learning one prophetic little song there:

> When I went to Lunnon town sirs,
>   Too rul loo rul
>   Too rul loo rul
> Wasn't I done very brown sirs?
>   Too rul loo rul
>   Too rul loo rul. (14)

The story of the green provincial "done brown" applies, as a prediction, to both Pip and Wopsle (whose great-aunt runs the school). The two countrymen who have the greatest pretension to learning and verbal talents are the same ones who feel cramped by the provincial life.

The final stage of Pip's systematic education is directed by Mr. Pocket. Pocket "knew more of my intended career than I knew myself, for he referred to his having been told by Mr. Jaggers that I was not designed for any profession, and that I should be well enough educated for my destiny if I could 'hold my own' with the average of young men in prosperous circumstances" (29). Unlike apprenticeship, this upper-class education is directed toward no specific occupation. There is, of course, no particular niche in the professional world that the gentleman is trained specifically to fill. In fact, the creature that Pip had seen as necessary is like a drone, with nothing to do but to loiter and dally and quarrel. Much later, confronted with the loss of his expectations, Pip says to himself, " 'I have been bred to no calling, and I am fit for nothing' " (41). Like the genteel Mrs. Pocket, Pip appears to have "grown up highly ornamental, but perfectly helpless and useless" (23). Pip, like David before he became a writer, has no vocation, no reason for existing in the world of work that Dickens's friend Carlyle extolled. Magwitch's conception, to which Pip gave his assent, was of a person who could simply "be," neither toiling nor spinning. The vapidity of Pip's education is demonstrated to both men when Magwitch asks Pip to read aloud to him random books in foreign languages.

Gentlemen do "spin" some things in this novel: words. One of the death masks in Jaggers's offices is of a gentleman. Wemmick says of him, " 'He forged wills, this blade did, if he didn't also put the supposed testators to sleep too. You were a gentlemanly cove, though ... and you said you could write Greek. Yah, Bounceable! What a liar you were! I never met such a liar as you!' " (24). A hint of something criminal and deceptive is associated with the power to use words. In Wemmick's "crime museum" Pip is shown "several manuscript confessions written under condemnation ... 'every one of 'em lies, sir' " (25). Orlick's loyalty to Compeyson (Magwitch's mortal enemy) is related to his ability to put words to protean uses. As Orlick says to Pip, vaunting the power of his "masters": " 'Some of 'em writes my letters when I wants 'em wrote—do you mind?—writes my letters, wolf! They writes fifty hands; they're not like sneaking you, as writes but one' " (53). And Magwitch says, " 'Compeyson's business was the swindling, handwriting forging, stolen bank-note passing, and suchlike' " (42). If there is any gentleman's vocation, it is not forging metal, as Joe does, but forging words. The Prince of Darkness is not only, as Joe says, a liar; he is also a gentleman.

As my discussion (in the Appendix) of *Oliver Twist* and *A Child's History* suggests, Dickens no doubt felt that the writing of fiction, which made it possible for him to live a gentlemanly life, was a faintly criminal activity. This is implied in much of Dickens's work. He intimates that, at the very least, the artist (as in his portrait of Skimpole in *Bleak House*) could be as worthless as the gentleman proper. There is certainly a suspicion of language rooted deep in Dickens's art, which might reflect a subconscious guilt about the verbal creation of "airy nothings." With language the artist has "a knife that can cut both ways" (to paraphrase Dostoyevsky). The border between the honest work and the forgery, between the fiction and the lie, is a vague one, at times, and fiction writers perhaps know this better than any other word users. Dickens seemed to realize that, if he was to use language, with all its deceptive capabilities, he had to transform it into an instrument of truth. He did this partly by showing up the lies that lurk in the rhetoric of men of all callings.

Herbert Pocket, discussing Compeyson (ironically Magwitch's model for Pip), says,

> "I have heard my father mention that he was a showy man. . . . But that he was not to be, without ignorance or prejudice, mistaken for a gentleman, my father most strongly asseverates; because it is a principle of his that no man who was not a true gentleman at heart, ever was, since the world began, a true gentleman in manner. He says, no varnish can hide the grain of the wood; and that the more varnish you put on, the more the grain will express itself." (22)

A true gentleman would display an integrated character in which the externals of behavior would not belie the inner self. The "inner man" always eventually betrays himself, anyway; disguise is never completely successful. (Pip and Herbert have a great deal of difficulty disguising Magwitch, when the time for escape comes.)

It happens that, just as Pip acquires the externals of the gentlemanly role, events conspire to force him to end the long-held distinction between the "secret criminal" living within his breast and the innocence of his exterior. When Pip publicly, in court, displays his association with the criminal Magwitch, his sense of guilt becomes externalized. Secrecy is no longer, as it had once been, part of the dynamism of his development. Much of his life had been sustained by his manipulation of the guilt-free sartorial façade which he and his tailor conspired to present. (Gentility is the picture of innocence; when Compeyson and Magwitch were originally sentenced to prison, the "gentleman," well-spoken, well-dressed, received the lighter sentence.) Pip, the manufactured gentleman, by standing near the prisoner's dock and holding Magwitch's hand, where the "audience . . . pointed down at this criminal or at that, and most of all at him and me" (56), denies his own total innocence and that his clothes and speech completely define him. He confesses his own secret guilt before the multitude. We have seen how criminals were brought into the light before the gaze of the crowd on several occasions in *Oliver Twist*. All that is secret will be revealed; and everything that is buried inside the self will rise to the surface. Because of this inescapable mechanism, the protagonist of *Great Expectations* changes and abolishes discontinuities between his objective and his subjective self. Pip, throughout the "second stage" of his expectations, developed a personality which took itself too narrowly for what it wanted others to take it to be. The guilty aspect of himself he tried to bury even to self-regard, so that the part, the exterior, could be taken for the whole. This was the cramped fiction of himself Pip tried to live with. For him at last to reveal publicly what had been hardly admissible to himself means that, perhaps somehow by the operation of witnesses, he has brought to the surface a missing element of his self-image. The self-image has become complex, compacted as it is of both a gentlemanly (in a radically different sense than he thought earlier) and a criminal aspect, but fully definable as neither. The double process of regeneration and degeneration thus reveals itself in all its complexity. The double process shows that Dickens is using a developmental perspective in order to account for the presence of good and bad in a single person.[26] An image at the trial scene reveals Dickens's implication that good and evil people exist on one plane of life in the world, not as in the two radically separate spheres we saw in *Oliver Twist*. In fact, good and evil people might be one and the same, depending ultimately on the perspective in which they are judged: "The sun was striking in at the great windows of the court ... and it made a broad shaft of light between the two-and-thirty condemned prisoners and the judge, linking both together, and perhaps reminding some among the audience how both were passing on, with absolute equality, to the greater Judgment that knoweth all things and cannot err (56)."

Notes

1. *The Varieties of Religious Experience: A Study in Human Nature* (New York: New American Library, 1958), p. 78. James borrows the term from Francis W. Newman's *The Soul: Its Sorrows and Its Aspirations* (1852).
2. Forster, *Life of Charles Dickens,* 2:285.
3. Johnson, *Tragedy and Triumph,* p. 982.
4. *Great Expectations,* ed. R. D. McMaster (New York: The Odyssey Press, 1965). All further references will be to this edition.
5. "The Moving I: A Study of Point of View in *Great Expectations,"* in *Assessing Great Expectations,* ed. Richard Lettis and William E. Morris (San Francisco: Chandler Publishing Co., 1963), pp. 195, 197.
6. "Irony is the principal mode of *Great Expectations,"* according to Sylvia Bank Manning, *Dickens as Satirist* (New Haven: Yale University Press, 1971), p. 192.
7. A contemporary reviewer of *Great Expectations* (Edwin P. Whipple, *Atlantic Monthly,* September 1861) made some of the most astute observations I have ever encountered on this novel. Dickens, he said, "does not record, but invents; and he produces something which is natural only under conditions prescribed by his own mind." Whipple went on to admire "the poetical element of the writer's genius, his modification of the forms, hues, and sounds of Nature by viewing them through the medium of an *imagined mind"* (italics mine). In *Dickens: The Critical Heritage,* ed. Philip Collins (New York: Barnes and Noble, 1971), pp. 429-30.
8. More precisely, Garis, *Dickens Theatre,* calls it a "set-piece of traditional moral self-discovery," p. 203.
9. *Dickens the Novelist* (Norman, Okla.: University of Oklahoma Press, 1968), p. 301.
10. Compare Pip's use of his name with the attempts of Joyce's young Stephen Dedalus to locate himself in relation to other people and to the cosmos, as shown in his inscription of the flyleaf of his geography book *(Portrait,* p. 16):

> Stephen Dedalus
> Class of Elements
> Clongowes Wood College
> Sallins
> County Kildare
> Ireland
> Europe
> The World
> The Universe.

11. "The Structural Study of Myth," in *Structural Anthropology* (Garden City, N.Y.: Anchor Books, 1967), p. 216.

12. As Leach puts it: " 'How is it that human beings are on the one hand animals (natural) and on the other hand not-animals (cultural)?' " "The Legitimacy of Solomon," in *Genesis as Myth and Other Essays* (London: Jonathan Cape Editions, 1969), pp. 38-39.

13. Hardy, "Change of Heart in Dickens' Novels," p. 182.

14. In his edition of *Great Expectations* (41 n.) McMaster finds a specific reference to the catechism, and it too is associated with Pip's thoughts at the graves of his parents. Pip says: "I have a lively remembrance that I supposed my declaration that I was to 'walk in the same all the days of my life' laid me under an obligation always to go through the village from our house in one particular direction" (41).

15. *Confessions,* pp. 30-31. See also the marvelous passage in Gosse, *Father and Son* (New York: W. W. Norton, 1963), pp. 32-35, where the parents' incapacities and fabrications awaken the child to his sense of their nonomniscience. In James's *What Maisie Knew* the same pattern occurs, with the child, who is moved from household to household, from the home of her father to that of her mother, thus becoming able to see the falseness of both of them, by contrast.

16. *Confessions,* pp. 42-43.

17. *Saint Genet: Actor and Martyr,* trans. Bernard Frechtman (New York: Mentor Books, 1964), p. 26.

18. For instance, Dorothy Van Ghent, *The English Novel: Form and Function* (New York: Harper & Row, 1961), pp. 136-37; and Julian Moynahan, "The Hero's Guilt: The Case of *Great Expectations,*" in *Assessing Great Expectations,* pp. 153 ff.

19. Moynahan, "The Hero's Guilt," p. 161.

20. Karl P. Wentersdorf, "Mirror-Images in *Great Expectations,*" *Nineteenth-Century Fiction* 21 (December 1966): 222.

21. Dupee, *Selected Letters,* p. 186.

22. Dickens was of course in many respects Kafkaesque, and vice versa, as Mark Spilka has shown in *Dickens and Kafka: A Mutual Interpretation* (Bloomington: Indiana University Press, 1963).

23. Wentersdorf, "Mirror-Images in *Great Expectations,*" pp. 203-24. See also Moynahan, "The Hero's Guilt," and Van Ghent, *Form and Function.*

24. There is more to this *Hamlet* episode: When Joe tells Pip about the play, he mentions the Ghost. " 'If the ghost of a man's own father cannot be allowed to claim his attention, what can, sir?' " (217). The ghost, who spoils Hamlet's present by reminding him of duties based on past crimes, "represents" Magwitch as well as Havisham. The former had appeared at the grave of Pip's father like a man risen from the dead and will appear again to torment Pip, after Pip has written him off as probably dead. Also, this relation of the play to Pip's life explains a curious slip one critic has made in discussing it. Sylvère Monod (*"Great Expectations* A Hundred Years After," *Dickensian* 56 [1960]: 137) assumes that Compeyson (also a ghost out of Pip's past) is in the audience during the performance of *Hamlet,* though he in fact does not appear until the next time Pip attends a performance by Wopsle (not of *Hamlet*). It would have been better in terms of symbolic density if Dickens had contrived the scene the way Monod assumed he did.

25. John Henry Cardinal Newman, *The Idea of a University* (New York: Rinehart Editions, 1966), p. xxxviii.

Notes

26. Edmund Wilson, "Dickens: The Two Scrooges," in *The Wound and the Bow* (New York: Oxford University Press, 1965), p. 54, claims that "Dickens' difficulty in his middle period, and indeed more or less to the end, is to get good and bad together in one character."

"Pip and Miss Havisham." From *Great Expectations*.

FIVE

"A Cobweb Meant Expectation": Pip and the Act of Confession

Many readers, but notably Robert Garis, find in *Great Expectations* a novel at once theatrical and parabolical; others, such as Q. D. Leavis, see the novel as being far indeed from "theatre" or "fairy tale," especially in that its hero is supposedly "representative of the ordinary man" of Victorian times (the assumption being that we have an historical method for ascertaining what is representative).[1] "This is the End of the Second Stage of Pip's Expectations"—the solidity of the borderline drawn around his developmental scheme no doubt lends support to assertions that Dickens is offering little more than a conventional parable, of the "Seven Ages of Man" variety. I contend that this is not genuine parable, nor is it genuine representative art, but, in a quite special way, it is a form of artifical and abstract fiction. It is fiction—not theatre—for even though the mists rise and fall, like curtains in a Dickens theatre, further punctuating the stages of Pip's progress, the theatrical metaphor obscures an art that reminds us of theatre perhaps because we have no special concepts or terminology for handling a temporal art that is artificial and abstract. I choose the words *artificial* and *abstract* here not because I wish to insist on a terminology, but mainly because they are themselves artificial and abstract (in the sense of nonreferential) enough to allow the sense in which I use them to emerge from context. We can appreciate these qualities of *Great Expectations* if we try to see how Dickens has intensified his life-long explorations of the significance of art and the imagination. In earlier chapters I discussed the pervasive interest these novels reveal in the power of the word, the power, especially, of fictions. By examining the final stages of Pip's career, I hope to show what Dickens's most remarkable fiction has to tell us about itself, once it takes us into its confidence.

I. Healing the Split in the Self

Just before the novel announces the end of the second stage of Pip's expectations, Magwitch arrives to confront Pip in his chambers, thus precipitating the series of events that extends as one long identity-crisis for Pip, who suddenly becomes aware of the hidden forces in his life. Pip's notion of his role had been infinite in one direction, as he surmised a future; but the surmise was made possible only by a process of repressive exclusion: to the extent that the past could be forgotten, the future could expand. In the past were certain embarrassing things: the impotent body of the child that was a reproach to the very notion of bodyhood and animality itself; the criminality of the self that could overcome bodily impotence only by sporadic violence and deception. Pip's dream of the future, his belief that he was becoming a necessary being, was based on the repudiation of the body (and its replacement with the sartorial image) and the denial of guilt. Now, with Magwitch, Dickens makes a quite abstract point: Magwitch returns neither because Pip has a neglected body nor because Pip has a neglected guilt. Magwitch returns because Pip has forgotten. We know or can guess at possible unconscious motives for Pip's forgetting, but such obvious motives are not important; the point is that there is a gap in the self. When Jonathan Bishop writes that "Pip ought to have grown up to become a writer, and be called 'Philip,' "[2] he no doubt, in making this interesting assertion, is aware of the pun. The speck or dot or "pip" must indeed become "filled up" (not the way Oliver was, however), and I contend (contrary to Bishop's claim that Pip does not grow up)[3] that Dickens's interest in pursuing the consequences of his expanding theory of memory prompted him at last to imagine a completed hero. In saying this, I admittedly find more to approve in Pip than most critics do. Actually, I mean that Pip is complete in a quite technical sense: the later stages of his development reveal that he achieves the objectification that

Pip and the Act of Confession

Dickens could not imagine for David Copperfield. Whether this objectification is associated with a form of life that realist critics could find dull or dismal is beside the point. Pip's life is Dickens's most elaborate essay in imaginary psychology, a psychology that can be usefully viewed as independent of the social circumstances of the nineteenth century, no matter how many correspondences we might be able to find between them (assuming that we really could know the relation of social circumstances to character psychology, an assumption common to many critics and yet seldom examined with any rigor).

The sudden rude juxtaposition of Magwitch and Pip forces the young man temporarily to live his present as well as his future in a new relation to his past. The advent of Magwitch is announced by a powerful ill-wind, like the storm in which Steerforth dies. And like many storms occurring in literature, it threatens to scramble the fixed, quotidian reality, the carefully built-up schema of civilized response, in order to clear the way for the intrusion of primordial images of fear and desire. This storm is like a wind of memory, as well: "If the wind and the rain had driven away the intervening years, had scattered all the intervening objects, had swept us to the churchyard where we first stood face to face on such different levels, I could not have known my convict more distinctly than I knew him now" (39). The most painful thing about having to recognize this part of his past is that his own animality,[4] and, in general, his body, so repulsive to this civilized gentleman, must now be confronted. "I had seen him with my childish eyes to be a desperately violent man . . . I had heard that other convict reiterate that he had tried to murder him . . . I had seen him down in the ditch, tearing and fighting like a wild beast" (39).

> He ate in a ravenous way that was very disagreeable, and all his actions were uncouth, noisy, and greedy. Some of his teeth had failed him since I saw him eat on the marshes, and as he turned his food in his mouth, and turned his head sideways to bring his strongest fangs to bear upon it, he looked terribly like a hungry old dog. (40)

Pip had been ashamed of his own brute nature ever since his vulgarity had been ridiculed by an upper-class girl who had fed him "like a dog" at Satis House. Somehow all the years of education should have put him out of reach of such animality, exuding now from a man claiming to be his second father. Has not Pip come a long way from the time when he and Joe would divide a buttered loaf of bread between them? Has not Herbert Pocket taught him how to use a knife and fork correctly—so well that Pip can be ashamed of Joe's manners?

Actual society is moderately ashamed of what Erich Auerbach calls the "creaturely" aspect of civilized man.[5] Communal eating becomes ritualized into "dining," partly in order to conceal the fact that man has a body he must keep alive by filling his mouth with matter, grinding it to a pulp, swallowing it down in a bolus. On almost every occasion in *Great Expectations* where eating is shown, an undercurrent of animality is suggested: at the Christmas dinner with its latent cannibalism (a theme visible again in Miss Havisham's declaration that she will be the dinner for her rapacious relatives); at the Pockets', where the baby is constantly in danger, at table, from sharp objects, while the servants wage continual culinary war and the butcher threatens; at Jaggers's dinner, where the boys squabble and are shown the hands of a presumed murderess. Behind the ritual of dining together lies the imperfectly concealed brutality of a "dog-eat-dog" world.

Magwitch forces a confrontation with origins and the past, a confrontation of the gentlemanly fiction with the criminal fiction (demanding a reciprocal adjustment of viewpoint, so that the fictions can vanish), a deeper confrontation between the chthonic (animal, nonhuman) self and the civilized self, and finally, linked to all this, a confrontation of the bodily self with the inner self. Handling these suddenly intensified oppositions demands a crisis of some proportions, a crisis of adulthood certainly more significant than the one offered in *Copperfield.* Pip begins at first, when Magwitch appears, to learn the connections of things, the relation between the overworld of Havisham and the underworld of Magwitch. For the connections to be clear, everything must come into consciousness, nothing can be excluded, as before. Solving the intellectual problem posed by the "abyss between Estella in her pride and beauty, and the returned transport whom I harboured" (43) means suddenly noticing everything offered to immediate perception: Pip studies with new eyes the lineaments of Molly, Jaggers's sinister servant, who is in reality Estella's mother. Seeing everything, both of the past and of the present, is one of the steps to psychic integration; a demystified world will be the outward and visible sign of the inner complex unity. The plot, which links the Havisham and Magwitch worlds in complex ways (so complex that students, I notice, are often incapable of explaining these links) and shows these realms as coextensive, is itself a temporal symbol of Pip's psychic movement from complex nonintegration to complex integration.

Dickens makes much of the necessity for a physical ordeal for Pip and others as if to correct any idea, derivable from *Copperfield*, that all ordeals are intrinsically of the imagination or are emotional. Certain of the final events of the novel show the relation of the "wound" (which Dickens envisages with the clarity of a Hemingway) to the imagination. Examination of these will, I hope, correct the views of some critics who are convinced that Dickens's heroes never have very profound experiences of their own. Jonathan Bishop, for instance, thinks that Pip assumes, in essence, a Copperfieldian standoffishness to experience, and that is why he does not grow.[6] (In *Copperfield* violence occurred only for the hero-as-child.)

In his final encounter with Miss Havisham, which is the next important event after the arrival of Magwitch, Pip endures the scorching initiates often undergo in their ordeals, but which we should not take altogether too symbolically. This is the most violent moment in Pip's life—that is, of his violence against others. The description of the fire stresses this: since Miss Havisham does not die in flames but rather from "nervous shock," Pip indeed has a hand in killing her. "I . . . closed with her, threw her down, and got [the coats] over her . . . we were on the ground struggling like desparate enemies, and . . . the closer I covered her, the more wildly she shrieked and tried to free herself" (49). (In the David Lean film of *Great Expectations,* the director has added the interesting touch of showing Pip as accidentally responsible for knocking a coal out of the fire—thanks to the firmness with which he closes the door on leaving—which ignites Miss Havisham's cobwebby and thus highly inflammable gown.) Pip is burned on both hands, and his left arm is incapacitated.

The second important moment in the crisis is Pip's imprisonment by Orlick, when he comes closer to death than ever before. As so many potent acts are, this is an act of darkness in a desert place. In every respect Pip is far away from the comfortable and civilized daylight life he has enjoyed over the years. The captivity occurs near enough to childhood haunts, to the place where he met Magwitch, to implicate his origins. Because of the wounded arm, Pip, bound to the ladder, suffers greater bodily pain than ever before and as well comes to imagine his own death. He uses these last minutes (in which, like Fagin in his last hours alive, his mind, "with inconceivable rapidity, followed out all the consequences of such a death" [53]) to pursue his guilty thoughts, which have been awakened as much by the accusations of Orlick as by the danger he is in: "The death close before me was terrible, but far more terrible than death was the dread of being misremembered after death. And so quick were my thoughts that I saw myself despised by unborn generations" (53). "Softened as my thoughts of all the rest of men were in that dire extremity; humbly beseeching pardon as I did, of Heaven; melted at heart, as I was, by the thought that I had taken no farewell, and never now could take farewell, of those who were dear to me, or could explain myself to them, or ask for their compassion on my miserable errors; still, if I could have killed him, even dying, I would have done it" (53).

I have mentioned the sense in which Orlick's accusations can be taken as symbolically true. But with the subtlety of his late art Dickens shows us in this enigmatical figure, so much discussed by critics of the novel, a new aspect of the process of doubling. In *Copperfield* Steerforth's sins were symbolically David's, until David saw himself in the final mirror, at which point Dickens showed he was beginning to discover the complexities of symbolic agency. With Orlick we have a similarly two-edged situation. We admit Orlick's accusations to a point, but we also see their preposterousness. Our symbolic viewpoint shifts, if we read this episode thoughtfully, into a literalist one: We then do (or should) recognize finally that it is not Pip who sees Orlick as his double, but Orlick who falsely takes Pip as his double. That is, Orlick is involved in the narcissism of seeing himself in others and others in himself. Their confrontation does not seem so much to awaken Pip to guilt by symbolic contagion or association as to remind him of his actual offenses. In this crisis Pip's heart "softens," and he is able to admit to the hard-hearted offenses he had been unable to feel the wrong of before. He feels the desire also to confess to the people he has sinned against. (Miss Havisham had earlier done the same to him.) He later does ask Joe and Biddy for pardon, which they grant him, just as he had forgiven Miss Havisham. This sort of two-sided activity cannot take place—there is no need for it—in fictions where symbolic appropriations and doublings are shown as the typical state of affairs. The acts of asking for and granting pardon are the primal acts of communication for Dickens's characters, toward the end of this novel. These acts are essentially confessions, which can occur only where there is an acknowledgment of the existence of others and of mutual responsibility for life's evils, along with self-consciousness and the awareness of one's precise role in a total time-scheme of offenses and errors.

In the strain of this crisis Pip loses track of time, and, while he busies himself with past and future, he feels once again (for a Dickens character in danger) that intensely personal sense of time. "I could have summed up years and years and years while he said a dozen words" (53). After he is rescued by friends and Trabb's boy he also says: "I had a strange and strong misgiving that I had been lying there a long time—a day and a night—two days and nights—more" (53). This subjective time is relatively uncommon in literature before the nineteenth century. But Thomas De Quincey, whose representations of subjective states are remarkably similar to those in *Copperfield,* had vividly expressed the same experience in *Confessions of an English Opium Eater.* "Sometimes I seemed to have lived for seventy or a hundred years in one night; nay, sometimes had feelings representative of a duration far beyond the limits of any human experience."[7] While De Quincey seems to represent such experience of pure duration as regressive, Dickens places them in a progressive, developmental light.

Dickens makes much of Pip's mental life during his imprisonment, by evoking some of the hallucinatory states of mind that characterize a man (as Dickens sees it) who is experiencing his individuality at its highest pitch. He notes that Pip sees images of the past and future as if they were present; Pip says of Orlick that "what he did say presented pictures to me, and not mere words. In the excited and exalted state of my brain, I could not think of a place without seeing it, or of persons without seeing them. It is impossible to overstate the vividness of these images" (53). Thus Pip discovers in pain (with death impending) the hisness of his body, while discovering the reality of time, a new kind of time that is not "expectation," which can present past images immediately, as in *Copperfield*. "I saw ... I saw ... I saw" (53), says Pip.

After his release Pip has a new sense of obligation to almost everyone, including Magwitch. In the subsequent pages time, especially the present and the looming future, acquires a greater urgency than elsewhere. The immediate objective in the future (a future diminished considerably since the destruction of his dream) saves Pip temporarily from physical and mental collapse. He does not fall ill, he says, because of "the unnatural strain upon me that to-morrow was. So anxiously looked forward to, charged with such consequences, its results so impenetrably hidden though so near" (53). (He now also understands, better than before, the tricks that time can play with the best of plans.) When he leaves in the boat with Magwitch for his next ordeal—by water this time—he is able to move toward freedom from the imprisoning role of gentleman, into a blank future whose indeterminacies he accepts:

> Of all my worldly possessions I took no more than the few necessities that filled the bag. Where I might go, what I might do, or when I might return, were questions utterly unknown to me; nor did I vex my mind with them, for it was wholly set on Provis's safety. I only wondered for the passing moment, as I stopped at the door and looked back, under what altered circumstances I should next see those rooms, if ever. (53)

This is not simple repudiation of the past; it is acceptance of a future without expectation, of a future without infinite progress. Dickens with some subtlety reminds us here of Pip's original departure from his childhood bedroom.

With Magwitch in the boat, as they are attempting to leave England behind, Pip discusses freedom, and thereby discloses something more of the developmental implications of imprisonment. Prior to *Great Expectations,* as we have seen, Dickens often tried to use imprisonment developmentally. Indeed, *Little Dorrit* (1857) was an explicit—perhaps too explicit—attempt to show growth in the shadow of the prison walls. In that novel, however, and in *A Tale of Two Cities,* the prison defeated certain of the central figures (Old Dorrit and Old Manette), while it was unconvincingly offered as contributing to the education of others, including Little Dorrit. Here is Dickens's more subtle meditation, based on the contrast between Pip's symbolic and Magwitch's actual imprisonment:

> "If you knowed, dear boy," he said to me, "what it is to sit here alonger my dear boy and have my smoke, arter having been day by day betwixt four walls, you'd envy me. But you don't know what it is."
> "I think I know the delights of freedom," I answered.
> "Ah," said he, shaking his head gravely. "But you don't know it equal to me. You must have been under lock and key, dear boy, to know it equal to me—but I ain't a-going to be low."
> It occurred to me as inconsistent that, for any mastering idea, he should have endangered his freedom and even his life. But I reflected that perhaps freedom without danger was too much apart from all the habit of his existence to be to him what it would be to another man. (54)

The last part of this passage shows that Pip is beginning to acquire some access to other people. What helps him to understand Magwitch is his own, different knowledge of imprisonment and his subsequent escape from many prisons, including the one that Orlick contrived for him. Freedom in all its danger is illuminated by the experience of bondage. This is again part of the familiar logic of works that explore the development, the essential temporality of the self: bad experiences are as necessary to growth as good ones; one could even say that not to experience imprisoning evil means not to have a complete self. Dickens's controlling idea, essential to his emergent imaginary psychology, is that there can be no complete self without "hard times." His later fiction shows that times are always hard for everyone (not excepting the central characters), and his novelistic conception of maturity is based on the acceptance of hard times, and, thus, of time itself. Critics who affirm that Dickens's characters could never grow up complete (in such a society as he depicts) perhaps fail to grasp this essential developmental logic, however faulty this logic might be when applied to the lives of real people. It would, incidentally, be essential to a critique of humanism to examine this structuralist, *Bil-*

dungsroman logic, which traditionally shows good coming out of evil, as in almost every fictional or "nonfictional" account—Augustine's, Bunyan's, Rousseau's, Wordsworth's, Charlotte Brontë's, Newman's, Sartre's, and so on—we might glance at. The supposition that this logic has or might have little value in application to real lives might possibly transform some humanist assumptions. For undeniably there is a widespread belief, drawn initially from the earliest documents of our culture (the Bible, Homer's epics, Greek tragedy), that suffering is essential to growth. Study of real human development (if it is independently possible) might actually disqualify this assumption or pathos of the imagination. One of the achievements of *Great Expectations* is that its structure does reveal the fictiveness of this assumption. Quite simply, it does this by offering it as true within its frame and then disqualifies that truth by disclosing the fictiveness of the frame. The revelation, however, is not a disproving: it merely invites us to test the familiar literary assumption that good comes out of evil in the world not of art but of the life that becomes visible once art has shown us its own artificiality.

When Magwitch dies, Pip is left wholly to himself, "afraid to think of any future" (55), and he thereupon falls into a fever in his rooms in the temple. "Then there came one night which appeared of great duration, and which teemed with anxiety and horror" (57). The disturbance of Pip's habitual orientation, which had begun with the great chthonic wind that brought Magwitch, now becomes a total unraveling of consciousness in hallucination and dream. This feverish disruption of the continuity of conscious life is the most severe for Pip. It is more emphatically a death and rebirth than the overly rhetorical "wandering in the desert" and attendant mental disturbance of David Copperfield near the end of his story. Again Pip's experience replicates De Quincey's: "I had the torments of a man passing out of one mode of existence into another, and liable to the mixed or the alternate pains of birth and death. The issue was not death, but a sort of physical regeneration."[8] "What a resurrection," De Quincey's narrator says, "from its lowest depths of the inner spirit."[9]

Prior to his regeneration, Pip plumbs the lower depths of the self, in hallucination. But his dreams and hallucinations have meaningful structures. The first of them sums up, in a kind of fictive miniature, the three earlier stages of the protracted crisis: the Magwitch-stage, the Havisham-stage, and the Orlick-stage.

> Whether I had found myself lighting the lamp, possessed by the idea that he was coming up the stairs, and that the lights were blown out; whether I had been inexpressibly harassed by the distracted talking, laughing, and groaning of some one, and had half suspected those sounds to be of my own making; whether there had been a closed iron furnace in a dark corner of the room, and a voice had called out over and over again that Miss Havisham was consuming within it; these were things that I tried to settle with myself and get into some order, as I lay that morning on my bed. But the vapour of a limekiln would come between me and them, disordering them all. (57)

A later hallucination, on the other hand, is unrelated to specific events of Pip's life, but consists instead of a further displacement from them, an expressionist fantasy on the destiny-and-determinism motif:

> That I often lost my reason, that the time seemed interminable, that I confounded impossible existences with my own identity; that I was a brick in the house wall, and yet entreating to be released from the giddy place where the builders had set me; that I was a steel beam of a vast engine, clashing and whirling over a gulf, and yet that I implored in my own person to have the engine stopped, and my part in it hammered off; that I passed through these phases of disease, I know of my own remembrance, and did in some sort know at the time. (57)

This is a cry against the mechanism—or, as it is put by Dickens, the architecture—in which Pip's life has been bound; against the imprisoning fiction of destiny that made him a callous snob. In the callousness itself, the hardness, the deadening of the animal impulses is embedded the notion of *thingness* that tortures Pip at last. Growing up has meant, until this crisis, the acquisition of the gentleman's carapace, the mineral self that is a fortress of exclusion at the same time it is a prison. Pip is now at the center of his transformative crisis, at a point where coming to terms with himself will involve, as well, coming to terms with other people.

II. Healing the Split from Others: Theory of Memory Continued

There is another form of objectification than that dreamed of by Pip during his fever, in which the self simply is threatened with becoming an object. This higher objectification, as envisaged by Dickens, is reached by confession, in the sense of bringing the hidden depths of the self into the view of other people. In court, beside Magwitch, Pip had confessed to the anonymous public; next he has to confide in Joe. For part of the opposition between what Pip was (namely, like Joe) and what he has come to be is an opposition between Joe and Pip. Again, as with Magwitch, by integrating his origins with his present self he can abolish the illusory distance between himself and another person from his past.

First of all, during Pip's sickness, we see a rapid recapitulation of childhood and growth on almost literally a bodily level. For Pip is as weak as a child and must "learn to walk" again as he gathers strength:

> I was slow to gain strength, but I did slowly and surely become less weak, and Joe stayed with me, and I fancied I was little Pip again.
> For the tenderness of Joe was so beautifully proportioned to my need that I was like a child in his hands. He would sit and talk to me in the old confidence, and with the old simplicity, and in the old unassertive protecting way, so that I would half believe that all my life since the days of the old kitchen was one of the mental troubles of the fever that was gone. (57)

(The word *old* in this passage takes on the sentimental honorific value that—as Sylvére Monod points out[10]—it took in *Copperfield* from the beginning.) But this is not just a bodily repetition of growing up; it is also an occasion of verbal recall—a second level of repetition. This recall comprehends both pleasant and unpleasant events. Joe and Pip discuss "Tickler" and all the childhood pain associated with that instrument. What they achieve between them, Pip and Joe, is the laying of the ghosts of the past, which can be done only by deliberate remembering and verbalizing. In this second childhood, all that was suppressed before is touched upon delicately and elliptically, but so that all differences are brought to light as much as need be in honest speech. But Joe's subsequent departure (after they spend a last pleas-

Pip and the Act of Confession

ant Sunday together: Dickens has finally changed the meaning of what had been a "Murdstone" day) indicates that Pip cannot think of the years between childhood and adulthood as mere vapors. One does not rise above one's past, like a Lawrentian phoenix. One somehow carries the past along with oneself at the very time of surpassing it. Evidently, to deny the past is to deny growth and the present. Further, while showing Pip repeating his early past in shared memory, Dickens suggests that past situations can never be returned to as in *Copperfield,* for here remembering is a form of true knowing, and this knowing is at some remove from reliving or attempting selfishly to appropriate the past. This removal is distinctly a temporal removal, so that, to the question "What does rebirth accomplish?" we might answer, with Dickens, that, for one thing, it distances the past. Rebirth is Dickens's most potent image of becoming, but to show this rebirth as a continuity is to show the past as formally operative in the most important moments of becoming, where memory acts as catalyst and even brings to birth new forms of consciousness.

The concluding events conform to the theory of memory outlined in *The Haunted Man* and partly explored in *Copperfield.* In the final crisis Pip encounters, and is haunted by, figures out of the past who force him to remember what he had wished to suppress. Magwitch reminds him of the sin he had once committed. As we know, when his guilty past had appeared to him before, he had tried to disown it. For instance, "the man with the file" at the Three Jolly Bargemen appeared to him a second time as he was on a coach, off to see Miss Havisham. Seeing this convict filled him with disgust: "I felt that a dread, much exceeding the mere apprehension of a painful or disagreeable recognition, made me tremble. I am confident that it took no distinctness of shape, and that it was the revival for a few minutes of the terror of childhood" (28). Again, after having been taken through Newgate by Wemmick, he experienced an arousal of bewildering thoughts about the crime he had associated with his past. "I consumed the whole time in thinking how strange it was that I should be encompassed by all this taint of prison and crime" (32). Awaiting Estella, he said (in a fine, ironic Biblical image), "I beat the prison dust off my feet as I sauntered to and fro, and I shook it out of my dress, and I exhaled its air from my lungs. So contaminated did I feel, remembering who was coming, that the coach came quickly after all, and I was not yet free from the soiling consciousness of [crime]" (32). Then he draws about himself his self-righteous image of purity. But when Magwitch appears, Pip, as he begins to recognize that he was "made" by an evil man, finds himself a participant in evil, and the surface of official innocence cannot be sustained. Deny the past and it returns with redoubled insistent force.

The theory of memory holds that the right kind of remembering is a precondition of growth, and this remembering, which can be initiated by outside forces, is largely willed. Forgetting, on the other hand, particularly a certain willful forgetting, makes for insensitivity, hardness of heart, dead moral impulses. But the right kind of forgetting is the ultimate goal, and it follows the right kind of remembering. These abstractions are fleshed out in the lives of Pip, Miss Havisham, and Estella.

Consider, as an illustration first of the wrong kind of remembering, Miss Havisham's mental arrest, which is one of many in the novel; the situation at Satis House ("Satis," "which is Greek, or Latin, or Hebrew, or all three . . . for enough") is a perverse equivalent of the state of mind that says of the passing moment, "Verweile doch, du bist so schön"; the enchantment of the heart that ends earthly strife and growth. Miss Havisham has compulsively hardened herself by lopping off her future. She will live it by proxy, by setting to work the faithful mechanism, Estella's glittering lapidary coldness, a mechanism which will perpetuate a past moment of betrayal even beyond Miss Havisham's own life. All else for her consists of daily reenactment of the past, thus elevating an "accident" of existence to an eternal principle of identity. Thus the famous standstill of time at Satis House: "I took note of the surrounding objects in detail, and saw that her watch had stopped at twenty minutes to nine, and that a clock in the room had stopped at twenty minutes to nine" (8).

> I began to understand that everything in the room had stopped, like the watch and the clock, a long time ago. I noticed that Miss Havisham put down the jewel exactly on the spot from which she had taken it up. As Estella dealt the cards, I glanced at the dressing-table again, and saw that the shoe upon it, once white, now yellow, had never been

Pip and the Act of Confession

worn. I glanced down at the foot from which the shoe was absent, and saw that the silk stocking on it, once white, now yellow, had been trodden ragged. Without this arrest of everything, this standing still of all the pale decayed objects, not even the withered bridal dress on the collapsed form could have looked so like grave-clothes, or the long veil so like a shroud. (8)

Pip easily sees the deathly character of arrested time. Miss Havisham's death-in-life is like Mrs. Clennam's in *Little Dorrit,* who is another self-immured person, a morbid instance of the compulsion to repeat the past which had been the dominant feature of David Copperfield's consciousness. Certainly David's obsessive thirst for "honey in the hive of memory" is almost as fatal as Miss Havisham's taste for the gall. Dickens's later emphasis, foreshadowed in *The Haunted Man,* embraces those who compulsively remember only the evil in life. He shows no character in *Great Expectations* wallowing in memories of the good times. Virtually every character has a preponderance of evil or ill-fortune in his past which he needs somehow to bring into relation with the good.

Pip and Estella, on the other hand, mainly practice the wrong kind of forgetting. Pip manages to forget the good and the evil in his past (except for Estella, who is really his image of the future), while Estella puts away from herself what little good there was in her early life, Pip's love. When Pip visits her at Satis House shortly after her return from finishing school abroad, their first meeting in a number of years, he is disconcerted to discover that she does not remember many of the things that had happened between them:

I showed her to a nicety where I had seen her walking on the casks that first old day, and she said with a cold and careless look in that direction, "Did I?" I reminded her where she had come out of the house and given me my meat and drink, and she said, "I don't remember." "Not remember that you made me cry?" said I. "No," said she, and shook her head and looked about her. I verily believe that her not remembering and not minding in the least, made me cry again, inwardly—and that is the sharpest crying of all.

"You must know," said Estella, condescending to me as a brilliant and beautiful woman might, "that I have no heart—if that has anything to do with my memory."

I got through some jargon to the effect that I took the liberty of doubting that. That I knew better. That there could be no such beauty without it.

"Oh! I have a heart to be stabbed in or shot in, I have no doubt," said Estella, "and, of course, if it ceased to beat I should cease to be. But you know what I mean. I have no softness there, no—sympathy—sentiment—nonsense." (29)

This is precisely the claim in Dickens's parable about the chemist Redlaw. The person best able to sin against the hearts of others will have no memory.

It is true that Estella has a memory of a certain kind. She has been a good student of Miss Havisham's and has learned to remember in the particularly vengeful fashion advocated by her mentor. Here is the exchange when Miss Havisham discovers that her ward's hard-heartedness extends to her, too:

"Did I never give her a burning love, inseparable from jealousy at all times, and from sharp pain, while she speaks thus to me! Let her call me mad, let her call me mad!"

"Why should I call you mad," returned Estella, "I, of all people? Does any one live who knows what set purposes you have, half as well as I do? Does any one live, who knows what a steady memory you have, half as well as I do? I who have sat on this same hearth on the little stool that is even now beside you there, learning your lessons and looking up into your face, when your face was strange and frightened me!"

"Soon forgotten!" moaned Miss Havisham. "Times soon forgotten!"

"No, not forgotten," retorted Estella. "Not forgotten, but treasured up in my memory. When have you found me false to your teaching? When have you found me unmindful of your lessons? When have you found me giving admission here," she touched her bosom with her hand, "to anything that you excluded? Be just to me. . . . I have never forgotten your wrongs and their causes. I have never been unfaithful to you or your schooling. I have never shown any weakness that I can charge myself with." (38)

Dickens reveals for us two extremes of behavior toward the past, and they can, as in the case of Estella, go together: excessive forgetting and excessive remembering. In both activities personality is narrowed because memory is selectively narrowed. While *The Haunted Man* and *Copperfield* dwelt on personalities initially committed to

Pip and the Act of Confession

excessive remembering, *Great Expectations* adds to this analysis the exploration of excessive forgetting, a further treatment of the second phase of *The Haunted Man,* though with additional subtleties. Dickens again asserts that true memory is a total structure and that it is "softening" to the person earlier made hard-hearted by a partial or specialized memory. Now memory plays a more important role than before in character change, in the process of conversion. We note this in both Pip and Estella. Before any healthy forgetting can occur there must be the right kind of remembering for both central characters. Essentially Pip has to remember the good and the bad, while Estella must remember the good, Pip's "heart."

In the final scene of the novel, in the "ruined garden" of Satis House, Pip sees a softened Estella. "The freshness of her beauty was indeed gone, but its indescribable majesty and its indescribable charm remained. Those attractions in it, I had seen before; what I had never seen before was the saddened softened light of the once proud eyes" (59). This softening is associated with an improved memory; for memory, in addition to physical suffering, has contributed to her complete education:

> "I have often thought of you," said Estella.
> "Have you?"
> "Of late, very often. There was a long hard time when I kept far from me the remembrance of what I had thrown away when I was quite ignorant of its worth. But since my duty has not been incompatible with the admission of that remembrance, I have given it a place in my heart."
> "You have always held your place in *my* heart," I answered....
> "To me, the remembrance of our last parting has been ever mournful and painful."
> "But you said to me," returned Estella, very earnestly, " 'God bless you, God forgive you!' And if you could say that to me then, you will not hesitate to say that to me now—now, when suffering has been stronger than all other teaching, and has taught me to understand what your heart used to be. I have been bent and broken, but—I hope—into a better shape." (59)

Pip also had to suffer in order to discover the healthy memory he exhibits when he tells Biddy, only a short time before this meeting with Estella, " 'I have forgotten nothing in my life that ever had a foremost place there, and little that ever had any place there'" (59). In all his life he did not grow so rapidly as when he was converted by suffering—by enduring the return upon him of a past he had tried to forget. The conversion was to a sense of community with other men, which was bolstered by his admission to others and to himself of his share in both the evil and the good that the Dickens hero, the castaway in time, helps to create.

The final identity crisis, then, is a crisis of remembering, and, once Pip remembers, memory itself, a long-time Dickensian obsession, becomes demystified, as we can see if we grant that the narrator of the novel is meant to be the adult Pip and not simply a theatrical mouthpiece. Dickens's controlling idea, applicable to his characters who change in a changing time, seems to be: "Repudiate your origins and you never escape them." The time-boundaries of the self cannot be denied. Thus, part of the ultimate project for the Dickens hero is to get free of origins while simultaneously acknowledging them. One remembers origins in order to forget them later. The crucial remembering is shown as taking place in the "writing" of *David Copperfield,* while the same remembering has presumably already taken place by the time the narration of *Great Expectations* begins. Mr. Pirrip's memories are not self-curatives; he remembers for the instruction of others.

What of the final condition of the Dickensian hero who has risen above all imprisoning fictions, the fiction of the past, of the future, of woman, of other people? He is released from the infinite cycles that Copperfield would never wish to escape, but which would have been imprisoning indeed for Pip. The hero at the end of *Great Expectations* asserts the linear time-boundedness of life and lives it in "tragedy and triumph." With all his final expectations granted when it is really too late to be satisfied, he is almost a parody of Augustine's God, who, in his perfection, has "neither memory nor expectation."

Notes

1. Leavis, *Dickens the Novelist,* p. 427.
2. *Something Else* (New York: George Braziller, 1972), p. 185.
3. Ibid., p. 183.
4. Many commentators mention the problem of animality—Garis, for instance, puts it into the perspective of Freud's *Civilization and Its Discontents* —but I do not believe that the problem has been adequately explored in relation to the growth of Pip, in relation to his temporality, in particular, and his relation to origins, even more particularly.
5. *Mimesis: The Representation of Reality in Western Literature,* trans. Willard Trask (Garden City, N.Y.: Anchor Books, 1957). Auerbach, among other things, sees in the development of Western literature a progressive tendency to take the "creaturely" aspect of man seriously.
6. Bishop, *Something Else,* p. 183.
7. *Confessions of an English Opium Eater* (London: Everyman's Library, 1964), p. 234.
8. Ibid., p. 247.
9. Ibid., p. 179.
10. Monod, "*Great Expectations* A Hundred Years After," p. 337.

"My Musical Breakfast." From *David Copperfield*.

CONCLUSION

Dickens and the Art of Confession

We have considered features of *Great Expectations* which, particularly when viewed in relation to the two other novels, help expose the thoroughgoing abstractness and artificiality of the novel. All novels are artificial, but this one makes artificiality its message. The simultaneous projection of linear, future-directed fictions and the exposure of them in Pip's experience is one sign of this kind of construction. In no other Dickens work are two opposed and yet continuously overlapping developmental patterns offered at once for the same character. "A poet," wrote Theodore Roethke: "someone who is never satisfied with saying one thing at a time." Thanks to the structure resulting from the doubling of developmental patterns, which we interpret as narrative being conscious of itself, *Great Expectations* does not even give us one time at a time. The double contrast of child and criminal and child and normative adult is another artificial feature of this novel, when it is seen in conjunction with the complex treatment of time as an imaginary system. The better able Dickens was to raise to visibility novelistic psychology as structure (as in the unfolding of the theory of memory and the stages of growth) or to sharpen the reader's awareness of the pure artificiality of the familar novelistic gestures (plot, subsidiary characterization, setting, and so on), then the better able he was to offer the abstract play of art as an alternative to literal images of an individual's life. Twentieth-century reprints of this novel help further to suspend conclusions about traditional or univocal meanings, for the novel is now usually printed with both the original ("unhappy") and the revised ("happy") endings.

There is, then, an abundance of material in *Great Expectations* which supports the view that the work is at once ethically neutral, messageless about life, and yet still significant as an aesthetic confession, a confession about, and by means of, art. And if we look at those places in the novel where general statements about "life" are made, or again at those events which seem to have message import, we discover effectively contrived virtual entities behind which an emptiness seems to lie. Consider those passages which affirm (as does Pip's frequent use of the term *destiny*) that a powerful hidden causality is at work in Pip's life. Just after Pip has met Miss Havisham for the first time, the narrator, with his retrospective privilege, has this to say:

> That was a memorable day to me, for it made great changes in me. But it is the same with any life. Imagine one selected day struck out of it, and think how different its course would have been. Pause you who read this, and think for a moment of the long chain of iron or gold, of thorns or flowers, that would never have bound you, but for the formation of the first link on one memorable day. (9)

"Pause you who read this"—the narrator is evidently telling an exemplary tale, and he cannot refrain from drawing conclusions from time to time about life in general or about the similarity of his own mind to his reader's. The use of the second-person form of address is quite rare in this novel, and thus we might expect it to be used at times when the author wishes to bring something well into the foreground. To the extent that this novel has conditioned us to expect a radical distinction between what takes place within the novel and what takes place outside, perhaps in our own lives, this form of address, which seems to reach out of the fictional frame to us, must appear as a veritable contamination, or a mixing of frames of reference. Why does Dickens have his narrator confuse boundaries that ordinarily he keeps intact? No doubt he does this as another way of stressing the existence of boundaries; the strategic violation brings to mind the distinction between the work and ourselves which we had all along tacitly assumed. Furthermore, if we look at the supposed content of the narrator's statement, we discover additional reasons for bringing it into the foreground. For the passage presents us with a contradiction between a form of speech and a claim about meaning which makes us question the ultimate use of any generalizations that emanate from the narrator.

The speech is rueful and quietly admonitory. By asserting that a small step can influence the remainder of one's life for good or ill, the passage appears to warn the reader about the dangers of taking a misstep the way, perhaps, Pip has done. But this would prove to be an empty act of speech if it were true that nothing could be done to prevent such missteps or to repair the damage afterwards. Pip was unable to avoid the problems posed by his meeting with Miss Havisham and Estella, because when he took his initial step he could conceive neither of alternative choices nor of the consequences of choice. If he had known the consequences in advance he might not have begun to forge his chain, but because he lives in time imagined as linear and irreversible, he of course must choose blindly. Blind acts initiate chains of events that are themselves inescapable. These chains, incidentally, are memory chains. They bind because memory preserves the links. This psychological determinism derives from the theory of memory as outlined in *The Haunted Man*. In that story identity itself was held together by an "intertwisted chain of feelings and associations, each in its turn dependent on ... recollections" of both positive and negative experiences. In this passage from *Great Expectations* the identity similarly formed (out of "iron or gold ... thorns or flowers") cannot be dissolved, as in the earlier story, by the action of a mysterious power which cancels memory. Imagination (rather than magic) and memory are the powers ranged against each other here. The narrator invites his reader to pause, to scan his or her own memories, to "imagine" a "memorable day" struck out of the whole chain, and from this point to construct an alternative history, another life, a path of freedom perhaps.

But this alternative identity, even if it signifies a path of freedom, is obviously a momentary and evanescent gift of an imagination powerless to alter the consequences of actions, powerless to modify the enslaving memories. Imagination cannot offer a new identity, only the idea of a new identity, an idea having no consequences beyond a momentary beguilement. To imagine the person one would have become if one had not become oneself: that is the aesthetic idea which Henry James dramatizes in "The Jolly Corner." There James plays with the paradoxes created when a character attempts actually to carry out at length the kind of project that Dickens's narrator asks us to pause briefly to think about.

Of course Mr. Pirrip's bourgeois notion of the limitations of imagination when faced with the power of memory quite oversimplifies the structure of imagining and remembering that Dickens's works had been articulating over nearly a quarter of a century. The imagination permits Dickens's characters to step outside these memories (as in the moments of crisis in *Copperfield*), and once this chain is broken they can begin to imagine other ways of living, other people, and so on. Even though the memory is a considerable power, the imagination, in its own appropriate times, does have real consequences for growth. Clearly, the relative incompleteness and obtrusiveness of the trusted narrator's ideas in *Great Expectations,* when he attempts to summarize life or to speculate about meaning, ought to be a warning against relying on particular internal statements as interpretations of what happens in the novel. A novel cannot be itself and interpret itself at the same time. General statements within the novel about meaning are perhaps in the nature of things narrower than the novel itself, so that, if it is a statement about meaning we are after, it must come from outside, from us. Thus when we speak of Dickens's "theory of memory," the term covers more accurately what we can *make* explicit as discourse than what already exists in explicit statements by Dickens. By focusing on the points in his works where he clears the way for imaginary improvisation and free construction—as in childhood and criminality, moments of crisis, moments of remembering, and so on—we can perceive his meaning most directly. Though they offer guidelines to interpretation, his explicit statements of portions of his theory of memory are comparatively limited, either because they are derived after the fact from earlier writing or because they are prior to acts of composition which swallow them up while changing and deepening them. And if the responsibility for summarizing the meaning of these novels really does lie outside the novels themselves, at the door of the interpreter, this is reason enough for excusing the writer's withdrawal into artifice; for why should unassigned interpretations be allowed to parade as his own message about life? If interpretation does no more than to display the author's strategy of presenting artifice as a substitute for representation of or instructions about life, it has done no harm and might have done some good. No artist wants to be thought responsible for literary seduction, for creating real Emma Bovarys.

In passages like the one cited above, and in other features of his novel, Dickens is hinting at something he cannot tell us directly (because we cannot hear it properly unless we work out the logic in our own minds). He is confessing that his narratives are pure shows (not theatre, but novelistic phenomena). Now it would take, one would imagine, a very contemporary audience—certainly not the audience we are told about of the nineteenth century—to enjoy fictions if they felt that no generalizations, no morals, could be drawn from them. To turn Robert Garis's argument around: It is not because it is exemplary and instructive that Dickens's novel is theatrical; it is theatrical because it is noninstructive with regard to real life. Yet is not the empty assertion of *Great Expectations* (if that is the case) itself a lesson of great interest about the nature of art—namely that it does not teach us living?

Let us note another passage, which also implies a determinism (though not psychological) and the suggestion that knowledge of the complex laws of causality comes too late to do any good. The passage appears just when the narrator is preparing the reader for the second advent of Magwitch, which initiates the final series of critical events in Pip's life:

> In the eastern story, the heavy slab that was to fall on the bed of state in the flush of conquest was slowly wrought out of the quarry, the tunnel for the rope to hold it in its place was slowly carried through the leagues of rock, the slab was slowly raised and fitted in the roof, the rope was rove to it and slowly taken through the miles of hollow to the great iron ring. All being made ready with much labour, and the hour come, the sultan was aroused in the dead of night, and the sharpened axe that was to sever the rope from the great iron ring was put into his hand, and he struck with it, and the rope parted and rushed away, and the ceiling fell. So, in my case; all the work, near and afar, that tended to the end had been accomplished; and in an instant the blow was struck, and the roof of my stronghold dropped upon me. (38)

It is noteworthy that, to make this point, Dickens places a borrowed fable (from James Ridley's *Tale of the Genii*) within his own story, as if to offer his reader another (in addition to Pip's feverish dreams and hallucinations) narrative miniature for contemplation at just the moment when a new phase of his novel is ready to begin. This one is a retrospective evaluation of Pip's life, but, for someone actually reading along, at this point in the story it produces a sudden figure-ground shift; it is like seeing a photographic negative of its course so far. The passage evokes a far more significant invisible causality than the psychological determinism seen in the one quoted above, for this chain reaches back beyond that "memorable day" mentioned in the first passage, to the original encounter with Magwitch. Psychological determinism allies itself thematically with the Havisham story; mechanical determinism is rooted in the Magwitch story. This is understandable, for the Magwitch story is not really psychological. It reaches back to the very frame of the novel, and, like the plot as a whole, remains for a good bit of the time distinctly separate from the mind of the hero. In fact, the above fable could refer either to Pip's manipulation by Magwitch or to Dickens's manipulation of the events of the novel or to both simultaneously. The evocation of an unknown artificer and a sultan who is really in a secondary role as victim suggests that the principle reference of the fable is to the author and his hero. Thus the causality evoked there is really that of the elegant plot Dickens has contrived in *Great Expectations*. And indeed this causality is not a plausible reconstruction of the way things appear to happen in any known world; it embodies artifice, a plot. The two main causal chains that the narrator calls to the reader's attention—the Pip-Magwitch sequence and the Pip-Havisham-Estella sequence—are connected to one another in a way that the reader perceives as a plotted connection only. Nobody could pretend that real life, with all its seeming determinacies and indeterminacies could produce such a remarkable linkage of the two strands of Pip's experience.

Specifically, the intrusion here of Dickensian coincidence—visible in the remarkable connection of the Havisham and the Magwitch plots—is of a totally different order from that in *Oliver Twist* (where coincidence was used to express a view in which essence is seen as always preserved unchanged throughout existence) or in *Copperfield* (where coincidence was used as symbol of a consciousness busy fixing its own essence in a threatening flux of time—by multiplying the sacred occasions in which that essence originated). To understand Dickens's use of coincidence—as a phenomenon—in *Great Expectations,* we might think again about Pip and his mistaken belief that Miss Havisham is his benefactress. Is it not strange that Dickens makes so much of the fact that Pip was mistaken about the source of his expectations? Does it not seem unfair to Pip that his error and subsequent disillusionment result from his assumption that he lives in a world of reasonable causes and concords? The most natural unconditioned assumption in the world would be that Miss Havisham is the source of his expectations. She is the only wealthy person he has ever met, she takes an interest in him, and so forth. For Pip to have guessed that anyone else could be the source of his expectations would be for him to assume that he lived in a veritable dream world— or a novel. It actually would have been akin to madness for him to have drawn any other conclusion (if, that is, he were a real person, not a novelistic invention). But Dickens does not seem to want to show us a Pip becoming educated by learning how the world truly functions—even on special occasions. Clearly Pip himself is an invention, and we can gain little for our own lives from meditating on the meaning of his progress; except, perhaps, a sense of difference, a sense that fictive characters may not necessarily act or develop the way real people do.

The Dickens narrative of time and growth is a confession about fiction-making itself. It would be difficult to imagine another kind of work that could take up the same task except in the form of a first-person developmental fiction. The role of fictions must be seen temporally and developmentally. And it would be hard to conceive of a novel of time and radical growth (childhood to adulthood) that did not have to examine at some length the role of fictions. At any rate, for Dickens, the problems of growth and time were bound up imaginatively with the entire question of the nature and meaning of the activities of art-making and art-consuming. Consider, hypothetically, the artist himself as he develops: A good many artists begin their careers with a readiness to believe in the power, the usefulness, the goodness, the essential reality of fiction-writing as a legitimate human activity. In Dickens's case, there was every reason for believing in the power of words. A shabby-genteel young man dreams up a mere story, and suddenly it is as if an anonymous duckling becomes transformed, by its own powers alone, into a swan—Charles Dickens becomes wealthy and admired. Temporarily, this confirms the potency of words, of fictions. Then the artist, dreaming on his own works, begins, within his work itself, to explore the potency of fiction-making; he begins to explore the source of his seemingly self-created power. At this point, at least insofar as we can learn from Dickens's writings, the author begins to discover his audience and, perhaps, his confessional burden.

As an artist contrives means of challenging his own belief in fictions, he imagines that his readers have become his accomplices as well as his judges and (sometimes) victims. Was it not the reader's naive readiness to exalt fictions and fiction-makers that perpetuated the narcissism of the author, and thereupon brought about his desire for a further understanding of his own work? Except in a few instances (where some readers accused Dickens of slandering real people by putting them in novels) Dickens originally heard his readers as merely the sound of applause. The reader applauded the first novels, but the reader's increasing sophistication—generated by the novelist himself, as he again and again attempted to renew his magical power—created more and more pressing problems of artistic faith for the writer, who eventually became aware (on some level) of playing a confidence-game whose stakes were rapidly mounting. Thus we can imagine a more desperate game of keeping a step ahead of an audience whose developing intelligence comes to be measured, for the artist, by his own sense of inauthenticity and artificiality. This is almost a vicious circle. Perhaps, however, the act of communication can restore the deviant artist, the artist as Daedalean maze-maker, to the community from which he has progressively been establishing his moral distance, perhaps even while writing moral fictions. Thus Dickens writes *Great Expectations,* and his expectation (he no doubt discovers) is to close the gap between himself and his readers—readers whose literary inclinations his own exertions have helped shape. Only a difficult and indirect art can make contact with such a reader. The reader cannot be asked merely to consume the work, as one might

Dickens and the Art of Confession

a fairy tale; it must educate him, or rather prompt the reader's self-education into what will matter for him in art.

Great Expectations is Dickens's most generous confidence game. His generosity towards his well-formed readers will not permit him the luxury of constructing representations, as in *Oliver Twist,* or uncritical fictions (myths), as in *Copperfield.* Like Milton, like Stendhal, he doubtless wants a fit reader, not a gull for whom confession would have no savor and with whom confidence would be no privilege. Who is this reader? He must be somebody who has already read Dickens's earlier works; somebody who brings to each text a knowledge of its pre-texts. And, since self-interpretation is impossible even for Dickens, the reader must be willing actively to interpret. Dickens enjoyed a rare privilege as a writer, and we must assume he was aware of it enough for us now to take it into account. He could assume that almost every member of his audience had read almost all of his works at approximately the time of first issue. Every one of these readers could read the latest Dickens novel with a certain expectation. Even as his present-day readers we expect and look for a difference between each novel and the others that will still preserve our sense of the totality of Dickens's *oeuvre.* The possibilities of differential understanding are obvious and intriguing. On the other hand, if we were to read, say, *Copperfield* only, we would be like a reader of Kierkegaard who has read only the first volume of *Either/Or.* To read only the various depositions of volume one is to remain mystified, because one remains without a structured knowledge that embraces the times and changes and shifting frames in Kierkegaard's work. But the reader of both volumes is equipped to understand either one; and of course only that reader can grasp both. This holds true for the reader of *Copperfield* and *Great Expectations.* The boundaries are sharply drawn, by time and art, between them; but they are both developmental fictions. They require the differential study that can lead to the form of truth of the whole.

"Fagin in the condemned Cell." From *Oliver Twist*.

APPENDIX

Confidence Game: *Oliver Twist, A Child's History,* and the Failure of Autobiography

This sketch of the Dickens imagination is not so much biographical as a reconstruction of an important "drama" constituting Dickens's never-completed autobiography. My general intent in offering this reconstruction—in the form of a decoding of a seemingly innocent and nonautobiographical (and nonconfessional) pair of texts—is to show the veritable perversity of Dickens when it came to treating facts of his own life. He simply could not do it directly. Instead, either consciously or unconsciously he embedded his autobiography (fragmentary as it was) in *Oliver Twist, A Child's History of England,* and doubtless elsewhere as well. His confession proper was completed in his developmental novels, his personal histories of other, fictive beings. His autobiography was encoded in the fragments I examine below. The exposure of this confidence-game will, I hope, support my previous analysis of his fictional confessions.

Many critics have spoken rather slightingly about Dickens's lack of a world-historical perspective—that is, his lack of an objective comprehension of the past on its own terms. Unquestionably, Dickens's attitude toward history is important to assess when considering his development of notions of time, growth, fiction, and identity. It is especially important because the past provided Dickens with one of his most interesting fictions: one that gave him an indirect means of confessing a certain bewilderment about his own personal past. In probing the sources of his newly achieved identity as a writer, Dickens not only was compelled to begin thinking developmentally about his life, and, consequently, about his characters, he was also thereby obliged to confess to a mental conflict that had a direct connection with his astonishing fiction-making powers. In particular, Dickens was ambivalent about what might be termed the "power of symbols," and he used the fictions that were currently making him a wealthy man as instruments for exploring just this issue: How can the mere words (the fictions) that I invent have the power to change my external life, to make me, for instance, a wealthy and respected man?

Consider further the importance of "word power" from the point of view of a man interested in social reform, in constructive behavior in what E. M. Forster called the "outer world of telegrams and anger." To write about the New Poor Law is hopefully to abolish it. To create a workhouse in a story is hopefully to close down the real ones. Dickens's prefaces (especially those in the "Cheap Edition") sometimes reflect his notions about a possibly reciprocal relation between the real world and the world of the imagination, as we can see in the "Preface to the Cheap Edition" (1850) of *Oliver Twist,* where Dickens plays quite lengthily with the notion of fiction negating reality. The preface was written more than a decade after the novel, and thus is a more explicitly philosophical meditation than would have been possible in the days when Dickens was just beginning to feel the power of his fictions. (He was a man becoming wealthy and loved by "dreaming up" impoverished and abandoned children.) In the preface Dickens takes on a man for having said, before a large gathering, that Jacob's Island "ONLY *existed in a work of fiction, written by Mr. Charles Dickens ten years ago* [roars of laughter]". Not only is this a disclaimer of novelistic accuracy, it is an attack on fiction itself. "When I came to read this," Dickens writes,

> I was so much struck by the honesty, by the truth, and by the wisdom of this logic... that I resolved to record the fact here, as a certain means of making it known to, and causing it to be reverenced by, many thousands of people. Reflecting upon this logic, and its universal application; remembering that when FIELDING described Newgate,

The Failure of Autobiography

the prison immediately ceased to exist; that when SMOLLETT took Roderick Random to Bath, that city instantly sank into the earth; that when SCOTT exercised his genius on Whitefriars, it incontinently glided into the Thames; that an ancient place called Windsor was entirely destroyed in the reign of Queen Elizabeth by two Merry Wives of that town, acting under the direction of a person of the name of SHAKESPEARE; and that Mr. POPE, after having at a great expense completed his grotto at Twickenham, incautiously reduced it to ashes by writing a poem upon it;—I say, when I came to consider these things, I was inclined to make this preface the vehicle of my humble tribute of admiration to SIR PETER LAURIE. But, I am restrained by a very painful consideration—by no less a consideration than the impossibility of *his* existence. For SIR PETER LAURIE having been himself described in a book (as I understand he was, one Christmas time, for his conduct on the seat of Justice), it is but too clear that there CAN be no such man!

Perhaps because Dickens began to get quite carried away with himself in this fantasy, Forster deleted from the manuscript the following paragraph, which sounds almost murderous, as if Dickens were beginning to think he *could* exterminate a man with his words:

If any person, in a diseased appetite for notoriety, should henceforth assume the name and title of SIR PETER LAURIE that person will please to take notice ... that he is dead.

Interest in symbolic agency, in the powers of language (especially fictions) no doubt influenced Dickens's way of dealing with history. As any reader of Forster's *Life* will acknowledge, Dickens could appreciate how his personal past helped to shape him into the man he was. But as for the greater forces that, as we say, "shape history," it appears that Dickens did not feel the need to represent them in any truly sophisticated way. *Barnaby Rudge* (1841), which deals with the Gordon Riots of 1780, was carefully researched, as John Butt and Kathleen Tillotson have shown,[1] and generally faithful to the facts that Dickens had available. Yet such fidelity does not in itself indicate an objective approach to history. Steven Marcus has emphasized that Dickens was drawing an analogy between the "No-Popery" uprisings and the Chartist agitation of his own day.[2] That is, Dickens was indirectly writing about his own times and using events of the past no doubt partly as a protective screen, partly as a Carlylean lesson, as in *Past and Present*. *A Tale of Two Cities* (1859), Dickens's only other novel set in a time when he himself was not alive, is far less a genuine representation of past events than was *Barnaby Rudge*. Taylor Stoehr's masterful reading of the novel shows how Dickens's "passion for order" in effect transformed history into a version of personal history.

Stoehr's general thesis is based on his recognition that Dickens's "mind was of that special sort (sometimes called 'compulsive,' though perhaps misleadingly so) which organizes experience . . . according to such powerfully overriding principles that every item of conscious life has its place in the scheme and is related by rule and code to every other item, as in a gigantic filing system."[3] If this is correct, we would expect Dickens's apprehension of history to correspond to these ordering principles. I should like to illustrate here the operation of Dickens's remarkable "code," which reveals the curiously subjective manner in which he approached history. The analysis will also show how, for Dickens, novelistic details which at first seem purely arbitrary and inexplicable at once reveal and conceal autobiography, and, behind autobiography, reveal the elements of a genuine—though perversely indirect—confession. Dickens's fictive use of the past as an instrument for expressing current personal issues shows us yet another aspect of his creative deformation of time. In order to explore Dickens's method the critic must make a devious zigzag of his own: he must use at least one later work as an aid to interpreting an earlier one.

Everybody remembers the famous exchange between Aunt Betsey and David Copperfield about Mr. Dick, the affable madman who spends most of his adult life trying to write "a Memorial about his own history."

> "Did he say anything to you about King Charles The First, child? . . . That's his allegorical way of expressing [himself]. He connects his illness with great disturbance and agitation, naturally, and that's the figure, or the simile, or whatever it's called, which he chooses to use." (14)

David learns that "Mr. Dick has been for upwards of ten years en-

The Failure of Autobiography

deavouring to keep King Charles the First out of the Memorial; but he had been constantly getting into it, and was there now." This peculiarity has been much discussed, but what I should like to reveal here is a striking instance of the way the "King Charles situation" appears elsewhere in Dickens's works. We shall discover, I think, that there is good reason for concluding that Dickens himself connected if not illness at least a mental conflict of his own "allegorically" with that "great disturbance and agitation" which, two hundred years before Dickens wrote the passages just quoted, featured as its central "trauma" the beheading of Charles I. To trace this connection, one must follow a labyrinthine path through Dickens's works and English history; for just as Mr. Dick cannot directly verbalize the cause and circumstances of his illness (which originated in his sister's desertion of him), so it appears that Dickens also had to write about himself indirectly.

Most readers of *Oliver Twist* will admit to seeing a few confessional or even autobiographical elements in it; but nobody, so far as I have been able to ascertain, makes any strong confessional-autobiographical claims about the novel. What surprises me, however, is that nobody seems to have noticed or explored its complex pattern of allusion to personages and events in seventeenth-century Parliamentary politics. It is this pattern which, in fact, leads us to discover the autobiographical-confessional dimension of the novel. Many readers are aware of Dickens's extensive use of variants or traces of his own name in his novels (Mr. *Dick* with his *Charles* head for example), which provide initial clues about his manner of indirect confession. Dickens both reveals and disguises himself in such names as "Charles Darnay," "Winking Charley," "Charlotte," "Richard Doubledick," and, yes, "Dick Swiveller." But sometimes whole clusters of names will appear and, as names, create in their resonance patterns of allusive drama. In *Oliver Twist* we find only one Charles: Master Charley Bates, the laughing urchin from Fagin's den, who, on an occasion illustrated by Cruikshank, gives Oliver "a lively pantomimic representation" of hanging (18). Though a minor character, he is still the only one who succeeds in turning from crime to an honest life. More puissant than "Little Dick," the waif who expires before the engines of Mr. Brownlow's benevolence can catch him up, Master Bates (and

193

let us hope there is no Dickensian pun meant here) lives on into fictive infinity as "the merriest young grazier in all Northamptonshire" (53). (He is the only merry person who comes out well in the novel.)

But consider some other names in this novel, names which evidently were not chosen randomly by Dickens. Foremost, of course, is "Oliver." Where did Dickens get it? He had no friends, relatives, or even acquaintances by that name. (He did admire Oliver Goldsmith, certainly, and I hope elsewhere to trace Goldsmith's influence on this work.) And what about other names? Let me offer two short lists. On the right are several prominent names from the novel; on the left, placed sinistrally in hopes of causing a tremor of recognition in my readers, are names of men prominent in the sixty years between the accession of Charles I (1625) and the death of Charles II (1685). I give only the significant parts of the names.

Historical Persons	*Fictional Characters*
Brownlow	Brownlow
Dawkins (Admiral)	Dawkins (Artful Dodger)
Grimstone	Grimwig
John Claypole	Noah Claypole
Elizabeth Claypole	Charlotte Claypole
Monk (General)	Monks (Oliver's half-brother)
Oliver Cromwell[4]	Oliver Twist

One can see how, given this family of names, the names of other historical and fictional characters emerge, by a process of association perhaps similar to Dickens's own, as candidates for the list. Thus we might pair, with some justification, the names "Dick Cromwell" (Cromwell's son) and "Little Dick," and so on. If at least part of my point be granted, let us not pause here to reflect on say, Dawkins, Brownlow (Speaker in Barebone's Parliament), and Sir Harbottle Grimstone. (Grimstone was also a Speaker, but, in the main, according to Oliver Goldsmith, "a royalist in his heart,"[5] he was no better a friend to Oliver Cromwell than Mr. Grim*wig* is at first to Oliver Twist—the latter saying he will "eat his head" if Oliver is not proven a thief). We find these names, incidentally, in Goldsmith's *History of*

The Failure of Autobiography

England, which, as British Museum records attest, was charged out to Dickens in 1830, seven years before he began *Oliver Twist.*[6] We have no record of his reading any other history of England during that interval. At any rate, the names I wish to focus on are Charles, Oliver, Claypole, and Monk[s]. Dickens is evidently playing a rather intricate game, in this novel, using fictive and real names as counters. My claim is that Dickens internalized a complex patch of national history as material for what we might call a psychomachia, in which Roundhead and Cavalier (as well as certain ambiguous figures) represent the inner forces in conflict. Since Dickens himself wrote directly about the historical period being considered by us, we have some very important clues about the nature of the conflict—a conflict which shapes his art to an extent we can here only begin to estimate.

A Child's History of England, written in 1853, fifteen years after *Oliver Twist,* is about as subjective as history can be, revealing, I think, more about its author than about England's past. In fact it is remarkable that Dickens could take so many liberties after having just read Thomas Keightley's avowedly Protestant, but nevertheless sober and fair-minded, history of England.[7] True, Dickens did not write this work out by hand, as he did all his other works; he dictated it, evidently as a form of relaxation, in the intervals of working on *Bleak House* (a work whose similarities to *Oliver Twist* would suffice, in the recounting, to delay us in our central mission).[8] In this casual mode of composition we have something close (perhaps as close as Dickens ever got) to free-association, in which Dickens used history as material for fantasy, and, thereby, self-disclosure.

In *A Child's History* Dickens represents the Charles I–Oliver–Charles II sequence as an historical triad, bearing resemblances, one feels, to the tableau of Christ hung up between two thieves. Dickens was not notably fond of kings and counsellors, but his treatment of the two Charleses verges on real intemperance, while, all things considered, Cromwell gets off very lightly indeed. There are many examples of Dickens's willingness to overlook Cromwell's peccadilloes, but notice that he accords the notorious massacre at Drogheda one brief paragraph. Instead of letting the children of England hear about Cromwell's permitting a good many Irish children (and their mothers) to be put to the sword, as they huddled in the cathedral for sanctuary, Dickens in effect draws his reader's attention to Cromwell's prose style. Off-duty, as it were, the sympathetic chronicler of the sufferings of little "Jo" (*Bleak House*) can record with grim satisfaction that, at Drogheda, "there were numbers of friars and priests among them, and Oliver gruffly wrote home in his despatch that these were 'knocked on the head' like the rest."[9]

Dickens appreciated the blunt phrase, indeed; and as we can see in his account of Charles the First's career, a man of many glib words was not thought to be quite so admirable. Dickens stresses the point that, if only the word of Charles "could have been relied upon, his history might have had a different end" (342). "The King . . . never could be straightforward and plain, through one single day or through one single sheet of paper" (352). In short the king was a great liar. Consider what Charles, thus branded, might have meant for Dickens, a fiction writer who protested so often (as in "The Author's Preface to the Third Edition" of *Oliver Twist*) that he himself always told "the stern and plain truth." Dickens's friend Carlyle, following popular tradition, describes Cromwell, who is one of his heroes, as "the inarticulate Prophet; Prophet who could not *speak*. Rude, confused, struggling to utter himself, with his savage depth, with his wild sincerity."[10] And so in the first phase of this drama, in spite of his "reputed confusion of speech,"[11] the simple man exterminates the prevaricating king. It is not irrelevant here to recall that ancient connection between story-telling and beheading established in a book that Dickens loved, *The Arabian Nights*. Charles I told too many lies, hence his beheading; but Scheherazade and Charles Dickens must keep on telling stories in order to stay alive.

In the second act, or phase, of this symbolic drama Charles II appears, in *A Child's History,* as one of the world's most abandoned profligates. In almost every paragraph he bears the famous label stuck on him by the Earl of Rochester: "the Merry Monarch." Dickens repeats this tag until it strains the reader's patience. Further, he attempts to transform this "Merry Monarch" into a veritable Typhoid Mary of the 1665 plague and a Mrs. O'Leary's cow of the 1666 London fire—a fiddling Nero, reveling while London burns (394-97). The only thing Dickens forgives this dignitary is his affair with little Nell Gwyn, "who really had good in her" (392). Dickens approvingly cites

The Failure of Autobiography

Charles's deathbed cry, "Do not let poor Nelly starve" (411). Dickens, like Charles II, was married to a Catherine: hence perhaps his sympathy for little Nells and Nolls. Aside from his general condemnation of Charles's sensuous indulgence, Dickens singles out some of his crimes for special reproach. Notably, he waxes indignant over the symbolic execution of Cromwell, which was supposedly permitted by Charles. The defunct Protector's corpse was yanked from its grave in Westminster Abbey, hanged at Tyburn, and later beheaded. Very few historians record that final detail, but Dickens had a fine symbolic sense: *He* knew why the malefactors would find it amusing to celebrate the anniversary of Charles the First's beheading by in turn beheading (posthumously) the original beheader. Now, according to Dickens, another sacred head fell during the reign of the "Merry Monarch," for Charles had the additional "villany to order the execution of OLIVER PLUNKET" (407). Plunket was a pious, good, and exceedingly unlucky man, but one might ask, considering the many victims of the Titus Oates affair, why Dickens chose this man (rarely mentioned, except in detailed histories) to stand as example of the king's ferocity. Perhaps the name *Oliver* itself dictated his choice, or perhaps some even more complicated unconscious connections are involved (Catherine of Braganza was a major defender of Plunket, before his downfall). In his rage against such crimes by Charles, Dickens exclaims that, "though he had had ten merry heads instead of one, he richly deserved to lose them by the headsman's axe" (398). And so Dickens, too, indulges in the same decapitation fantasy that impelled evildoers to violate the corpse of Cromwell. Thus, in Dickens's story, all three of these rulers of England get beheaded in one way or another: actually, posthumously, and then fictively. We might agree that, by this sort of association, they form an imaginative unit for Dickens.

Now to another sequence, which leads us through *A Child's History,* and the corpus of received history as well, back to *Oliver Twist.* When Cromwell was nearing death, Dickens tells us, his "mind was greatly troubled" because "his favourite daughter" Elizabeth Claypole "lay very ill." She died a few weeks after her father did in 1658, and, says Goldsmith, "on her deathbed upbraided him with all those crimes that led him to trample on the throne."[12] Dickens links Cromwell's death firmly to the "death of his beloved child" and in turn links her death closely to the fact that she had "lately lost her youngest son" (386). In his rapid, compressed account a strongly implied causality appears: a child dies, hastening its mother's death, which in turn hastens its grandfather's death. Three generations topple like dominoes. Elizabeth, incidentally, was married to John Claypole, a man who comes down to us on his page of the *Dictionary of National Biography* as "a debauched ungodly cavalier," who gave his father-in-law considerable trouble. If we now recall that Dickens's own parents were also named Elizabeth and John, we immediately glimpse a possible reading of national history in terms of personal history. And, quite remarkably, I think, the name of the fatal child born to John and Elizabeth Claypole was Oliver.

Thus, in parallel with the Charles I-Oliver-Charles II sequence, we have another, more intimate though equally fatal, sequence: Oliver Claypole-Elizabeth Cromwell Claypole-Oliver Cromwell. In Dickens's novel the "Charles-variant," Charlotte Claypole (who may or may not be actually married to her consort, Noah Claypole) appears in an obnoxious form. If, as certainly seems possible, Dickens has *Charlotte* in mind as coded substitution for the word *Elizabeth* and we view the substitution in the light of the above sequence, it can be written (dispensing with surnames): Oliver-Charlotte-Oliver. The apparent process of association using historical cues has led us to extract two reversed mirroring sequences (Charles-Oliver-Charles and Oliver-Charlotte-Oliver), which suggest a deeply buried complication within Dickens—a complication all the more significant by virtue of its indirect expression in two works at two different times in Dickens's life. The first sequence—if it could in fact be separated in our minds from the second—would have to be described as linked to a basic ambivalence about lying and truth-telling; the second involves the psychic disruption associated with betrayal, particularly betrayal of one sex by another within the same family. The blacking warehouse, where he was forced to work during a short portion of his childhood, was of course a prison and a hell to which Dickens often returned in his imagination. His mother was very nearly responsible for seeing to it that the child stayed in that prison. As he later said to Forster, his sole confidant, "I know how all these things have

The Failure of Autobiography

worked together to make me what I am: but I never afterwards forgot, I never shall forget, I never can forget, that my mother was warm for my being sent back."[13] We should not underestimate this statement. If we look at the Elizabeth figure in *Oliver Twist*, again Charlotte Claypole, we see one of Dickens's most unpleasant females. She sides with Noah, her lover, during Oliver's rebellion against his early oppressors. Reading the scene we easily detect a family drama of primal importance. Dickens seems to have known that betrayal (similar to Mr. Dick's in *Copperfield*) made him what he was, a man having the doubleness of vision necessary for great fiction-writing, but he also knew the cost of losing the simple, truthful identity that he tried to represent in the characters of Oliver Twist and Oliver Cromwell, neither of whom is very convincing. Dickens confesses as much in giving the former his interesting last name: for the twist is the secret sign of exiled Cain, of Oedipus, of the duplicitous artist. And truly, an atmosphere of guilt surrounds Oliver Twist even though he does nothing sinful at all. But we have seen, in the case of Oliver Claypole, who by merely expiring could become both matricide and regicide, that, in the Dickensian universe, doing nothing is impossible. Even the airy nothings created by artists are potentially dangerous offspring of dangerous men. Dickens arrived at a complex notion of symbolic agency, as it were, which virtually eliminates power-distinctions between giant historical figures and the most passive of daydreamers. He would modify this view later.

Let us consider Oliver's evil half-brother, Monks, if we wish to understand this further. He is the secret agent of the novel, closest in knowledge to the omniscient narrator himself, and seems always to act without acting in his own person. He is at the center of all mystery and plots involving identity. The use of the name *Monks* should dispel many reservations about what I claim Dickens is doing with these historical names. The real Gen. George Monk's role in English politics is also mysterious and complex; starting as an ally of Charles I, he sided later with Cromwell, and then abandoned Cromwell's incompetent son—Dick—in favor of Charles II. As Dickens says, "General Monk got the army well into his own hands, and then in pursuance of a secret plan he seems to have entertained from the time of Oliver's death, declared for the King's cause. He did not do this openly..." (387). Thus began the abominable reign of Charles II.

In the novel, Monks is dragged into daylight and finally loses all the power and mystery originally comparable to that of the actual Monk. Dickens well understood the dramatic possibilities in evoking a power which works mysteriously and underground. We see this also in his creation of Fagin, who is Monks's agent, and who himself works invisibly and indirectly, by means of expendable instruments. When he, too, is hauled into daylight and tried before the gaze of the English multitude, he becomes for that crowd (which seems as great as all of England) the most horrible thing they can *see* —for what they see is an ultimate isolation and agony for which even their desire for justice is responsible. In fact, Fagin figures in an ambiguously moral revenge-cycle of perpetual violation that is all too human. (Compare the Charles I-Oliver-Charles II cycle of beheadings.) It is not difficult to see how Fagin, too, could be associated with Dickens's deepest personal-historical fantasy.

Reading back from *A Child's History,* we discover some harder evidence for viewing Fagin as a part of all this. Dickens recounts a well-known symbolic event, occurring during the trial of Charles I: "The King was sentenced to death that day.... The silver head of his walking-stick had fallen off when he leaned upon it, at one time of the trial. The accident seemed to disturb him, as if he thought it ominous of the falling of his own head; and he admitted as much, now it was all over" (369). ("All over"! Again we are tempted to accuse Dickens of a rather remarkable pun.) Compare this event to two others that occur while Fagin is being sentenced to death—by hanging, not by decapitation, which makes these events all the more important as clues to Dickens's deeper fantasies of beheadings. "He looked up into the gallery.... There was one young man sketching his face in a little notebook. He wondered whether it was like, and looked on when the artist broke his pencil-point, and made another with his knife." And again, on the same page: "Even while he trembled, and turned burning hot at the idea of speedy death, he fell to counting the iron spikes before him, and wondering how the head of one had been broken off, and whether they would mend it, or leave it as it was" (52). We could dwell at length on that young artist (of the shabby courtroom reporter sort, no doubt) capturing Fagin's head,

The Failure of Autobiography

which we can indeed by now think of in connection with the head of Charles I.

Fagin is called the "merry old gentleman" throughout the novel, and, as I mentioned before, is a master of disguises and lies, as well as the potential destroyer of Oliver, even though Oliver in fact helps to destroy him. Thus he behaves in the novel much as Dickens thought both Charleses behaved in history. Stephen Marcus emphasizes the consanguinity of Oliver Twist and Fagin as "opposite[s] and counterpart[s],"[14] but in Marcus's inability to discover the third structure—English history—which mediates between the novel and Dickens's personal history, Fagin eludes him as deftly as he eludes Edgar Rosenberg, who protests that in order to understand Fagin "one should have to command some ultimate psychology."[15] Rosenberg is right, and this psychology could never be commanded were not one able, eventually, to recognize the Dickens code, which embodies a quite unique form of symbolic multivalence. Fagin evidently plays a part in the primal Dickens trauma which, as Marcus says, "figures in some central way in every novel he wrote."[16] Here the trauma appears as an imaginative scheme of Caroline violation, reparation, and revenge, the whole scheme bodying forth a portion of Dickens's psychic history. It involves creativity and autonomy as these appear in a context of imaginary parricide, and a consequent guilty self-destructiveness, tempered by an underlying sense of a maternal—and perhaps therefore cosmic—betrayal.

One of the truly horrific scenes in literature, more horrible than any mere execution scene could be, occurs in Fagin's cell, just before his death, a scene part of which I discussed in Chapter One. Oliver enters and in effect bids farewell to a condemned mentor-father, as many of the circumstances suggest. This is something very like a restaging of the visits Cromwell paid to the imprisoned Charles I at Hampton Court. Charles's subsequent escape from the palace (which was graced, by Dickens's time, with its appropriately symbolic maze-garden) was the final proof that the King "could not be trusted," and this sealed his death warrant. Cromwell's part in this escape is, I believe, still an impenetrable historical mystery. Did Oliver aid Charles? Evidently, but why? Did he really want Charles to escape to the Continent or was he actually setting him up for the kill? Dickens's

A Child's History, at least, defends Cromwell as having good intentions (365), but the ambiguities surrounding Oliver Twist's visit with Fagin are insistent enough for us to conclude that what we might call the "Oliver-principle," as it figured in Dickens's personal meditations, might not be blameless.

Kind old Mr. Brownlow has a different look to him as he leads the trembling boy into the cell, despite even the hardened turnkey's advice that " 'It's not a sight for children.' " Brownlow answers rather lamely that, " 'as this child has seen him in the full career of his success and villany, I think it well—even at the cost of some pain and fear—that he should see him now' " (52).[17] This seems to have been the pedagogical aim of *A Child's History,* as well. One of its most moving illustrations shows "Charles the First Taking Leave of His Children" the night before his execution. We see the only genuine moment of Charles's experience, when he has, at the end of an infamous career, become softened by the prospect of departure from his children. Goldsmith's *History* shows the same scene—iconographically a long-time favorite—but in a much harsher light. In Fagin's cell, Oliver is apparently reenacting not only Hampton Court but also that famous moment of filial leave-taking.

The descent into the cell establishes a relation between Fagin and Oliver that Dickens could never make explicit without sacrificing his valuable pretense that Oliver never dirties his hands—never acts, in fact. But the first words Fagin says when he sees Oliver are, " 'Good boy, Charley—well done,' " before he takes a second look and adds: " 'Oliver, too.' " Charley Bates, soon to become the "merry young grazier" is not there, however: Fagin's hallucination of a double Charles-Oliver, though, is sufficient to reveal Dickens's own symbolic doublethink. Fagin, who was in a way Oliver's first protector, again displays an ambiguous care that, in Dickens's experience, is characteristically fatherly. " 'Take him away to bed!' cried the Jew." Fagin goes on to say of Oliver, " 'He has been the—the—somehow the cause of all this.' " From Oliver, Fagin's deranged mind moves—by a kind of direct logic we often hear as madness in a world of indirect speech —to Noah Claypole (now named Morrice Bolter): " 'Bolter's throat as deep as you can cut. Saw his head off!' " (52)[18] Pleading with Oliver to help him escape from the prison, he says, " 'Say I've gone to

The Failure of Autobiography

sleep—they'll believe *you*. You can get me out, if you take me so.' " The narrator concludes his scene: "Oliver nearly swooned after this frightful scene, and was so weak that for an hour or more, he had not the strength to walk" (52). The many images of sleeping and swooning, associated both with Fagin and with Oliver, serve to bind them together within the context of two notions of escape: escape through passivity and escape through a "sleep" that is also inexorable punishment. Cruikshank's perceptive and brilliant illustration of Fagin shows him alone in his cell with a conspicuous hat upside-down on the bench beside him. This hat serves as a proleptic image of decapitation (an equally conspicuous hat appears beside Charles I, in the illustration mentioned above from *A Child's History*), for it is seemingly this fate, and not hanging, that we can now imagine Dickens as sending him to.

The psychic conflict in Dickens, whose personal fantasies and their imaginative projections into *Oliver Twist* can now, I think, be at least partly understood, remains still only partly understandable—the novel is only a twisted fragment of a confession whose remarkable indirection asks for much more thoroughgoing attempts at decoding its verbal surface. As an early form of Dickens's lifelong "confession" it is little better than a child's history, told to himself, which permits a few people to eavesdrop. As hindsight helps us to understand, Dickens's contemporary readers would probably have needed, as an aid to decipherment, the later *Child's History of England*. Eventually, though, Dickens came to use devices that, in *Copperfield* and *Great Expectations,* made possible more direct confessions, more satisfactory revelations, of personal (and interpersonal) conflicts. And these later works communicate his discovery that such conflicts, when viewed developmentally and impersonally in fictional forms, can be the basis for confessions about the nature of both the fiction-making activity and its product, the novel per se. Such confession reveals the limits of Dickens's art, not only (as we might expect) to himself but to his readers as well.

Notes

1. *Dickens at Work,* p. 85. "He adds, but never falsifies."
2. *From Pickwick to Dombey,* pp. 169-212. Marcus owes a great deal to Butt and Tillotson for his discussion.
3. *The Dreamer's Stance,* p. 13.
4. Two entries in a book on English names support the possibility of a semantic relationship between *Cromwell* and *Twist* (1) "Cromwell, the *crooked* well," with *well* meaning "spring or *source."* S. Baring-Gould, *Family Names and Their Story* (Philadelphia: J. B. Lippincott, 1910), p. 174 (my italics). Deviousness and indirection might be seen as historically associated with this name whose root means "twist." Baring-Gould says on another page (364) that "at the Restoration the name of *Cromwell* was odious, and it underwent a slight change so as to disguise it. But what a descent there is from Thomas Cromwell, Earl of Essex, and Oliver, the Lord Protector, to Mr. Vincent *Crummles,* in whose company Nicholas Nickleby acted Romeo." Cromwell's own son Dick, when he returned from his sojourn on the Continent, lived in England under an assumed name.
5. Oliver Goldsmith, *The History of England from the Earliest Times to the Death of George II* (London, rpt. 1824), 2:191.
6. T. W. Hill, "Books that Dickens Read," *The Dickensian* 45 (1949): 82.
7. See Johnson, *Tragedy and Triumph,* p. 727.
8. Ibid.
9. *A Child's History of England* (New York: Harper & Brothers, n.d.), p. 374. All subsequent references will be to this edition, with page numbers cited parenthetically in my text.
10. Thomas Carlyle, "The Hero as King," in *English Prose of the Victorian Era,* ed. Charles Frederick Harrold and William D. Templeman (New York: Oxford University Press, 1938), p. 203. Goldsmith's *History* mentions Cromwell's verbal "obscurity" (2: 181).
11. Carlyle, "The Hero as King," p. 203.
12. *History,* 2:182.
13. Forster, *Life of Charles Dickens,* 1:32.
14. *From Pickwick to Dombey,* p. 359.
15. *From Shylock to Svengali: Jewish Stereotypes in English Fiction* (Stanford, Calif.: Stanford University Press, 1960), p. 20.
16. *From Pickwick to Dombey,* p. 363.
17. Marcus remarks that this is "an appallingly gratuitous and tasteless lesson in virtue," ibid., p. 69.
18. Noah Claypole: need I discuss the literal meaning of this name and its function in a context of decapitation-fantasies?

Bibliography

I list here only those books that were particularly useful in the preparation of this study. I have not tried to include numerous other works consulted, such as specialized articles on Dickens.

I. Books About Dickens

Butt, John, and Tillotson, Kathleen. *Dickens at Work.* London: Methuen & Co., 1957.
Cockshut, A. O. J. *The Imagination of Charles Dickens.* London: William Collins Sons & Co., 1961.
Collins, Philip. *Dickens and Crime.* Bloomington: Indiana University Press, 1968.
Ford, George H. *Dickens and His Readers: Aspects of Novel Criticism since 1836.* Princeton, N.J.: Princeton University Press for the University of Cincinnati, 1955.
Garis, Robert. *The Dickens Theatre: A Reassessment of the Novels.* Oxford: Clarendon Press, 1965.
House, Humphry. *The Dickens World.* London: Oxford University Press, 1941.
Kincaid, James R. *Dickens and the Rhetoric of Laughter.* Oxford: Clarendon Press, 1971.
Leavis, F. R., and Leavis, Q. D. *Dickens the Novelist.* Harmondsworth, Middlesex, and Baltimore, Md.: Penguin Books, Pelican Books, 1972.
Marcus, Steven. *Dickens: From Pickwick to Dombey.* New York: Basic Books, 1965.
Miller, J. Hillis. *Charles Dickens: The World of his Novels.* Cambridge, Mass.: Harvard University Press, 1965.
Monod, Sylvère. *Dickens the Novelist.* Norman: University of Oklahoma Press, 1968.
Spilka, Mark. *Dickens and Kafka: A Mutual Interpretation.* Bloomington: Indiana University Press, 1963.
Stoehr, Taylor. *Dickens: The Dreamer's Stance.* Ithaca, N.Y.: Cornell University Press, 1965.
Welsh, Alexander. *The City of Dickens.* Oxford: Clarendon Press, 1971.

Wilson, Edmund. *The Wound and the Bow.* New York: Oxford University Press, 1965.

II. The Novel, Confessional Narrative, Theory of Literature, and General Background

Abrams, M. H. *Natural Supernaturalism: Tradition and Revolution in Romantic Literature.* New York: W. W. Norton & Co., 1971.
Ariès, Philippe. *Centuries of Childhood: A Social History of Family Life.* Translated by Robert Baldick. New York: Random House, Vintage Books, 1962.
Axthelm, Peter. *The Modern Confessional Novel.* New Haven, Conn.: Yale University Press, 1967.
Bachelard, Gaston. *On Poetic Imagination and Reverie: Selections from the Works.* Translated by Colette Gaudin. New York: Bobbs-Merrill Co., Library of Liberal Arts, 1971.
―――. *The Poetics of Space.* Translated by Maria Jolas. New York: Grossman Pubs., Orion Press, 1964.
Barthes, Roland. *Critical Essays.* Translated by Richard Howard. Evanston, Ill.: Northwestern University Press, 1972.
―――. *Mythologies.* Selected and translated by Annette Lavers. New York: Hill and Wang, 1972.
―――. *S/Z.* Translated by Richard Miller. New York: Hill and Wang, 1974.
―――. *Writing Degree Zero: and, Elements of Semiology.* Translated by Annette Lavers and Colin Smith. Boston, Mass.: Beacon Press, 1970.
Bates, E. Stuart. *Inside Out.* Oxford: William Blackwell & Sons, 1936.
Beebe, Maurice. *Ivory Towers and Sacred Founts: The Artist as Hero in Fiction from Goethe to Joyce.* New York: New York University Press, 1964.
Bergson, Henri. *An Introduction to Metaphysics.* Translated by T. E. Hulme. New York: Bobbs-Merrill Co., Library of Liberal Arts, 1955.
Bishop, Jonathan Peale. *Something Else.* New York: George Braziller, 1972.
Bloom, Harold. *The Anxiety of Influence: A Theory of Poetry.* New York: Oxford University Press, 1973.
Bloom, Harold, ed. *Romanticism and Consciousness: Essays in Criticism.* New York: W. W. Norton & Co., 1970.
Booth, Wayne C. *The Rhetoric of Fiction.* Chicago, Ill.: University of Chicago Press, 1961.
Brooks, Peter, ed. *The Child's Part.* Yale French Studies, no. 43. New Haven, Conn.: Yale University Press, 1969.
Brown, Norman O. *Love's Body.* New York: Random House, 1966.
Bruner, Jerome Seymour. *On Knowing: Essays for the Left Hand.* New York: Atheneum Publishers, 1965.

Bibliography

Buckley, Jerome H. *Season of Youth: The Bildungsroman from Dickens to Golding.* Cambridge, Mass.: Harvard University Press, 1974.

———. *The Triumph of Time: A Study of the Victorian Concepts of Time, History, Progress and Decadence.* Cambridge, Mass.: Harvard University Press, Belknap Press, 1966.

———. *Victorian Temper: A Study in Literary Culture.* London: George Allen and Unwin, 1952.

Cage, John. *Silence; Lectures and Writings.* Middletown, Conn.: Wesleyan University Press, 1961.

Cassirer, Ernst. *The Philosophy of Symbolic Forms.* Vol. 2, *Mythical Thought.* Translated by Ralph Manheim. New Haven, Conn.: Yale University Press, 1955.

Church, Joseph. *Language and the Discovery of Reality: A Developmental Psychology of Cognition.* New York: Random House, Vintage Books, 1966.

Collingwood, Robin George. *The Idea of History.* New York: Oxford University Press, Galaxy Books, 1956.

Coveney, Peter. *The Image of Childhood: The Individual and Society: A Study of the Theme in English Literature.* With an introduction by F. R. Leavis. Rev. ed. Baltimore, Md.: Penguin Books, 1967.

Culler, Jonathan. *Structuralist Poetics.* Ithaca, N.Y.: Cornell University Press, 1975.

Dilthey, Wilhelm. *Meaning in History: Dilthey's Thoughts on History and Society.* Edited by H. P. Rickman. London: George Allen and Unwin, 1961.

Douglas, Mary. *Purity and Danger: An Analysis of Concepts of Pollution and Taboo.* London: Routledge and Kegan Paul, 1966.

Dunne, John S. *A Search for God in Time and Memory.* London: Macmillan & Co., 1970.

Ehrenzweig, Anton. *The Hidden Order of Art: A Study in the Psychology of Artistic Imagination.* London: Paladin, 1970.

Ehrmann, Jacques, ed. *Structuralism.* Garden City, N.Y.: Doubleday & Co., Anchor Books, 1970.

Eisenstein, Sergei. *Film Form.* Translated by Jay Leyder. New York: Harcourt, 1969.

———. *The Film Sense.* Translated by Jay Leyder. New York: Harcourt, 1947.

Erikson, Erik H. *Childhood and Society.* New York: W. W. Norton & Co., 1963.

———. *Identity: Youth and Crisis.* London: Faber & Faber, 1968.

———. *Young Man Luther: A Study in Psychoanalysis and History.* London: Faber & Faber, 1959.

Fanger, Donald. *Dostoevsky and Romantic Realism: A Study of Dostoevsky in Relation to Balzac, Dickens and Gogol.* Harvard Studies in Comparative Literature, no. 27. Cambridge, Mass.: Harvard University Press, 1965.

Gale, Richard M., ed. *The Philosophy of Time.* London: Macmillan & Co., 1968.

Girard, René. *Deceit, Desire, and the Novel: Self and Other in Literary Structure.*

Translated by Yvonne Freccero. Baltimore, Md.: Johns Hopkins University Press, 1965.
Goodman, Paul. *The Structure of Literature.* Chicago, Ill.: University of Chicago Press, 1954.
Gosse, Edmund. *Father and Son.* New York: W. W. Norton & Co., 1963.
Graubard, Stephen R., ed. *Myth, Symbol and Culture.* Issued as vol. 101, no. 1 of the Proceedings of the American Academy of Arts and Sciences. *Daedalus* (Winter 1972).
Guerard, Albert J., ed. *Perspectives on the Novel.* Issued as vol. 92, no. 2 of the Proceedings of the American Academy of Arts and Sciences. *Daedalus* (Spring 1963).
Guillén, Claudio. *Literature as System.* Princeton, N.J.: Princeton University Press, 1971.
Harvey, W. J. *Character and the Novel.* Ithaca, N.Y.: Cornell University Press, 1965.
Hegel, G. W. F. *The Phenomenology of Mind.* Translated by J. B. Baillie. New York: Harper & Row, Harper Torchbooks, 1967.
──────. *Reason in History: A General Introduction to the Philosophy of History.* Translated by Robert S. Hartman. New York: Bobbs-Merrill Co., Library of Liberal Arts, 1953.
Holland, Norman N. *The Dynamics of Literary Response.* New York: Oxford University Press, 1968.
Holloway, John. *The Victorian Sage: Studies in Argument.* New York: W. W. Norton & Co., 1953.
Hunter, John Paul. *The Reluctant Pilgrim: Defoe's Emblematic Method and Quest for Form in "Robinson Crusoe."* Baltimore, Md.: Johns Hopkins University Press, 1966.
Husserl, Edmund. *The Phenomenology of Internal Time-Consciousness.* Translated by James S. Churchill. The Hague: Martinus Nijhoff, 1964.
Jakobson, Roman, and Halle, Morris. *Fundamentals of Language.* Janua Linguarum: series minor, 1. The Hague: Mouton, 1956.
James, William. *The Varieties of Religious Experience: A Study in Human Nature.* New York: New American Library, 1958.
Jameson, Fredric. *The Prison-House of Language: A Critical Account of Structuralism and Russian Formalism.* Princeton Essays in European and Comparative Literature. Princeton, N.J.: Princeton University Press, 1972.
Kawin, Bruce F. *Telling it Again and Again: Repetition in Literature and Film.* Ithaca, N.Y.: Cornell University Press, 1972.
Kermode, Frank. *The Sense of an Ending: Studies in the Theory of Fiction.* New York: Oxford University Press, 1966.
Kierkegaard, Søren. *Repetition: An Essay in Experimental Psychology.* Translated by Walter Lowrie. New York: Harper & Row, Harper Torchbooks, 1964.
──────. *The Point of View for My Work as an Author: A Report to History and*

Bibliography

Related Writings. Translated by Walter Lowrie. Newly edited with a preface by Benjamin Nelson. New York: Harper & Row, Harper Torchbooks, 1962.

Lacan, Jacques. *Écrits.* Paris: Éditions du Seuil, 1966.

———. *The Language of the Self: The Function of Language in Psychoanalysis.* Translated by Anthony Wilden. Baltimore, Md.: Johns Hopkins University Press, 1968.

Laing, R. D. *The Divided Self: An Existential Study in Sanity and Madness.* Baltimore, Md.: Penguin Books, 1965.

Langbaum, Robert. *The Poetry of Experience: The Dramatic Monologue in the Modern Literary Tradition.* New York: W. W. Norton & Co., 1963.

Leach, Edmund. *Genesis as Myth and Other Essays.* London: Jonathan Cape, 1969.

Lévi-Strauss, Claude. *The Savage Mind.* Chicago, Ill.: University of Chicago Press, 1966.

———. *Structural Anthropology.* Garden City, N.Y.: Doubleday & Co., Anchor Books, 1967.

McConnell, F. D. *The Confessional Imagination: A Reading of Wordsworth's "Prelude."* Baltimore, Md.: Johns Hopkins University Press, 1974.

Macksey, Richard, and Donato, Eugenio, eds. *The Languages of Criticism and the Sciences of Man: The Structuralist Controversy.* Baltimore, Md.: Johns Hopkins University Press, 1970.

Macmurray, John. *The Form of the Personal.* Vol. 1, *The Self as Agent.* London: Faber & Faber, 1957. Vol. 2, *Persons in Relation.* London: Faber & Faber, 1961.

Mehlman, Jeffrey, ed. *French Freud: Structural Studies in Psychoanalysis.* Yale French Studies, no. 48. New Haven, Conn.: Yale University Press, 1972.

Merleau-Ponty, Maurice. *The Primacy of Perception and Other Essays.* Translated by James M. Edie. Evanston, Ill.: Northwestern University Press, 1964.

Meyerhoff, Hans. *Time in Literature.* Berkeley and Los Angeles: University of California Press, 1960.

Miller, J. Hillis. *The Form of Victorian Fiction: Thackeray, Dickens, Trollope, George Eliot, Meredith and Hardy.* Notre Dame, Ind.: University of Notre Dame Press, 1968.

———. *Thomas Hardy: Distance and Desire.* Cambridge, Mass.: Harvard University Press, Belknap Press, 1970.

Miyoshi, M. *The Divided Self.* New York: New York University Press, 1969.

Morris, John N. *Versions of the Self: Studies in English Autobiography from John Bunyan to John Stuart Mill.* New York: Basic Books, 1966.

Muir, Edwin. *The Structure of the Novel.* London: Hogarth Press, 1963.

Neumann, Erich. *The Origins and History of Consciousness.* Translated by R. F. C. Hull. 2 vols. New York: Harper & Row, Harper Torchbooks, 1962.

Ogden, C. K. *Bentham's Theory of Fiction.* Paterson, N.J.: Littlefield, Adams & Co., 1959.

Olney, James. *Metaphors of Self: The Meaning of Autobiography.* Princeton, N.J.: Princeton University Press, 1972.

Orme, J. E. *Time, Experience and Behaviour.* London: Iliffe Books, 1969.

Ortega y Gasset, José. *The Dehumanization of Art and Other Writings on Art and Culture.* Translated by W. R. Trask. Garden City, N.Y.: Doubleday & Co., Anchor Books, 1956.

———. *Mediations on Quixote.* Translated by Evelyn Rugg and Diego Marín. New York: W. W. Norton & Co., 1961.

Pascal, Roy. *Design and Truth in Autobiography.* London: Routledge and Kegan Paul, 1960.

Piaget, Jean. *The Child's Conception of Time.* Translated by A. J. Pomerans. New York: Ballantine Books, 1971.

———. *The Language and Thought of the Child.* Translated by by Marjorie Gabain. New York: New American Library, Meridian Books, 1955.

———. *Play, Dreams and Imitation in Childhood.* Translated by C. Cattegno and F. M. Hodgson. New York: W. W. Norton & Co., 1962.

———. *Six Psychological Studies.* Translated by Anita Tenzer and David Elkind. New York: Random House, Vintage Books, 1968.

———. *Structuralism.* Translated by Chaninah Maschler. New York: Basic Books, 1970.

Poulet, Georges. *The Interior Distance.* Translated by Elliott Coleman. Ann Arbor: University of Michigan Press, Ann Arbor Paperbacks, 1964.

Poulet, Georges. *The Metamorphoses of the Circle.* Translated by C. Dawson and Elliott Coleman. Baltimore, Md.: Johns Hopkins University Press, 1966.

———. *Studies in Human Time.* Translated by Elliott Coleman. Baltimore, Md.: Johns Hopkins University Press, 1956.

Ricoeur, Paul. *The Symbolism of Evil.* Translated by Emerson Buchanan. Boston: Beacon Press, 1969.

Said, Edward W. *Joseph Conrad and the Fiction of Autobiography.* Cambridge, Mass.: Harvard University Press, 1966.

Sartre, Jean-Paul. *Baudelaire.* Translated by Martin Turnell. New York: New Directions, 1950.

———. *Literary and Philosophical Essays.* Translated by Annette Michelson. New York: Macmillan Co., Collier Books, 1962.

———. *Saint Genet: Actor and Martyr.* Translated by Bernard Frechtman. New York: New American Library, Mentor Books, 1964.

———. *Search for a Method.* Translated by Hazel E. Barnes. New York: Random House, Vintage Books, 1968.

Saussure, Ferdinand de. *Course in General Linguistics.* Edited by Charles Bally and Albert Sechehaye. Translated by Wade Baskin. London: Peter Owen, 1960.

Sayre, Robert F. *The Examined Self: Benjamin Franklin, Henry Adams, Henry James.* Princeton, N.J.: Princeton University Press, 1964.

Bibliography

Schiller, Friedrich. *On the Aesthetic Education of Man.* Edited and translated by Elizabeth M. Wilkinson and L. A. Willoughby. Oxford: Clarendon Press, 1967.
Scholes, Robert. *Structuralism in Literature: An Introduction.* New Haven and London: Yale University Press, 1974.
Shumaker, Wayne. *English Autobiography: Its Emergence, Materials, and Form.* Berkeley and Los Angeles: University of California Press, 1954.
Strachey, Lytton. *Queen Victoria.* New York: Harcourt, Brace and Co., 1921.
Tillotson, Kathleen. *Novels of the Eighteen-Forties.* Oxford: Clarendon Press, 1954.
Trilling, Lionel. *Sincerity and Authenticity.* Cambridge, Mass.: Harvard University Press, 1972.
Van Ghent, Dorothy. *The English Novel: Form and Function.* New York: Harper & Row, 1961.
Vogler, Thomas A. *Preludes to Vision: The Epic Venture in Blake, Wordsworth, Keats, and Hart Crane.* Berkeley and Los Angeles: University of California Press, 1971.
Watt, Ian. *The Rise of the Novel: Studies in Defoe, Richardson, and Fielding.* Berkeley and Los Angeles: University of California Press, 1957.
Williams, Raymond. *Culture and Society, 1780–1950.* New York: Columbia University Press, 1958.
Wittgenstein, Ludwig. *Philosophical Investigations.* Translated by G. E. M. Anscombe. Oxford: Basil Blackwell & Mott, 1958.

Index

Abrams, M. H., 108
Adolescence, 132–35
Adulthood, xiv, 18–19, 40–41, 115, 118, 125, 162. *See also* Adolescence; Childhood
Adventure, 5–6, 39–40. *See also* Picaresque
Agnes (*David Copperfield*), 37, 51–52, 90, 100, 102–4, 105–7, 111
Animality, 125, 135, 144, 160, 161–62, 169, 177 n.4
Arabian Nights, 196
Art, and artificiality, 80, 83, 159–60, 168, 179–80, 182, 184; abstract, xx, 50, 159–60, 179; mimetic, 50, 55, 83; nondidactic, xx–xxi, 180–83. *See also* Dickens, Charles, art of
Artful Dodger (*Oliver Twist*), 18, 21, 22
Artist, the, 142, 151, 199; development of, xvii, 186–87; as hero, xvii, xx, 78, 83, 90; narcissism of, 79–80, 90–91, 186
Auden, W. H., 108
Auerbach, Erich, 162
Augustine, Saint, 168, 176; *Confessions*, 8, 22, 43, 70 n.15, 110, 168
Autobiography, xiv–xv, 34, 37–38, 45, 66–67, 83; David's, 61, 65–66, 83, 100, 103, 110; Dickens's, 57, 83; Dickens's, coded, 189–203 passim

Bachelard, Gaston, 42, 44; *The Poetics of Space*, 42
Balzac, Honoré: *Cousine Bette*, 127; *Eugénie Grandet*, 127; *Illusions Perdues*, 127
Barnaby Rudge, 31 n.35, 191–92
Bates, Charley (*Oliver Twist*), 193–94, 202
Becoming, 7, 12, 15, 17, 18, 19, 59, 88, 108, 116, 119, 141–44, 171. *See also* Development; Growth
Bede, the Venerable, 124
Beginnings, 2, 3–5, 33–34, 115–16, 117–18. *See also* Origins
Bergson, Henri, 10
Betrayal, 172, 198–99, 201
Betsey, Aunt (*David Copperfield*), 50, 65, 99, 100, 107, 192
Bible, the, 108
Bishop, Jonathan, 160, 162
Bleak House, 57, 151, 195, 196
Body, the, 43, 75, 76, 77, 81, 82, 84, 86, 87, 133–35, 140, 144, 160, 161, 166
Book of Common Prayer, 128
Borges, Jorge Luis, xviii, 87
Brontë, Charlotte: *Jane Eyre*, 76–79, 113 n.3, 133, 168
Brontës, the, 55
Brownlow, Mr. (*Oliver Twist*), 10, 12, 13, 18, 24, 193, 202
Brownlow (speaker in Barebones's Parliament), 194

Bruner, Jerome, 24
Bunyan, John, 168
Burke, Kenneth, 41
Burns, Elizabeth A., 82
Butler, Samuel: *Ernest Pontifex*, 33, 49, 108
Butt, John, 191

Cannibalism, 134, 161
Carker (*Dombey & Son*), 31 n.35
Carlyle, Thomas, 2, 102, 146, 150, 196; *Past and Present*, 192
Carstone, Richard (*Bleak House*), 99
Chance, 10, 51–52, 184–85
Change, 5–6, 13, 14, 15, 37, 40, 46, 53, 54, 56, 73, 74, 81, 89–90, 94, 105–6, 107, 109, 115, 119, 125, 127, 141, 142, 175, 176
Charles I, 65, 193, 195–96, 200–202, 203
Charles II, 195, 196–97
Charlotte (*Oliver Twist*), 198, 199
Cheerybles, the (*Nicholas Nickleby*), 18
Child, the, xxi, xxii, 1–3, 7, 40, 42–43, 111, 115, 122–23, 179; "battered," 134; and the mirror, 76–77, 79; unchildlike, 18, 59
Childhood, xiv, 1–4, 18, 40–44, 62, 66, 74, 82, 83, 115, 118–19, 121, 125, 133, 170, 180; equated with innocence, 18, 19, 62, 149; good and evil in, 83, 128; transition to adulthood from, 18, 37, 40, 79, 80, 100, 124–25, 128, 143, 171, 185. *See also* Adulthood
Child's History of England, 151, 189–203 passim
Chuzzlewit, Jonas (*Martin Chuzzlewit*), 31 n.35
City, the, 51–52, 70 n.23, 143–44; as prison, 139
Claypole, Elizabeth, 194, 197–98

Claypole, John, 194, 198
Claypole, Noah (*Oliver Twist*), 22, 198–99, 202; the name, 194, 198, 205 n.18
Claypole, Oliver, 198, 199
Clennam, Mrs. (*Little Dorrit*), 61, 173
Clothes, 8, 21–22, 43, 140, 144, 146, 151, 160
Cockshut, A. O. J., 15
Coincidence, 10, 30 n.18, 51–52, 184–85
Collingwood, R. G., 36
Compeyson (*Great Expectations*), 151, 152, 156 n.24
Concealment, 17, 20–22, 124, 152; and language, 22–23, 151; power of, 199; and reemergence, 17, 124, 152
Confession, xiv, xvi, xx, 34, 36, 57, 65–66, 67, 90–91, 110–11, 121, 122, 129, 132, 138, 152, 165, 170, 180, 186–87; Dickens's, xiv, xvii, 57, 67, 189, 192–93, 203; Mr. Dick's, 65
Confessional narrative, xiii, xiv–xvi, xviii, xx–xxii, 36, 65, 90–91, 108, 180; and autobiography, xiv, xv–xvi, 34, 36; and time, 34; and truth, xiii, xiv, xv–xvi, 20, 122
Conrad, Joseph, 53, 54, 55; *Lord Jim*, 108
Consciousness, xxi, 6, 25, 33, 34, 36, 40, 42, 50, 52, 55–56, 73, 79, 83, 88, 108–9, 115, 144, 162, 168, 171, 185; first, 33, 39; growth of, 73, 144, imaginary, 53, 54, 79–80, 155 n.7; and language, 94
Copperfield, David (*David Copperfield*), xviii, xix, 7, 34–67 passim, 74–111 passim, 115, 118–23, 124, 125, 130, 161, 168, 176, 192; birth of, 34–35, 39; childhood of,

41–47, 61–62; education of, xvii, 78, 81, 95–97, 107, 149; growing up of, 79–81, 83, 88–89, 96; as hero, 35–36, 38, 39–40, 83, 98, 100, 105, 107; identity of, 40, 41, 85–89, 93–94, 102, 104; immaturity of, 52, 81, 85, 110; obsession with the past of, 41, 48–49, 50–52, 60–62, 82, 99–107, 109, 142–43, 173; search for self of, 37, 38, 83, 84–85, 88–89, 98, 100, 103, 110, 111, 115, 130

Coveney, Peter, 29 n.3

Crackit, Toby (*Oliver Twist*), 21, 22

Crashaw, Richard, 143

Criminal, the, xxi, xxii, 18–20, 24–25, 162, 179; mentality of, xxi, xxii, 17, 20, 24, 28; world of, 8, 17, 22, 24, 28, 37, 126

Criminality, 18–19, 126, 135, 138–39, 152, 160, 171, 182; convergence with innocence of, 126; imagined, 16, 77, 125, 126, 138, 145–46

Crocodile Book, 45, 49

Cromwell, Oliver, 195–96, 197–99, 201–2; the name, 205 n.4

Dandy, the, 21–22, 31 n.31, 86–87, 146

David Copperfield, xiv, xvi, xxii, 3, 9, 18, 21, 25, 28, 33–67, 73–111, 107, 115, 116, 118–21, 124–25, 136, 146, 162, 163, 170, 171, 176, 182, 185, 187, 203; the title, 39–40

Death, 28, 46, 50, 87, 124–25, 164, 168; in life, 50, 124, 173; and the mirror, 87; and rebirth, 124, 168

Decapitation, 196, 197, 200–201, 203

Deception, 86, 127, 129, 131–32, 150, 160. *See also* Lies

Dedlock, Lady (*Bleak House*), 54

Defilement, 46, 60

Degeneration, 136–37, 140, 152

De Quincey, Thomas, 168–69; *Confessions of an English Opium Eater*, 165

Destiny, 34–36, 52, 100, 136–38, 140–42, 169, 180

Determinism, 169, 181, 183–84

Development, xiv, xvi, xvii, 8, 40, 48, 55, 81–82, 127, 140, 153, 160 –61. *See also* Becoming; Growth

Developmental narrative, xiii, xiv, xviii–xix, 1, 3, 13, 19, 21, 24, 28, 34, 37, 39, 40–41, 104, 123, 140, 153, 159, 167, 185, 187, 189

Dick, Mr. (*David Copperfield*), 65, 111, 192–93, 199

Dickens, Charles, 116, 142; art of, xxi, 50, 53, 64, 90, 116–17, 155 n.7, 159–60, 164, 179, 181–84, 185–87, 195, 203; Blacking Warehouse, its effect on, 15, 66, 198–99; and confessional writing, xiii–xv, xviii, xxii, 22, 57, 65, 67, 110, 117, 189; death of sister-in-law, its effect on, 66–67; "doubleness," in late style of, 133, 136, 152, 164–65, 179, 199, 202; and his readers, 186–87; and Romanticism, 81; and social reform, 190–91; suspicion of words by, 95, 98, 151, 196; theatrical devices, use of by, 54–55

Disguise, 21–22, 86, 93–94, 147, 151–52, 201

Dombey and Son, 57, 140

Dora (*David Copperfield*), 61, 84, 86 –87, 94, 101

Dostoyevsky, Fyodor, 54, 55, 151; *The Double*, 90

217

Doubles, 88–89, 90, 164, 202
Dreams, and dreaming, 55, 66–67, 85, 147, 168, 169
Dualism, 8–9, 42–43, 45, 70 n.15

Earle, John: *Microcosmography*, 40
Eating, 52, 134, 161–62
Eden, 42, 47
Eliot, George, 34, 54, 73, 127; *Mill on the Floss*, 133
Eliot, T. S., 32
Emily (*David Copperfield*), 51, 101, 102, 110, 126
Erikson, Erik, 13
Eroticism, 78, 86, 87, 88. *See also* Sexuality
Estella (*Great Expectations*), 131, 144, 172, 173–75
Evil, 19, 45–46, 60–61, 65, 66, 69 n.4, 98, 104, 109–10, 126, 135, 138, 168, 173; and David, 46, 60, 61, 66, 75; equated with adulthood, 18–19; -good dichotomy, 19, 45, 59, 60–61, 83, 125, 153, 173; and language, 95; and Oliver, 16–17; and Pip, 126, 135, 138–39, 167, 172
Experience, 1, 6, 7–8, 17, 18, 19, 39, 40, 43, 69 n.4, 85, 108–9, 115, 126, 144, 163; and development, 59–60

Fagin (*Oliver Twist*), 13, 14–15, 17, 20, 22, 24, 52, 200–203; last night alive of, 25–28, 91, 121, 164, 200–203
Father figures, 12–13, 43, 46, 76, 82, 123–24, 162, 201–2; and imaginary parricide, 201
Fiction, and fiction-making, xv, xvii–xix, xx–xxi, 1, 22, 34, 37, 40, 77, 90, 95, 115–16, 159, 180; David's, 45, 90, 93–94, 95, 98; Dickens's, 151, 160, 185–87, 190, 196, 199, 203; Pip's, 132, 141, 152, 179; reality negated by, 190–91
Fielding, Henry: *Tom Jones*, 3, 10, 18, 91
Flaubert, Gustave: *Madame Bovary*, 80
Forgetting, 100, 160, 172, 173–75
Forster, E. M., 190
Forster, John, 39, 59, 66, 116, 142, 191, 199
Freud, Sigmund, 55; *Three Contributions to the Theory of Sex*, 133
Future, the, 3, 7, 13, 27–28, 58, 71 n.43, 74, 144, 172; David and, 34, 50, 98–99, 100–102, 104–6; Oliver and, 7, 11, 13, 14; Pip and, 115–16, 139, 142–43, 160–61, 165–66, 168, 173

Gargery, Joe (*Great Expectations*), 128, 130, 132, 134, 148, 162, 165, 170–71
Gargery, Mrs. Joe (*Great Expectations*), 128, 129, 137–38, 140, 149
Garis, Robert, 53–57, 121, 159, 183
Genet, Jean, 22, 137
Gentleman, image of the, 142, 143–48, 150–52, 162, 166, 169
"George Silverman's Explanation," 38
Gide, André, 108, 133
Goethe, J. W. von, xiv
Goldsmith, Oliver, 194, 197; *History of England*, 194–95, 202; *Vicar of Wakefield*, 91
Gosse, Edmund, 75
Great Expectations, xiv, xvi–xviii, xix, xx, xxii, 3, 9, 10, 18, 21, 22,

24, 28, 33, 37, 43, 45, 48, 52, 54–55, 67, 90, 106, 109, 115–53, 159–76, 179–81; as abstract fiction, xvi, xvii–xviii, 159–60, 179; irony in, 120–21; thematic concern in, 121

Greene, Graham, 55

Growing up, xvii, xviii, 3, 16, 18, 41, 125, 126, 160, 167, 169, 170; narratives of, 22, 56, 80, 85, 91, 147

Growth, xiii, xiv, xviii, xxi, 1–2, 8, 19, 22, 37, 73–74, 77, 79, 80, 98, 109, 132–33, 140, 142–43, 161, 167, 170–72, 179, 182, 185, 190; and memory, 74; and suffering, 104, 167–68, 175–76. *See also* Becoming; Development

Guilt, 28, 54, 75, 77, 82, 110, 135, 138–39, 145–46, 149, 152, 160, 165, 171, 199, 201

Gummidge, Mrs. (*David Copperfield*), 101

Hamlet, 147, 156 n.24

Hardy, Barbara, 127

Hardy, Thomas: *Jude the Obscure*, 108

Haunted Man, The, 57–58, 66, 83, 100, 171, 173, 174–75, 181

Haunting, 17, 48, 55, 124; of the present by the evil past, 17, 26, 46, 58, 66, 99, 102, 124, 171

Havisham, Miss (*Great Expectations*), 61, 65, 127, 131, 161, 163, 165, 172–73, 185

Headstone, Bradley (*Our Mutual Friend*), 46

Heep, Uriah (*David Copperfield*), 46–47, 98

Heidegger, Martin, 21, 88

Heredity, 12–13, 14, 18–19, 33, 41

Hero, the, xix, xx, 5, 10–11, 19, 33, 35–36, 37, 39–40, 42, 60, 76, 81–83, 85, 101, 107–9, 111, 115–16, 121, 140–41, 160, 163, 176; as pilgrim, 102, 108–9, 115

Hirsch, E. D., 108

History, Dickens and, 189–90, 191–92, 194–201; and personal history, 192, 198, 201

Hoffmann, E. T. A., 90

"The Holly Tree," 66

House, the, as prison, 76, 92, 139; as shelter, 42, 43–44, 46–47, 49, 51, 87–88, 107; "inside" and "outside," 42, 43, 76, 85, 87–88; violation of, 43, 46, 76, 88

Identity, xviii, xix–xx, xxi, 1, 4, 19, 20–22, 25, 34, 36, 40, 60, 77, 85–88, 115, 120, 122–23, 130–31, 144–52, 160, 169, 172, 181–82, 190, 199; autochthonous, 4, 88, 125; crisis of, 13, 14, 19, 74–75, 118, 133, 160, 169, 176; false, 21, 131; and imagination, 74, 181–82; and language, 23; and memory, 58–60; and name, 3, 22; in possessions, 20–21; and time, 12, 28, 59, 93. *See also* Twist, Oliver

Imagination, xxii, 4, 16, 18, 26, 39, 40, 74–75, 77, 78, 88, 90, 91, 92–93, 99, 141, 142, 146, 160, 162, 181–82

Imprisonment, 25–28, 75, 91–92, 139, 164, 165, 171, 198; and escape, 139–40, 167, 201, 202–3; and psychic growth, 15, 84, 140, 165–67; and time, 25, 26–28, 84, 91–92, 121, 139, 165–66

Individuality, 28, 111, 130, 138, 165

Inner life, 24, 39, 53–56, 110, 127, 163, 195; and dreams, 55. *See also* Psychology; Self, inner and outer

Innocence, 24, 135, 152; convergence of, with criminality, 126, 152–53, 172; equated with childhood, 18, 19, 124, 149; fears of contamination of by evil, 16–17, 88, 109–110, 126, 172, 202

Isolation, 15–16, 25, 26, 84, 91–92, 130, 138, 200

Jaggers (*Great Expectations*), 161, 163

James, Henry: *The Ambassadors*, 127; "The Jolly Corner," 182; *Portrait of a Lady*, 105; *What Maisie Knew*, 108, 156 n.15

James, William, 115

Jaspers, Karl, 54

Johnson, Edgar, 57, 116

Jonson, Ben, 23

Joyce, James: *Portrait of the Artist as a Young Man*, 44; *Ulysses*, 85, 101

Kafka, Franz, 54, 55, 60, 107, 146

Keightley, Thomas, 195

Kierkegaard, Søren, xiii, xv, 59, 187

Kincaid, James R., 3

Lacan, Jacques, 76–77, 79, 80

Langbaum, Robert, 80–81

Language, 22–23, 38, 43, 91, 92–97, 120, 122–23, 149–51, 191; and criminality, 22–23, 150–51; and evil, 95, 150–51; false, 95–97, 106; and identity, 23, 94, 144; secret, 22–23, 95–96; and time, 91. *See also* Words, power of

Lawrence, D. H., 33, 41; *The Rainbow*, 33; *Women in Love*, 108

Leach, Edmund, 125

Leavis, Q. D., 159

Lean, David, 163

Lévi-Strauss, Claude, 125

Lies, and lying, xv, xvi, 20, 22, 97, 98, 129, 131–32, 146, 149–50, 151, 196, 201; Dickens's ambivalence about, 198

Linkinwater, Tim (*Nicholas Nickleby*), 52

Little Dorrit, 167, 173

Magwitch, 122, 124–26, 127–28, 129, 134, 135, 139, 140, 145, 152, 156 n.24, 160, 161–62, 166, 167, 168, 170, 171, 184

Mallarmé, Stephane, 79–80

Mann, Thomas, 33–34

Marcus, Steven, 7, 191, 201

Marshall, William H., 53

Martha (*David Copperfield*), 51, 110

Maylie, Rose (*Oliver Twist*), 10, 24

Memory, xxii, 12, 25, 26, 33–34, 39, 41, 47, 49, 50–51, 55–56, 57–66, 74, 82–83, 91, 99, 103, 109–10, 115, 160, 161, 170–72, 174–76, 179; in *The Haunted Man*, 57–60, 171, 174; and imagination, 74, 82, 91, 110, 142, 181–82; morbid, 65, 67, 172–73, 174–75; theory of, xxii, 56, 59–60, 65, 66–67, 74, 83, 109–10, 160, 171–72, 175, 179, 181, 182

Merleau-Ponty, Maurice, 79, 81, 82

Micawber, Mr. (*David Copperfield*), 97–98, 99, 100–101

Miller, J. Hillis, 11, 97

Mirror, 45, 76–80, 81, 82, 83, 84–86, 87–89, 90, 98, 146–47, 164; Pip and, 146–48; window as, 82, 87, 88, 89

Index

Monism, 8–9, 60
Monks (*Oliver Twist*), 24, 199–200; and General Monk, 199–200
Monod, Sylvère, 121, 170
Moynahan, Julian, 138
Muir, Edwin, 10
Murdstone, Mr. (*David Copperfield*), 45, 46, 70 n.20, 74–76, 77, 81–82, 86, 87, 124–25
Myth, of development, 136; the Dickens hero's, 10, 60–61, 66, 71 n.43, 107–9, 115, 116, 141–42

Names, 3, 22, 36, 39, 121–23, 155 n.10, 193–95, 197–98; Dickens's, 45, 193–94; historical, in *Oliver Twist*, 193–95, 198, 199
Nancy (*Oliver Twist*), 17, 22, 24
Narcissism, xix–xx, 74, 78, 80–81, 82, 83–86, 87, 88, 110, 111, 164; and aestheticism, 80, 83, 84, 86
Narrator, xx, xxi, 4, 5, 6, 7, 8, 11, 23, 36, 37–38, 50, 55, 56, 80, 92; in *David Copperfield*, 35, 37–38, 39, 40, 50, 53, 56, 60, 63, 85, 87, 106, 119–21; in *Great Expectations*, 55, 118, 119–21, 145, 176, 180–81; omniscient, 5, 34, 119; relationship to hero, xx, 5, 63–64, 118, 119–20
Nature, 103–4
Needham, Gwendolyn, 73, 102
Newman, John Henry, Cardinal, 148, 164
Nietzsche, Friedrich: *The Use and Abuse of History*, 100
Novalis, 108, 111

Objectification, 80, 81, 161, 170; in psychic development, 126
Objectivity, 77, 80–81, 83, 84, 86, 87, 88, 92, 130, 161; narrator's, in *Great Expectations*, 119–21
Odyssey, The, 108
Old Curiosity Shop, 12
Oliver Twist, xiv, xvi, xxii, 1–28, 33, 34, 37, 39, 41, 48, 49, 52, 59, 60, 103, 115, 116, 118, 126, 130, 135–36, 137, 141, 146, 151, 152, 153, 185, 187, 190–203 passim; and Dickens's autobiography, 189, 193–203; title of, 4–5
Omer, Mr. (*David Copperfield*), 50, 51
Ordeals, 14, 19, 139, 163–64, 166, 168
Origins, 3, 9, 10, 19, 33–34, 47, 49, 107, 116, 123, 125, 131, 141, 162, 164, 170, 176, 177 n.4; autochthonous, 3, 9, 125
Orlick (*Great Expectations*), 138–39, 150–51, 164–65
Ortega y Gasset, José, xxi
Orwell, George, 43

Partlow, Robert B., 119, 120
Past, the, 7, 13, 41, 47–48, 63–64, 66, 71 n.43, 99–104, 105–6, 107, 109, 121, 123, 142–44, 160–61, 162, 165–66, 170–73, 190, 192; changeless, 13, 14, 51, 99, 115; reappearance of, 17–18, 26, 27, 46, 58, 62–63, 65, 66, 82, 99, 102, 156 n.24, 171–72, 176; segmented, 60–62, 100
Peggotty (*David Copperfield*), 45, 49–50, 107
Perception, xxii, 4, 27, 39, 40, 49, 127, 162; contaminated by memory, 27, 49, 64, 83; contaminated by imagination, 74
"Personal history," 3, 25, 34–36, 39–40, 133, 189, 192, 198. *See also* Confession

Picaresque, xvii, 6, 13, 39, 91
Pickwick Papers, xxi, 1, 91
Pip (*Great Expectations*), xviii, xix, 7, 67, 115–53 passim, 159–76 passim; as "complete" hero, 160–61; education of, 148–50; expectations of, 115, 116, 141–42, 146, 166, 176, 185; and external pressures, 127, 131, 136–37, 144; identity of, 115, 122–23, 130–31, 144, 145–48, 152, 160, 169–70; origins of, 123, 125, 131, 141, 164, 170
Plot, 10, 35, 184; improbabilities of, 36; "mythic," 24
Pocket, Herbert (*Great Expectations*), 145, 150, 151
Poe, Edgar Allan, 79
Possessions, 20–21, 49–50
Poulet, Georges, 59
Present, the, 26, 27–28, 50, 58, 62, 64–65, 71 n.43, 74, 82, 100–101, 102–3, 107, 139, 142–43, 144, 161, 163, 166, 171. *See also* Future; Past
Psychic growth, 36, 43, 57, 73, 74, 77, 109, 110, 126, 167; psychic integration, 163
Psychology, fictional, xxi, xxii, 53–57, 59–60, 73, 74, 77, 79–80, 102, 122, 161, 167; of crime, xxi, 16, 17–18, 20–21, 24–26, 54

Raleigh, John Henry, 98–99
Rank, Otto, 80
Rebirth, xix, 8, 46, 124, 136, 152, 169
Redlaw (*Haunted Man*), 57–59, 100, 174
Regeneration. *See* Rebirth
Repetition, 13, 35, 78, 139, 170; David's, 41, 46, 48, 50, 52–53, 60–61, 63, 66, 69 n.4, 107; Mr. Dick's, 65; and stasis, 53, 82, 107
Resurrection, threatened, 43, 46, 124–25, 156 n.24
Ridley, James: *Tale of the Genii*, 184
Rilke, Rainer Maria, 44; *Notebooks*, 93, 108
Rites of passage, 21, 139
Ritual, 21, 52, 145, 146, 162
River image, 9, 30 n.17
Roethke, Theodore, 179
Romanticism, 81, 108
Rosenberg, Edgar, 201
Rousseau, Jean-Jacques, 2, 75, 94, 137, 144, 168; *Confessions*, 34, 129

Sartre, Jean-Paul, 80, 81, 95, 137, 168
Self, 7, 13, 34, 38, 58, 59, 60, 76–77, 111, 115, 122, 123, 144, 167; -alienation, 16, 25, 43–44, 64, 144; -awareness, 22, 24, 81; chthonic, 125, 162; -consciousness, 16, 24, 77, 98, 110, 119, 124, 130; -examination, 56–57, 60; inner and outer, xix, 7, 21, 53, 84, 86, 110, 127, 129–30, 151–52, 162; integrated, 60, 64, 167; and other, 19, 46, 76–77, 79, 80–81, 83, 88, 89, 90, 110–11, 130, 138, 146, 165, 169, 176; split in, 13, 81–82, 84, 85, 89, 130, 143, 160. *See also* Identity
Sexuality: adult, 102, 110; childhood, 133–35
Sikes (*Oliver Twist*), 25, 31 n.29
Sketches by Boz: "Astleys," 94; "A Visit to Newgate," 24, 84
Skimpole (*Bleak House*), 151
Space, 7, 11, 28, 42–44, 79, 85; the house as, 42–44, 51; inner, 25
Stasis, 1, 10, 12, 41, 48; in char-

Index

acterization, 3, 6, 7, 37, 53, 74, 82; of identity, 3, 9–12; in structure, 3, 8, 41–43, 53, 78, 82

Steerforth (*David Copperfield*), 84, 87, 88–89, 101, 110, 126, 164; as negative projection of David, 88, 164

Sterne, Laurence: *Tristram Shandy*, 2

Stoehr, Taylor, 55, 192

Strachey, Lytton: *Queen Victoria*, 49

Structure, xiii, xiv, xviii, 8, 9, 10, 33, 56, 107–8, 136, 168, 179; static, 41–43, 53, 78, 82

Subjectivity, 80–81, 84, 86, 88, 92, 144, 165

Suffering, 5, 54, 75–77, 85, 130, 175–76; as essential to growth, 104, 167–68

Summerson, Esther (*Bleak House*), 56, 75, 119

Symbols, power of, 74, 78, 79, 88–89, 190–91, 199. *See also* Words, power of

Tale of Two Cities, 167, 192

Tillotson, Kathleen, 191

Time, xviii, xix, xxi–xxii, 1, 10–13, 14, 17, 18, 25–28, 34–35, 45, 50, 52, 56, 57, 59, 74, 81, 82, 88, 91, 98, 104, 105, 107–9, 115, 116, 120, 121, 125, 142, 165–66, 167, 172, 179, 190, 192; arrested, 65, 82, 172–73; dislocation of, 25, 26 –27, 85, 91; as growth, xiii, 116, 132–33, 165, 176, 185; linear, 107–9, 176, 179, 181; present, 62, 139; subjective, 26–28, 57, 84, 91–92, 165. *See also* Future; Past; Present

Transformation. *See* Change

Truth, 20, 86, 87, 109, 120, 122, 168, 196, 198; and confession, xiii, xiv, xv–xvi, 20, 122; and language, 97, 98, 151

Twist, Oliver (*Oliver Twist*), xix, xxi, 6–8, 24, 34, 35–36, 37, 75, 77, 91, 118, 121, 123, 125, 127, 160, 163, 194, 199, 201–3; "education" of, 12–13, 14–17, 23; identity of, 4–5, 9–12, 14, 16, 23, 199; name of, 194–95, 197, 199, 205 n.4; origins of, 3, 9, 10

Uncommercial Traveller, 70 n.20

Violence, 75–76, 111, 127, 160, 163

"A Visit to Newgate," 24, 84

Wilson, Angus, 62

Woolf, Virginia: *To The Lighthouse*, 47

Wopsle (*Great Expectations*), 147, 150

Words, power of, 16, 38, 91, 92, 94–97, 123, 150, 160, 186, 190–91; tyranny of, 94–95, 149. *See also* Language

Wordsworth, William, 41, 57, 108, 168

Zola, Emile: *L'Assommoir*, 36